THE PELICAN BOOK OF ENGLISH PROSE

GENERAL EDITOR : KENNETH ALLOTT

A 361

VOLUME II : SEVENTEENTH-CENTURY PROSE

EDITED BY PETER URE

THE PELICAN BOOK OF ENGLISH PROSE

GENERAL EDITOR : KENNETH ALLOTT

VOLUME II

Seventeenth-Century Prose

· 1620–1700 ·

EDITED BY PETER URE

PENGUIN BOOKS

Penguin Books Ltd, Harmondsworth, Middlesex

U.S.A.: Penguin Books Inc., 3300 Clipper Mill Road, Baltimore 11, Md

CANADA: Penguin Books (Canada) Ltd, 178 Norseman Street,
Toronto 18, Ontario

AUSTRALIA: Penguin Books Pty Ltd, 762 Whitehorse Road,
Mitcham, Victoria

SOUTH AFRICA: Penguin Books (S.A.) Pty Ltd, Gibraltar House,
Regent Road, Sea Point, Cape Town

—

First published 1956

Made and printed in Great Britain
by The Whitefriars Press Ltd
London and Tonbridge

CONTENTS

CONTENTS

CONTENTS

CONTENTS

GENERAL INTRODUCTION

The Pelican Book of English Prose has the aim of bringing into focus for the ordinary reader nearly three hundred and fifty years of English prose: so that he may see for himself its variety and continuity in successive ages, the many purposes for which it has been employed (including the humbler ones), the prose styles thought expressive at different times, and the ruling interests and attitudes of particular periods with their associated changes of tone in the conduct of prose. This has involved some planning. An anthology is judged practically by what we can do with it. If it is to be read intelligently or used for study, not merely dipped into idly, it needs to support the reader's interest by a certain coherence and consistency of approach: that is to say, its contents must be properly arranged and introduced. The present anthology contains about 425,000 words of text exclusive of editorial matter and includes some three hundred writers who were at work between 1550 and 1880. These initial and terminal dates are plainly convenient: before 1550 prose cannot be read easily by the general reader without a glossary (and it will not be read, one suspects, with a glossary except by the serious student); after 1880 considerations of copyright become troublesome and begin to influence an editor's choice. The preliminary disposition of the material is in five volumes in chronological sequence, as follows:

I   Elizabethan and Jacobean prose (1550–1620)
II   Seventeenth-Century prose (1620–1700)
III Eighteenth-Century prose (1700–80)
IV   Prose of the Romantic Period (1780–1830)
V   Victorian prose (1830–80)

Each volume is self-contained and independently edited, but

the unity of the whole anthology is preserved by a 'horizontal' classification which cuts across the 'vertical' chronological division just described. The anthology, then, is sub-divided both chronologically and, within each volume, by an arrangement of subject-matter in accordance with the following scheme:

1. The Picture of the Age: Scene, Personality, Event
2. The Movement of Ideas: Reflection, Argument, Exhortation, Satire
3. The World of Imagination, Feeling and Comic Invention: Fiction, Historical and Occasional Writing
4. The Criticism of the Arts

The editors of the separate volumes have found this scheme, which took its final form only after several revisions, sufficiently flexible; and it is hoped that it may provide a useful framework for the reader and enable him to grasp more rapidly the distinguishing characteristics of prose in each period. It was the general editor's task to see that the agreed scheme was followed and to act as a clearing-house for the suggestions and criticisms of his colleagues. The sharing among six editors of the task of reading and selecting pieces for the five volumes of the anthology has probably been an advantage. It has meant a wider and more accurate coverage of the enormous area of English prose between 1550 and 1880; and it has allowed particular sections of prose to be undertaken by editors whose interests are centred in the periods for which they are responsible. The disunity that might have resulted from the arrangement has been carefully guarded against: both by the adoption of the agreed scheme and by other means of ensuring a common approach which have still to be described.

Some of these means were mechanical. It was decided that a substantial proportion of the passages in each volume, usually selected from the more important writers, should be long enough to furnish material for an hour's discussion if the anthology should be used as a textbook. It was also thought desirable that the introductory essays to the five volumes should be mainly concerned with the discrimination of prose styles, and that they should all contain frequent references to the authors and extracts introduced. Again, it was proposed that in each volume passages should be chosen where possible to shed light on each other, and it was agreed that the value of the whole work would partly depend on the number of the relationships of this kind it was possible to establish. A good deal of effort lies behind whatever success has been achieved. For example, a dozen passages in Volume II bear on any discussion of political and theological attitudes in the Great Rebellion, Volumes III and IV have some nicely mixed specimens of political writing and also groups of passages which touch on marriage and the position of women, Volume I gives us Nashe and Gabriel Harvey on Nashe, Volume V Dickens and Walter Bagehot on Dickens. There are also links between the volumes – it is not an accident that a passage by Carlyle in Volume V should refer to an incident in Mungo Park's African travels which is reproduced in Volume IV. Some of these correspondences lie on the surface, as in the examples chosen, but many are more esoteric and will not be apparent until the anthology is actively used. In each volume the order of the passages in the first section, 'The Picture of the Age', is chronological, but the order in the other three sections – for the sake of these correspondences – offers what F. T. Palgrave calls 'gradations of feeling or subject'. Such gradations may or may not combine with a modified chronological plan.

More important than any of these means of ensuring singleness of approach has been the community of feeling among the editors about what an anthology of prose should be called on to illustrate. *The Pelican Book of English Prose* is not a collection of the best passages of English prose, or even, exclusively, of the best passages of the authors included in it – a collection on either principle would produce an effect less representative than the one aimed at. A common objection to prose anthologies is that their editors do not choose passages typical of the authors represented because they put an undue weight on 'fine writing'. From some anthologies one would naturally conclude that historians reserved all their energies for depicting battle-scenes, or that Lyly, Sir Thomas Browne and Landor were considerably more important as writers of prose than Hooker, Dryden and Gibbon. In contradistinction our working-hypothesis has been that prose should not be too self-conscious, that the writers of the best English prose usually had more on their minds than the problems of style, and that much respectable prose in every age is unmindful of the school-master's ferula.[1] Consequently, in compiling this anthology, we have been guided by the following principles:

1. To choose passages primarily for the interest of their subject-matter (on the assumption, which has been justified, that such passages will inevitably illustrate all the prominent varieties of prose style).

2. To choose from a particular author not his most detachable pieces of fine writing, but passages which are typical of his normal manner when he is writing well.

3. To illustrate sparingly the 'purple passages' of English prose.

4. To include some prose at a pedestrian level of achievement for its documentary value (more particularly in the first section of each volume).

The editors consider that these methods of selection give a

---

1. The degree of self-conscious organization that is 'natural' varies, of course, from age to age, and, in any age, according to literary kind (for example, a declamatory style is more natural in a pulpit or from the hustings than in a diary or private letter).

more accurate cross-section of English prose than is obtained from most anthologies,[1] and that the loss in serious prose-artistry is negligible. Nothing that has been said should be taken to imply a settled antipathy to ornate prose, but it is fair to admit that the editors are suspicious of its self-conscious varieties after the Restoration (while recognizing with Newman that some 'verbiage' may be the natural expression of a generous 'fullness of mind').

The Text. Modernization has been rejected and passages are reproduced with the spelling and punctuation of the copy-texts (except for the silent correction of misprints and the conservative emendation of misleading punctuation). Thus Elizabethan prose retains its 'dramatic' or haphazard pointing except in special instances, and Keats's difficulties with spelling are left to appear. The only passages given in a modernized form are those first printed long after their original composition, e.g. an Elizabethan diary first published in the middle of the nineteenth century. Some unfamiliar words and phrases, which are naturally more frequent in Volumes I and II, are glossed briefly in footnotes where the context seems to require it – this is a matter that has been left to the individual editor's discretion – but no attempt has been made to supply a sense for all unusual words or to explain the many allusions.

The source of each passage is given at its foot, and the abbreviation of titles has been indicated (wherever possible the extended title has been preserved if of interest). First editions have usually been employed, but many passages included in the anthology were added by their authors to editions later

1. *The London Book of Prose* (1932), compiled by Professor Dobrée and Sir Herbert Read, is an obvious exception. Its excellence sets a standard for this kind of work.

than the first, or were revised through several editions, so that the preferred form of a passage may be found, for example, in a fifth edition. On the other hand, the unrevised version of a passage has sometimes been preferred by an editor for its freshness and unfamiliarity. The apparent anomalies in the choice of copy-texts are mostly explicable on such grounds, but there were a few occasions when a first edition would have been used if it had been available. The use of certain copyright material is acknowledged in a note at the end of each volume.

K. A.

INTRODUCTION

THE seventeenth century was a period in the use of language in prose when a demand for the plain and a taste for the subtle went together. These trends related directly to what men were seeking to do and know. The Elizabethan poet Sir John Davies had complained:

> All things without, which round about we see,
>   We seek to know, and how therewith to do;
> But that whereby we reason live and be,
>   Within ourselves, we strangers are thereto.

But Davies's successors exacted knowledge from things both within and without. In the essay and the biography – forms which had hardly existed before the new century began – there were developed, through introspection and psychological analysis, the scrutiny of personal motives and subtler ways of recording them. There was a new intensity in religious experience, perhaps most clearly seen in the technique of self-examination practised by the Puritans, their delicate balance of the outward and inward means of conversion, and their study of the regenerative process in the 'Lower Rooms of the Heart and the Inwards of the Belly'. 'Go not outside thyself,' commanded St Augustine, 'but return within thyself; for truth resides in the inmost part of man.' Others besides the Puritans obeyed him, and sought to establish a complex relationship with the God who, according to the Anglican John Hales, 'sets up an imperial throne in our understandings'. There is a new expressiveness in the sermon and spiritual autobiography of the age, vigorous and plain in Bunyan or Tillotson, ornate and exuberant in Taylor or Donne. Plenty of attention was paid to 'the things without' as well. As men observed, with the aid of their new microscopes and telescopes, the world of nature, their records were shaped into subtlety by the energy and uncertainty of the labouring mind, or into plainness by the wish to prevent mere words obscuring the 'things'. Lastly, the age was one of universal controversy, in which there flourished in abundance wit, satire, plain speaking or double dealing, the invective of pamphleteers or the coarse or allusive banter of gentlemen. We miss only two major forms in the immense variety of new and old ones: this is not, like the one that preceded it, an age of travellers, nor, like the one that followed it, of great novelists. The chief travellers of the period – if so they can be called – were the American settlers, who pass out of our ken; and the imagination of the period which produced *The Temple*, *Venice Preserved*, and *Paradise Lost*, was, outside the drama, not much exercised in prose fiction. So interwoven and various, however, are the kinds and manners of prose that it is hard to discern a chronological sequence in the evolution of its style. Broadly speaking, it may be agreed that between 1620 and 1660 the changes took the form of the jettisoning of much of the Elizabethan vocabulary and the diminution of excessive ornament and emphatic rhythm; and that in the post-Restoration period the style most in favour is lucid, easy, and – by contrivance, of course – desultory in appearance. The greatest prose-writer of the time – by which I mean perhaps only the one whom I read with the least expectation of enjoying in his prose the effects looked for in his heroic plays – is Dryden. Here is Johnson's description of the style of his prefaces:

They have not the formality of a settled style, in which the first half of the sentence betrays the other. The clauses are never balanced, nor the periods modelled: every word seems to drop by chance, though it falls into its proper place. Nothing is cold or languid; the whole is airy, animated, and vigorous; what is little, is gay; what is great is splendid . . . Though all is easy, nothing is feeble; though all seems careless, there is nothing harsh; and though since his earlier works, more than a century has passed, they have nothing yet uncouth or obsolete.

'By him', Johnson added, 'we were taught *sapere et fari*, to think naturally and express forcibly.' By any standard, Dryden's critical prefaces are a great achievement; the last of them, one of the freshest and most graceful, appeared in 1700, the year in which Dryden's death puts an end to the phase. I shall attempt here to sketch some of the forces which shaped the use of language in prose during the preceding eighty years and which may have helped to make such an achievement possible.

I

About 1600 controversy concerning prose-style appeared in a form which enabled writers to recognize its affinity to a similar controversy that had taken place in imperial Rome: a reaction against the rotund, balanced, and oratorical period, associated with Cicero, in favour of a more concise and flexible style, and one nearer to common speech; this was the manner associated with the *Epistles* of Seneca and the historical works of Tacitus. Erasmus had argued against the Ciceronian style, but it was not till 1575 and 1580 that the French humanist Muret successfully challenged the prevailing Ciceronianism by pointing to Seneca and Tacitus as better models. He was followed by the Dutchman Justus Lipsius, who edited these two authors, and, in the vernacular, by Montaigne. It was Montaigne who used the essay to study his strength and his weakness, making his own nature the root of his *moralia* and developing what has been called the psychological method. The formal extremes between which the controversy was conducted were, on the one hand, the various types of the new essay, which valued the figures of wit or thought, and used metaphor, aphorism, antithesis, and paradox, and, on the other, the speech proportioned according to rules of rhetoric derived from Cicero and Quintilian. Sidney used this latter form in his *Apologie for Poetrie* (c. 1580); if he had written twenty years later, he might have preferred to follow Montaigne. The oratorical style was marked by its use of similarities and repetitions of sound which were supposed to please and hold the attention. Montaigne in his essay on 'The Vanity of Words' attacked these 'big and rattling words' and thought that the 'sweet alluring and sense-entrancing sound of this harmonie' was fit only to deceive the common people. In England, Cornwallis, second only to Bacon as an essayist, made the issues clear in 1601 when he censured the Ciceronian rhetoric for its 'Tumbler's capers' and its habit of making three words do the work of one; and four years later Bacon himself continued the attack when he reviewed the style that seemed to him dominant during the preceding century:

... men began to hunt more after words than matter; and more after the choiceness of phrase, and the round and clean composition of the sentence, and the sweet falling of the clauses, and the varying and illustration of their work with tropes and figures, than after the weight of matter, worth of subject, soundness of argument, life of invention or depth of judgement.

Bishop Hall (1574–1656), called 'Our English Seneca', a conscious stylist whose long span of work unites Elizabeth's reign with Cromwell's, also set an important example, praising the Senecan style in 1608 for its brevity, which was 'very pleasing, even to the daintiest judgements . . . brevity makes counsell more portable for memorie & readier for use.'

The 'Senecan' style was the dominant style of the intellectual writers of the first half of the century. Many participated in a deliberate effort towards the anti-Ciceronian manner, preferring brevity, conciseness, energy, liveliness and strength in prose, and witty point-making to pleasing sound. There were many varieties of this style, according to where the theory or taste of its users rested the emphasis. It ranged from the excessively clipped and pointed manner of Felltham to the looser and more desultory style of Burton. Burton, in the Preface to the sixth edition of *The Anatomy of Melancholy* (1651), associates Seneca with an apology for his plainness: 'I call a spade a spade', he declares, 'I respect matter not words . . . I neglect phrases, and labour wholly to inform my reader's understanding, not to please his ear.' Felltham[1] exemplifies brevity and argues against 'long and distended clauses'. Thomas Randolph praised Felltham's style in verses which set out the anti-Ciceronian manner as many saw it:

> . . . the style being pure, and strong, and round;
> Not long, but pithy; being short-breath'd, but sound,
> Such as the grave, acute, wise Seneca sings –
> That best of tutors to the worst of kings.
> Not long and empty; lofty, but not proud;
> Subtle, but sweet; high, but without a cloud.
> Well-settled, full of nerves – in brief 'tis such,
> That in a little hath comprised much.

Neither Burton nor Felltham stand up very well nowadays to the test of continuous reading. Browne or Halifax, perhaps, survive this test better; far apart in time and spirit, they both illustrate the anti-Ciceronian manner. Here is an example from Browne, followed by one from Halifax:

The first day of our Jubilee is Death; the Devil hath therefore failed of his desires: we are happier with death than we should have been without it: there is no misery but in himself, where there is no end of misery; and so indeed, in his own sense, the Stoick is in the right. He forgets that he can die who complains of misery; we are in the power of no calamity while death is in our own.

1. See extract on p. 249.

The King [Charles II] did always by his Councils, as he did some-times by his Meals; he sat down out of form with the *Queen*, but he supped *below Stairs*. To have the Secrets of a King, who happens to have too many, is to have a King in Chains: He must not only, not part with her, but he must in his own Defence dissemble his dislike: The less kindness he hath, the more he must shew: There is a great difference between being *muffled*, and being *tied:* He was the first, not the last.

Here we have what Cowley called the 'dry chips of short lung'd Seneca', the curt style, advancing by jerks, with the sparing use of connecting *ands* and *buts*. Browne seems to be repeating the same idea in different words, as though he were striving to realize it ever more fully; Halifax advances by smart antitheses, a point made with each one. Both writers give the impression of the 'brain in counsell', as Cornwallis put it: they seem to be drawing upon a hidden store of aphorisms, polished and tested by experience. These examples represent extremes of the style, which prevailed in a looser form, especially in Browne:

In authentick draughts of Anthony and Jerome, we meet with thigh-bones and death's-heads; but the cemiterial Cels of ancient Christians and Martyrs, were filled with draughts of Scripture Stories; not declining the flourishes of Cypresse, Palms and Olive, and the mystical Figures of Peacocks, Doves, and Cocks. But iterately affecting the pourtraits of Enoch, Lazarus, Jonas, and the vision of Ezechiel, as hopeful draughts, and hinting imagery of the Resurrection; which is the life of the grave, and sweetens our habita-tions in the Land of Moles and Pismires.

Here, with more connectives in place, the effect is much less curt. The manner of such a passage has been compared by Professor Croll to a linked chain. Each period is loosely connected with its predecessor, and all are drawn onwards to a close which reaches vigorously after feeling. We proceed from casually placed details to the mood which contemplation of them induces. This mood Browne seems to uncover as he goes on, nor does he present us with tight little parcels of wisdom as in the short style. His eye is, indeed, often half-turned within; what helps to distinguish his manner, apart from his more elaborate vocabulary, from that of Cowley or Dryden, is its soliloquizing note. The later writers appear more aware of the presence of the reader, of how he may, as it were, intervene with his own objections or comments. Dryden, Boyle, and others, sometimes adopted the dialogue form as though to invite the reader, whom they assumed to be a person of intelligence and breeding, to join in the conversation too.

This turning outwards to the spectator is most clearly seen in the prose drama of the Restoration. Since what they wrote had to be spoken by actors on the stage, the dramatists, seeking to combine social grace with sprightly wit, were faced with special problems of rhythm, intonation and vocabulary; these they solved by drawing at least as much on the Jonsonian tradition of prose comedy, and on French example, as on the prevailing intellectual style. Through their modification of all these strains, they sometimes achieved melody, flexibility, and a fugitive note of tender lyricism, hovering on the edge of verse yet seeming to arise naturally out of the prose context. By contrast, their writing is elsewhere marked, as Professor L. C. Knights has said, in words borrowed from Arnold's strictures on Macaulay, by 'a hard metallic movement and a perpetual semblance of hitting the right nail on the head'. The vogue for antithetical point-making may bear some of the blame for this fault, but it may also perhaps take some of the credit for the fusion of gentle grace with aphoristic brevity which is the particular excellence of the best scenes in Etherege or Congreve.

This predominant Senecan style was rejected by such important writers as Milton before the Restoration and Clarendon after. When Clarendon, for example, composed the character studies for which his *History of the Rebellion* (1646–71) is specially renowned, he was little influenced by the Senecan 'character', with its short sentences beginning with *he* or *they* and its smart turns of wit, as these had been practised with great brilliance by Earle, kept alive by Butler,[1] and used in Clarendon's own day by Halifax in his *Advice to a Daughter*. Milton attacked 'Our English Seneca' himself when in 1642 he criticized his anonymous opponent, who may have been Hall's son, for his 'coy flirting style', the 'frumps and curtal gibes' of 'one who makes sentences by the statute, as if all above three inches long were confiscate':

[he] sobs me out half-a-dozen phthisical mottoes, wherever he had them, hopping short in the measure of convulsion-fits; in which labour the agony of his wit having escaped narrowly, he greets us with a quantity of thumb-ring posies. 'He has a fortune therefore good, because he is content with it.' This is a piece of sapience not worth the brain of a fruit-trencher.

Certainly the Senecan style developed its own kind of pert or quaint mannerisms and threatened at times to be as great a hindrance to the Baconian preference for matter above words as the Ciceronian style which Bacon had endeavoured to supplant in 1605. As early as 1623 he felt constrained to add a warning against Senecanism itself in so far as it ran the risk of becoming another distemper of learning and barren hunting after the fine placing of words.

II

Bacon's name reminds us how long a shadow he cast over the century. His influence is seen not only in this argument about two extremes of style but also in the view, which was becoming more and more articulate, that the duty of men when they wrote was not so much to choose between one style and ano-

1. See extracts on pp. 219 and 221.

ther as to prevent any style from hindering their obligation to impart instruction and describe the nature of things. The scientists, the divines, and the philosophers, who used prose as a means to ends which could be clearly distinguished from that of cultivating a style, were often suspicious of the traps planted by words; sometimes they lacked confidence that words could ever be disciplined for their special purposes. Bacon had compared words to 'a Tartar's bow, [which] do shoot back upon the understanding of the wisest, and mightily entangle, and pervert the judgement'; Hobbes in 1651 attributed the confusions of philosophers to their failure to learn from the mathematicians that they must define their terms; Locke, eighty-five years after Bacon, wrote:

If we would speak of things as they are, we must allow, that all the Art of Rhetorick, besides Order and Clearness, all the artificial and figurative application of words Eloquence hath invented, are for nothing else, but to insinuate wrong *Ideas*, move the Passions, and thereby mislead the Judgement; and so indeed are perfect cheat: And therefore however laudable or allowable Oratory may render them in Harangues and popular Addresses, they are certainly, in all Discourses that pretend to inform or instruct, wholly to be avoided.

Science and some aspects of religion were increasingly seen as efforts to 'speak of things as they are', and were often associated with the demand for a plain matter-of-fact style. It is hard to tell how far the plainer style of writers who were not primarily scientists or divines, such as Dryden, may be directly attributed to the pressure of these ideas. Throughout the period there existed a good deal of plain straightforward writing, neither conscious of artifice nor consciously divested of it: we may instance Pepys's account of his excursion to Epsom,[1] or contrast the way plain Thomas Raymond described his adventures in Holland in 1633[2] with the manner used by Elizabethan

1. See p. 53.
2. See p. 12.

voyagers not many decades earlier. That, of the two, Raymond's manner would have seemed preferable to Dryden may be due to the triumph of some spirit of the age of which science itself was but an expression. The anti-Ciceronians' preference for the spark of inward enlightenment instead of a harmony of sounds may have encouraged that spirit; it was fostered also by an impatient distaste for the wordish, and finally bloody, entanglements of the Civil Wars. There was, further, a distinction, ever more commonly made, between the language of poetry and that of prose, as well as a distrust, shown, for example, in Cowley's plea for a genuinely Christian poetry, for the kinds of ornament which had served them both. And there were social changes, as always. The writers most representative of these are the massed pamphleteers and journalists, from the radical Levellers such as Lilburne to the Tory L'Estrange; they addressed audiences who were not much concerned with prose style. In any complete account of the period's prose such factors would need to be carefully discriminated. But it so happens that science and religion were both central to the concerns of many thinking and writing men of the time. When, therefore, we find that both can be correlated with the widespread advocacy of a plain, disciplined and purposeful use of language in prose, it is hard to believe that the activity in these fields would not have spread outwards and affected the way words were used everywhere.

A number of writers, Hobbes and Boyle among the more illustrious, are heard expressing their dislike of ornate writing in the years before the incorporation of the Royal Society in 1662. Their attitude can be regarded as an example of the recurrent tendency, which was one aspect of the anti-Ciceronian movement and is common in any age, to call for renewed battle against 'luxury and redundance of speech'; or it can be directly related to the scientific interests of the writers concerned. The Royal Society, Baconian in temper and aims,[1] was anticipated by several proposals for similar foundations, but it is in connexion with the programme of the Society itself, when it finally came into being, that we get the plainest efforts towards a clearer style. 'In all the Reports of Experiments to be brought into the Society', runs an eighteenth-century statute, 'the Matter of Fact shall be barely stated, without any Prefaces, Apologies, or Rhetorical flourishes.' Anyone who consults the early volumes of the Society's *Proceedings* will note a general obedience to this dictate even before it was formulated. As Evelyn ruefully remarked in 1667 the members were 'sometimes the subject of satire[2] and the songs of drunkards', and in the same year Sprat's authorized defence of them sets out most clearly their stylistic programme:

Who can behold, without Indignation, how many Mists and Uncertainties, these specious *Tropes* and *Figures* have brought on our Knowledge? How many Rewards, which are due to more profitable and difficult *Arts*, have been still snatch'd away by the easy Vanity of *fine Speaking!* . . . I dare say, that of all the Studies of Men, nothing may be sooner obtain'd, than this vicious Abundance of *Phrase*, this Trick of *Metaphors*, this Volubility of *Tongue* . . . [the members of the Society] have therefore been more rigorous in putting in Execution the only Remedy, that can be found for this *Extravagance;* and that has been a constant Resolution, to reject all the Amplifications, Digressions, and Swellings of Style; to return back to the primitive Purity and Shortness, when Men deliver'd so many *Things*, almost in an equal Number of *Words*. They have exacted from all their Members, a close, naked, natural way of Speaking; positive Expressions, clear Senses; a native Easiness; bringing all Things as near the mathematical Plainness as they can; and preferring the Language of Artizans, Countrymen, and Merchants, before that of Wits, or Scholars.

This stylistic ideal was one which affected not only professed scientists but also the poets and preachers, who themselves

1. See extract from Sprat, p. 175.
2. See p. 186.

were sometimes members of the new Society. There is one particularly clear example of this wider influence: the changes made by Glanvill, between 1661 and 1675, in the three versions of his work on the new trends in philosophy,[1] in which he gradually prunes away the exuberant Browne-like style of his first version. 'To Sence the Sun stands still also; and no eye can perceive its Actual motion' was what he substituted in 1675 for this of 1661: 'If you will take the literal evidence of our Eyes; the *Aethereal Coal* moves no more than this *Inferior Clod* doth.' A more doubtful case is provided by the prose of Cowley between 1659 and 1667; he writes sometimes in the manner of Taylor, but other essays are models of easy prose like Dryden's. The expanding influence of the Society's demand for a 'close, naked, natural way of speaking' can be discerned, if less clearly, in the work of the preachers Barrow (a mathematician and early member) and Tillotson (member, 1672). According to Congreve, Dryden, who joined the Society in 1662, 'frequently owne[d] with pleasure that if he had any talent for English prose, it was owing to his having often read the writings of the great Archbishop Tillotson.'

The Royal Society's dislike of much current writing went together with speculation about the nature of language itself. The Baconian feeling that words were a 'Tartar's bow' led to the reflection that it was a pity they had to be used at all. In 1664 a committee, which included Dryden, Evelyn, Waller, and Sprat, was set up to consider 'improving the English tongue'; and there were proposals that there should be an English Academy to supervise the language. These came to nothing, but the committee was probably guided and influenced by Dr John Wilkins, the author of an *Essay towards a Real Character and a Philosophical Language* (1668). This book was the climax of several attempts to devise a universal

1. Represented in the extract on p. 174 in its second version (1665).

language; it sponsored a notation of hooks, curves, dots, and loops which referred directly to 'things' without the intervention of words. This was as far as the age went in preferring 'matter' over 'hunting the letter', and the scheme, like others since, collapsed through its own absurdity. Gulliver later on found the Professors of Laputa still busy about a plan for 'entirely abolishing all Words whatsoever', which entailed carrying around large bundles of *Things* instead.

III

It was this same John Wilkins[1] who concerned himself with the defects of preaching style in his *Ecclesiastes* (1646), and it is to the sermon as a form affecting the evolution of prose that we must turn now. The variety of sermons and sermon styles preached and practised is immense, and divines of rival persuasions were always happy to criticize each others' prose. It is not safe – although we might expect it to be – to make an easy discrimination between the styles of the two great parties, or to suppose that the Puritans and nonconformists were united in the advocacy of a plain and severe style, because they disliked ecclesiastical ceremony, and that the Arminians and Anglicans, because they approved of it, always cultivated a corresponding elaboration and beauty in their homilies. It is rather the case that on both sides advocacy of a plain style often took the form of a justifiable criticism of the rhetorical ingenuities of the opposite party. A survey is made difficult, too, because this division into two parties, if we try to apply it to the whole period, is unsound: not only are both sides split up into groups with their own habits of discourse, but the shifts of sectarian allegiances over the period confuse the tale. Nevertheless it is true that the plainer styles did triumph after the Restoration here as elsewhere. If a passage by Donne

1. See Burnet on Wilkins, p. 135.

is set beside one by Tillotson we can compare a cool address to the judgement – it was Tillotson who emphasized the *wisdom* of believing in God – with an appeal to the imagination. The change was due to other forces apart from the technical matters canvassed in the controversies over sermon style; but it may be useful to indicate a few of the things that were said in the course of them, without laying much stress on the party allegiances entailed.

The Puritan wing of thought probably had a start on its rivals in directing attention to the need for greater straightforwardness. The Pauline element in Calvinism led to an emphasis, as early as the middle of Elizabeth's reign, on Paul's 'Seeing that we have such hope, we use great plainness of speech' (2 Cor. 3: 12); but, although the Puritans generally subordinated art and artifice to doctrine and zeal, they were not indifferent to apt and significant words and evolved a sermon form that had its own characteristic dialectic. In the Commonwealth and Restoration they were attacked for their gaudy metaphors and allegories. The extract from Eachard on p. 248 indicates the kind of thing that was objected to; the style there castigated was disliked because, although the vocabulary might be plain enough, its range and illustrations were mean and low, 'canting' and 'enthusiastick'. Congregations could be very sensitive to sermon style (as witness Dorothy Osborne on p. 39). Thus, despite the Puritans' rejection of the 'metaphysical' manner and their consciousness of the needs of an unlettered audience, they did develop a specialized jargon and method; it was far removed from 'native Easiness' and became a target for dramatic satire from Jonson to Shadwell. It also contributed, in certain pages of Bunyan, to something so wonderful that all other writing of the age seems to fail by comparison.

The higher and more witty 'metaphysical' style of such Anglicans as Donne, Taylor, and Frank, which, following the example of the Jacobean Andrewes, prevailed in their church up to and into the Commonwealth, was soon criticized also – for example, by Wilkins, who wrote in 1646: 'To stuff a sermon with citations of Authors, and the witty sayings of others, is to make a Feast of Vinegar and Pepper'. An illustrious poet (and Anglican priest) may give testimony here. George Herbert, when he wrote, towards 1633, of what was required of a country parson before a rural congregation, objected to the method, practised by Donne, of splitting up the chosen text into tiny sections and developing each one independently:

The Parsons Method in handling of a text consists of two parts; first, a plain and evident declaration of the meaning of the text; and secondly, some choyce Observations drawn out of the whole text, as it lyes entire, and unbroken in the Scripture it self. This he thinks naturall, and sweet, and grave. Whereas the other way of crumbling a text into small parts, as, the Person speaking, or spoken to, the subject, and object, and the like, hath neither in it sweetnesse, nor gravity, nor variety, since the words apart are not Scripture, but a dictionary, and may be considered alike in all the Scripture.

Other things found fault with in the 'metaphysical' style were its 'metaphor-mongering', its witty antitheses, its love of Greek and Latin quotations, and its punning and quibbling. Eachard found it necessary to attack such mannerisms, along with the Puritan 'canting', as late as 1670, although Tillotson had printed his first sermon nearly ten years before. The 'great Archbishop' and other preachers – some of them probably influenced by the stylistic example of the Royal Society to which they belonged – agreed with the general principle of a moderate dissenter such as Baxter:

The Plainest words are the profitablest Oratory in the weightiest matters . . . the more I have to do with the ignorant sort of people the more I find that we cannot speak too plainly to them.

Religious, like scientific, truths were too important for the 'vanity of words' to be permitted to obscure them.

Thus it is, as Yeats put it, that 'the gyre ebbs out in order and reason'. In 1684 Bishop Burnet (1643–1715), whose long life bridges the gap between two centuries, surveyed the linguistic scene with a confident eye:

The English Language has wrought it self out, both of the fulsome Pedantry under which it laboured long ago, and the trifling way of dark and unintelligible Wit that came after that, and out of the coarse extravagance of Canting that succeeded this . . . We are now so much refined, that how defective soever our Imaginations or Reasonings may be, yet our Language has fewer Faults, and is more natural and proper, than it was ever at any time before. When one compares the best Writers of the last Age, with these that excel in this, the difference is very discernable: even the great Sir *Francis Bacon*, that was the first that writ our Language correctly; as he is still our best Author, yet in some places has Figures so strong, that they could not pass now before a severe Judg.

Dryden, writing to 'my dear friend Mr Congreve' in 1693, was not so satisfied: the new age of good manners and sound judgement might have tamed and refined the boisterous wit of 'long ago', but something seemed wanting:

> Our age was cultivated thus at length,
> But what we gain'd in skill we lost in strength.
> Our builders were with want of genius curst;
> The second temple was not like the first.

And to-day we are able to measure Burnet's confidence by a much longer historical perspective. The following pages show what was lost as well as what was gained.

PETER URE

THE PICTURE OF THE AGE:
SCENE, PERSONALITY, EVENT

DONNE'S ORDINATION AND PREACHING
(1615)

Now the *English Church* had gain'd a second St. *Austine*, for, I think, none was so like him before his Conversion: none so like St. *Ambrose* after it: and if his youth had the infirmities of the one, his age had the excellencies of the other; the learning and holiness of both.

And now all his studies which had been occasionally diffused, were all concentred in Divinity. Now he had a new calling, new thoughts, and a new imployment for his wit and eloquence: Now, all his earthly affections were changed into divine love; and all the faculties of his own soul, were ingaged in the Conversion of others: In preaching the glad tidings of Remission to repenting Sinners, and peace to each troubled soul. To these he applied himself with all care and diligence: and now, such a change was wrought in him, that he could say with *David, Oh how amiable are thy Tabernacles, O Lord God of Hosts!* Now he declared openly, *that when he required a temporal, God gave him a spiritual blessing.* And that, *he was now gladder to be a door-keeper in the house of God, then he could be to injoy the noblest of all temporal imployments.*

Presently after he had entred into his holy profession, the King sent for him, and made him his Chaplain in Ordinary; and promised to take a particular care for his preferment.

then] than (and so frequently throughout this volume)

And though his long familiarity with Scholars, and persons of greatest quality, was such as might have given some men boldness enough to have preached to any eminent Auditory; yet, his modesty in this imployment was such, that he could not be perswaded to it, but went usually accompanied with some one friend, to preach privately in some village, not far from *London*: his first Sermon being preached at *Paddington*. This he did, till His Majesty sent and appointed him a day to preach to him at *White-hall*, and, though much were expected from him, both by His Majesty and others, yet he was so happy (which few are) as to satisfie and exceed their expectations: Preaching the Word so, as shewed his own heart was possest with those very thoughts and joys that he laboured to distill into others: A Preacher in earnest; weeping sometimes for his Auditory, sometimes with them: alwayes preaching to himself, like an Angel from a cloud, but in none; carrying some, as St. *Paul* was, to Heaven in holy raptures, and inticing others by a sacred Art and Courtship to amend their lives; here picturing a vice so as to make it ugly to those that practised it; and a vertue so, as to make it be beloved even by those that lov'd it not; and all this with a most particular grace and an unexpressible addition of comeliness.

Izaak Walton

'Life of Donne' (1640) from *Lives* (1670). Text
from the revised second edition (1675)

THE HUNTING ARCHBISHOP

(1621)

ABOUT this time, a sad mischance befell *George Abbot* Archbishop of *Canterbury*, in this manner. He was invited by the Lord *Zouch* to *Bramshill* in *Hampshire* to hunt and kill a Buck; The Keeper ran amongst the Herd of Deer to bring them up to the fairer mark, whilest the Archbishop sitting on his Horse back, let loose a barbed-Arrow from a Crosbow, and unhappily hit the Keeper: He was shot through the Enmontery of the left Arm, and the Arrow dividing those grand auxiliary vessels, he died of the flux of blood immediately. Nature having provided, that all the large Vessels are defended externally by bones: He never spake after, as the person still alive at *Croydon*, who brought off his body, informed me, and died not of the ill dressing of the Wound, as some have printed it. This presently put an end to the sport of that day, and almost to the Archbishops mirth to the last of his life.

The fame of this mans death, flew faster than the Arrow that killed him: The Archbishops mischance, in many men met not with so much pity, as so sad a casualty did deserve: He was not much beloved by the inferiour Clergie, as over-rigid and austere: Indeed, he was mounted to command in the Church, before he ever learned to obey therein; Made a Shepherd of Shepherds, before he was a Shepherd of Sheep; Consecrated Bishop, before ever called to a Pastoral Charge; *which made*, say some, *him not to sympathize with the necessities and infirmities of poor Ministers*. As for the superiour Clergie, some for his irregularity and removal expected preferment, as the second Boule is made first, and the third, second, when that neerest the mark, is violently removed.

It is strange to see, how suddainly many men started up Canonists and Casuists in their discourse, who formerly had small skill in that profession. In their ordinary talk they cited Councels and Synods: some had up S. *Jerome's* speech, *Venatorem nunquam legimus sanctum*: others were busie with the Decree of the Councel of Orleance. . . *Episcopo, Presbytero, aut Diacono canes ad venandum, aut accipitres habere non licet*. Others distinguished of a three-fold hunting: 1. *Oppressiva*. 2. *Arenaria*. 3. *Saltuosa*. These maintained, that the two former

Enmontery] armpit

3

were utterly unlawfull, but the last might lawfully be used. Others distinguished of Homicide: 1. *Ex necessitate*. 2. *Ex voluntate*. 3. *Ex casu*. the case in hand. In a word, this accident divided all great companies into *pro* and *con*, for or against the Archbishops irregularity on this occasion, yet all the force of their skill could not mount the guilt of this fact higher than the fountain thereof. When all was done it was but *Casual Homicide*, who sought not for the man, but God was pleased to bring the Man to his hand.

Sir Henry Savill, the Archbishops old acquaintance as his contemporary in *Oxon*, repaired on his behalf to the Oracle of the Law, Sir *Edward Coke*, whom he found a bowling for his recreation. *My Lord*, said he, *I come to be satisfied of you in a point of Law*. *If it be a point of Common Law*, (said Sir *Edward Coke*) *I am unworthy to be a Judge, if I cannot presently satisfie you; but if it be a point of Statute Law, I am unworthy to be Judge, if I should undertake to satisfie you before I have consulted my Books*. *It is this*, (said Sir *Henry*) *Whether may a Bishop, Hunt in a Park by the Laws of the Realm? I can presently resolve you*, said the Judge, *He may hunt by the Lawes of the Realm by this very token, That there is an old Law* (let the young Students in that profession finde it out) *that a Bishop, when dying, is to leave his pack of Dogs* (called *Muta canum*) *to the Kings free use and disposal*.

The party, whom the Archbishop suspected his greatest Foe, proved his most firm and effectual Friend, even *Lancelot Andrewes* Bishop of *Winchester*: For when severall Bishops inveighed against the irregularity of the Archbishop, laying as much (if not more) guilt, on the act, than it would bear, He mildly checked them: *Brethren* (said he) *be not too busie to condemn any for Uncanonicalls according to the strictnesse thereof, lest we render our selves in the same condition* . . .

King James being Himself delighted in Hunting, was sorry any ill accident should betide the users thereof. But when He was assured, how deeply the Archbishop layed this casualty to his heart, He much pitied him, and said to A Lord, discoursing thereof, *It might have been My chance or thine.* So that not long after the A chbishop (who had lately retired himself to *Guildford Almes-house* of his own founding) returned to *Lambeth*, and to the performance of his Office, though some squeamish, and nice-conscienced *Elects* scrupled to be consecrated by him. He gave during his own life *Twenty pounds* a year to the *Man's Widow*, which was not long a Widow, as quickly remaried. He kept a Monethly-Fast on a *Tuesday*, as the day whereon this casualty befell; in a word, this Keeper's *death* was the Archbishop's *mortification.*

Thomas Fuller

*The Church-History of Britain from
the Birth of Jesus Christ* (1655)

SYMPTOMS OF LOVE: DANCING

(1621)

AMONGST other good qualities an amorous fellow is endowed with, he must learn to sing and dance, play upon some instrument or other, as without all doubt he will, if he be truly touched with this Loadstone of Love. For as *Erasmus* hath it, *Musicam docet amor & Poesin*, love will make them Musitians, and to compose Ditties, Madrigals, Elegies, Love Sonnets, and sing them to several pretty tunes, to get all good qualities may be had. *Iupiter* perceived *Mercury* to be in love with *Philologia*, because he learned languages, polite speech, (for *Suadela* her self was *Venus* daughter, as some write) Arts and Sciences, *quò virgini placeret*, all to ingratiate himself, and please his Mistriss. 'Tis their chiefest study to sing, dance; and without question, so many Gentlemen and Gentlewomen would not bee so well qualified in this kinde, if love did not incite them. *Who*, saith *Castilio*, *would learn to play, or give his mind to Musick, learn to dance, or make so many rimes, Love-Songs, as most do, but for womens sake, because they hope by that means to purchase their good wills, and win their favour?* We see this daily verified in our yong women and wives, they that being maids took so much pains to sing, play, and dance, with such cost and charge to their parents, to get those graceful qualities, now being married, will scarse touch an instrument, they care not for it. *Constantine agricult. lib.* 11. *cap.* 18, makes *Cupid* himself to be a great dancer, by the same token as he was capering amongst the Gods, *he flung down a bowl of nectar, which distilling upon the white Rose, ever since made it red:* And *Calistratus* by the help of *Dædalus* about *Cupids* statue made a many of yong wenches still a dancing, to signifie belike, that *Cupid* was much affected with it, as without all doubt he was. For at his and *Psyches* wedding, the Gods being present to grace the Feast, *Ganymede* fill'd *Nectar* in abundance (as *Apuleius* describes it) *Vulcan* was the Cook, the *Howres* were made all fine with Roses and Flowers, *Apollo* plaid on the harp, the *Muses* sang to it, *sed suavi Musicæ superingressa Venus saltavit*, but his mother *Venus* danced to his and their sweet content. Witty *Lucian* in that Pathetical Love passage, or pleasant description of *Iupiters* stealing of *Europa*, and swimming from *Phœnicia* to *Crete*, makes the Sea calm, the winds hush, *Neptune* and *Amphitrite* riding in their Chariot to break the waves before them, the Tritons dancing round about, with every one a Torch, the Sea-nymphs half naked, keeping time on Dolphins backs, and singing *Hymeneus*, *Cupid* nimbly tripping on the top of the waters, and *Venus* her self coming after in a shell, strawing Roses and Flowers on their heads. *Praxitiles* in all his pictures of Love, feigns *Cupid* ever smiling, and looking upon dancers; and in Saint *Markes* Garden in *Rome* (whose work I know not) one of the most delicious pieces, is a many of *Satyrs* dancing about a wench asleep. So that dancing still is, as it were, a necessary appendix to love matters. Young Lasses are never better pleased, than when as upon an Holiday after Evensong, they may meet their sweet-hearts, and dance about a *May*-pole, or in a Town-green under a shady Elm. Nothing so familiar in *France*, as for Citizens wives and maids to dance a round in the streets, and often too for want of better instruments, to make good Musick of their own voyces, and dance after it. Yea, many times this love will make old men and women, that have more toes than teeth, dance, – *John come kiss me now*, mask and mum; for *Comus* and *Hymen* love masks, and all such merriments above measure, will allow men to put on womens apparel in some cases, and promiscuously to dance, yong and old, rich and poor, generous and base, of all sorts. *Paulus Jovius* taxeth *Augustine Niphus* the Philosopher, *For that being an old man, and a publike Professor, a father of many children, he was so mad for the love of a yong maid (that which many of his friends were ashamed to see) an old gowty fellow, yet would dance after Fidlers.* Many laughed him to scorn for it, but this omnipotent love would have it so.

> *Hyacinthino bacillo*
> *Properans amor, me adegit*
> *Violentèr ad sequendum*
> Love hasty with his purple staffe did make
> Me follow, and the dance to undertake.

And 'tis no news this, no *indecorum;* for why? a good reason may be given of it. *Cupid* and *Death* met both in an Inne, and being merrily disposed, they did exchange some arrows from either quiver; ever since yong men dye, and oftentimes old men dote.

> *Sic moritur Iuvenis, sic moribundus amat.*

And who can then withstand it? If once we be in love, yong

or old, though our teeth shake in our heads like virginal Jacks, or stand parallel asunder like the arches of a bridge, there is no remedy, we must dance Trenchmore for a need, over tables, chairs, and stools, &c. And princum prancum is a fine dance.

Robert Burton
The Anatomy of Melancholy (1621). Text
from the revised sixth edition (1651)

GEORGE HERBERT'S MARRIAGE

(1629)

I SHALL now proceed to his Marriage; in order to which, it will be convenient, that I first give the Reader a short view, of his person, and then, an account of his Wife, and of some circumstances concerning both. – *He was for his person of a stature inclining towards Tallness; his Body was very strait, and so far from being cumbred with too much flesh, that he was lean to an extremity. His aspect was chearful, and his speech and motion did both declare him a Gentleman; for they were all so meek and obliging, that they purchased love and respect from all that knew him.* These, and his other visible vertues, begot him much love from a Gentleman, of a Noble fortune, and a near kinsman to his friend the Earl of *Danby*; namely, from Mr. *Charles Danvers* of *Bainton*, in the County of *Wilts* Esq; this Mr. *Danvers* having known him long, and familiarly, did so much affect him, that he often, and publickly declar'd a desire that Mr. *Herbert* would marry any of his Nine Daughters (for he had so many) but rather, his Daughter *Jane*, than any other, because *Jane was his beloved Daughter:* And he had often said the same to Mr. *Herbert* himself; and that if he could like her for a Wife, and she him for a Husband, *Jane* should have a *double blessing*: and Mr. *Danvers* had so often said the like to

Trenchmore] a lively country dance

Jane, and so much commended Mr. *Herbert* to her, that *Jane* became so much a Platonick, as to fall in love with Mr. *Herbert* unseen.

This was a fair preparation for a Marriage; but alas, her father died before Mr. *Herberts* retirement to *Dantsey*; yet some friends to both parties, procur'd their meeting; at which time a mutual affection entred into both their hearts, as a Conqueror enters into a surprized City, and, Love having got such possession govern'd, and made there such Laws and Resolutions, as neither party was able to resist; insomuch, that she chang'd her name into *Herbert,* the third day after the first interview.

This haste, might in others be thought a *Love-phrensie,* or worse: but it was not; for they had wooed so like Princes, as to have select Proxies: such, as were true friends to both parties; such as well understood Mr. *Herberts,* and her temper of mind; and also their Estates so well, before this Interview, that, the suddenness was justifiable, by the strictest Rules of Prudence: And the more, because it prov'd so happy to both parties; for, the eternal lover of Mankind, made them happy in each others mutual and equal affections, and compliance; indeed, so happy, that there never was any opposition betwixt them, unless it were a Contest which should most incline to a compliance with the others desires. And though this begot, and continued in them, such a mutual *love* and *joy,* and *content,* as was no way defective: yet, this mutual *content* and *love,* and *joy,* did receive a daily augmentation, by such daily obligingness to each other, as still added such new affluences to the former fulness of these divine Souls, as was only improvable in Heaven, where they now enjoy it.

Izaak Walton

'Life of Herbert' (1670) from *Lives* (1670). Text
from the revised second edition (1675)

Growing-up in Shropshire

(1620–30)

But though my Conscience would trouble me when I sinned, yet divers sins I was addicted to, and oft committed against my Conscience; which for the warning of others I will confess here to my shame.

1. I was much addicted, when I feared Correction, to lie, that I might scape.

2. I was much addicted to the excessive gluttonous eating of Apples and Pears; which I think laid the foundation of that *imbecillity* and Flatulency of my Stomach, which caused the Bodily Calamities of my Life.

3. To this end, and to concur with the naughty Boys that gloried in evil, I have oft gone into other men's Orchards, and stoln their Fruit, when I had enough at home.

4. I was somewhat excessively addicted to play, and that with covetousness, for Money.

5. I was extreamly bewitched with a Love of Romances, Fables and old Tales, which corrupted my Affections and lost my Time.

6. I was guilty of much idle foolish Chat, and imitation of Boys in scurrilous foolish Words and Actions (though I durst not swear).

7. I was too proud of my Masters Commendations for Learning, who all of them fed my pride, making me Seven or Eight years the highest in the School, and boasting of me to others, which, though it furthered my Learning, yet helped not my Humility.

8. I was too bold and unreverent towards my Parents.

These were my sins, which, in my Childhood Conscience troubled me for a great while before they were overcome.

In the Village where I lived the Reader read the Common-

Prayer briefly, and the rest of the Day even till dark Night almost, except Eating time, was spent in Dancing under a May-pole and a great Tree, not far from my Father's Door; where all the Town did meet together: And though one of my Father's own Tenants was the Piper, he could not restrain him, nor break the Sport: So that we could not read the Scripture in our Family without the great disturbance of the Taber and Pipe and Noise in the Street. Many times my Mind was inclined to be among them, and sometimes I broke loose from Conscience, and joyned with them; and the more I did it the more I was enclined to it. But when I heard them call my father *Puritan* it did much to cure me and alienate me from them: for I consider'd that my Father's Exercise of Reading the Scripture, was better than theirs, and would surely be better thought on by all men at the last; and I considered what it was for that he and others were thus derided. When I heard them speak scornfully of *others* as Puritans whom I never knew, I was at first apt to believe all the Lies and Slanders wherewith they loaded them: But when I heard my own Father so reproached, and perceived the Drunkards were the forwardest in the Reproach, I perceived that it was mere Malice: For my Father never scrupled Common-Prayer or Ceremonies, nor spake against Bishops, nor ever so much as prayed but by a Book or Form, being not ever acquainted then with any that did otherwise: But only for reading Scripture when the rest were Dancing on the Lord's Day, and for praying (by a Form out of the end of the Common-Prayer Book) in his House, and for reproving Drunkards and Swearers, and for talking sometimes a few words of Scripture and the Life to come, he was reviled commonly by the name of *Puritan*, *Precisian* and *Hypocrite*: and so were the Godly Conformable Ministers that lived any where in the Country near us, not only by our Neighbours, but by the common talk of the Vulgar Rabble of all about us. By this Experience

I was fully convinc'd that Godly People were the best, and those that despised them and lived in Sin and Pleasure, were a malignant unhappy sort of People: and this kept me out of their Company, except now and then when the Love of Sports and Play enticed me.

Richard Baxter

Reliquiæ Baxterianæ (1696)
From Part I, written 1664

SOLDIERING IN HOLLAND

(1633)

WEE had at this league a full plenty of all provisions out of the country and brought up the river by shipping of the States, and soe longe as money lasted wee had a merry life. As for my selfe I only wanted a good bed and sheetes. Parts of an old tent, which I had provided my selfe of one for my bed, being stuffed with straw, and ther, my pillow layd upon boughs supported with 4 cruches 2 foote from the ground, lying in my wascoate and drawers and stocking, covered with my cloathes, my cloake being the coverlett, sleeping excellently well, and in this leagur pretty free from lice.

At my first comeing before the towne my courage began somewhat to faile me, and, being younge and never being on on such an employment, wrought the more upon me. I remember I had an aurange tauny feather in my capp, and at first I thought that every great gun that was discharged towards our quarters had been aymed at it, the Spaniards not enduring that colour. But within few dayes I tooke my selfe to be a very gallant fellow, and had noe more dread of danger then if I had been in a fayre, only in the approaches I was not soe jocund though not attended with much feare. Once I was

leagure] camp

there when it was not my busines, and giving fier to a greate
gun or two at one of our batteries, there came a cannon bullett
from the enemy, tooke the topp of our worke and pashd us
soundly with the earth that flew about our eares. Many are
shott in peeping to see what the enemy doe betweene the
muskett basketts that stand on the topp of the breast worke
in the approaches, which are called keekers, for there little
rogues with feir-locks lying close to the grounde are ready to
dispatch such. Let but the topp of an old hatt appeare betweene
the basketts and you shall presently have 3 or 4 bulletts shott
into it. Our soldiers oftentymes bring pretty younge wenches
into the feild with them, which they have brought out of
their garrysons with them. I remember one of our souldiers
had such an one which lay with him in his hutt. One night
another soldier that had a mynde to be dealing with hir,
thincking hir husband had been on the gard (it being his
course) came confidently to the hutt, and entring claspe fast
hold aboute the mans neck, supposeing it to be the wench,
and began to kisse. But perceiveing his error made away as
fast as he could, and the fellow after him, giveing him very
nerely a prick or two on the breach with his sword, wherewith he escaped. Another wilde fellow who usually spent his
money 2 or 3 dayes before pay day had gott a greate marrow
bone and tyed it on the topp of his hutt over his head as he
lay in his bed. And in these fasting dayes he would often
rise up and smell on it saying twas very comfortable, with
calling earnestly for 'Pay day, O pay day, O sweete pay day,
come away, make hast' &c, and the night before he would
cry out, 'Oh I see pay day. Courage. Twil be here I am sure
to morrowe morneing.'

Thomas Raymond
Autobiography (1917). Written c. 1660

TABLE-TALK

(1634–54)

THE Court of England has much altered. Att a Solemne dancing, first you have the grave measures, then the Corantoes & the Galliards, & all this is kept upp wth ceremony, att length they fall to Trenchmore, & so to the Cushion Dance, Lord & Groome, Lady and Kitchin Maid, no distinction: So in our Court. In Queen Eliz: time, Gravitie & state was kept upp. In King James time things were pretty well But in K. Charles time there has binn nothing but Trenchmore & the Cushion dance, Omnium gatherum, tolly polly, hoyte come toyte.

*

The King calling his freinds from the Parliam^t because hee had use of them at Oxford, is as if a man had use of a little peece of wood, & hee runns downe into the Cellar & takes the spigott & in the meane time all the beere runns about the house. When his freinds are absent the King will be lost.

*

There was never a merry world since the ffairyes left danceing, & the parson left conjuring. The opinion of the Latter kept theeves in awe, & did as much good in a Country as a Justice of Peace.

*

I never converted but two, the one was Mr. Crashaw from writing ag[ains]t playes, by telling him a way to understand that place (of putting on woman's apparell) wch has nothing to doe with the business (as neither has it, that the fathers speake ag[ains]t playes in their time with reason enough, for they had reall Idolatry mix'd with their playes, haveing three Altars p[er]petually upon the Stage); the other was a Doctor of Divinity from preaching ag[ains]t painting, w^{ch}, simply in it selfe, is no more hurtfull then putting on my Clothes, or doeing any other thing to make my selfe like other folkes that I may not be odious or offensive to the Company. Indeed if I doe it with an ill Intenccōn, it alters the Case. Soe, if I putt on my gloves with an intenccōn to doe a mischeife, I am a villaine.

*

Tis ridiculous for a Lord to print verses, 'tis well enough to make them to please himself but to make them publick is foolish. If a man in a private Chamber twirles his Band string, or playes with a Rush to please himselfe 'tis well enough, but if he should goe into Fleet streete & sett upon a stall & twirle his bandstring or play with a Rush, then all the boyes in the streete would laugh att him.

*

When a protestant & a papist dispute, they talke like two madmen, because they doe not agree upon their principles. The only way is to destroy the popes power, for if hee has power to comand me, 'tis not my alledging reasons to the contrary cann keep me from obeying. For Example, if a Constable comand me to weare a greene suite to morrow & has power to make me, 'tis not my alledging a hundred reasons of the foolery of it cann excuse me from doeing it.

*

King James said to the ffly, have I three kingdomes & thou must needes fly into my Eyes? is there not enough to meddle withall upon the stage, or in law, or att the table, besides religion?

*

Wisemen say nothing in dangerous times. The Lyon you knowe call'd the sheep to aske her if his breath smelt; shee said Yes: hee bitt of her head for a foole. Hee call'd the Wolfe & asked him; hee said Noe; hee tore him in peeces for a flatterer. Att last hee called the ffox, and ask'd him: why, hee had gott a cold and could not smell.

John Selden
The Table-Talk of John Selden (1689). Text from
the Lincoln's Inn MS, as first printed 1927

In Canton

(1637)

A Pagode or China Church

WEE went to a Pagode of theirs, a reasonable handsome build-ing and well tyled. On the cheife place of the Altar sate an Image of a Woman of More then Ordinary bignesse, having on her head an ornament somewhat resembling an Imperiall Crowne. Nextt withoutt her, off from the Altar, stood 2 greatt statues of Mandareenes with Fannes in their hands, withoutt them 2 other Images of Mandareene, and outermost of all 2 evill Favoured ugly Feindlyke Figures. Of each of these there stood of each side one like a guard a good space [between] the 2 ranckes. Before the altar there burned a lampe and there stood Divers Frames, like greatt standing Cuppes of

4 or 5 Foote high, whereon they burne incense, pevetts, [etc.], perfumes, with many small Candles sticking in sundry places. There hung a bell within the said pagode of about 4 or 5 hundred-waght, off Cast Iron (or perhapps som other Mixture with itt), on which they strike on the outt side with a little woodden Clubbe; it resembled our Europe bells, but not soe broad brymmed.

Chaa, what it is.

The people there gave us a certaine Drinke called Chaa, which is only water with a kind of herbe boyled in itt. It must bee Drancke warme and is accompted wholesome . . .

A straunge way off invitation.

As wee returned toward our boate, some Chinois were going to their Pagode to Doe their superstition and to feast, it beeing the Morrow of the New Moone, and invited us along with them by Clapping their Fore Finger on the one side of their Nose, which as I was told is used sometymes as a familiar way of Invitation to eat, Drincke and bee Merry.

A Church built of oyster shells.

The walles of the said Pagode were built of extraordinary large and long Oyster shells, appcaring handsome to sight. In this poor Pagode were no Images, I say statues, only some few Defaced pictures hard to bee discerned.

The Manner of the Chinois ceremonies to their Images in their Pagodes.

Those thatt invited us were the Father and the sonne, who stood upright before the Altar, making Many bowings to the ground, with kneelings. The Father taketh 2 peeces of

pevetts] pastilles of incense   *Chaa*] tea

wood aboutt a spanne long and 2 Inches broad, bluffe or blunt att both ends, Flatt on the one side and rounding on the other, which hee threw uppe many tymes both together, and according as they Fell and lay (so I conceave), hee interpreted good or bad lucke to themselves. After, hee takes a Cuppe of wyne (as I Imagine), holding it first over his head and Muttring some certaine words, spills part therof on the ground; then takes hee another Cuppe, wherin was the head, liver and guizzard of a henne, Doing therewith as hee Did with the other, powring outt allsoe a little of the broath on the ground, Making as it were an offring of both unto their Saint before they tast it. Soe ended the Ceremony, a Fire beeing kindled and incense burning all the while before the altar. Then broughtt they us some henne cutt in smalle peeces and Fresh porcke Don in like Manner, giving us Choppsticks to eatt our Meat, butt wee knew not how to use them, soe imployed our Fingers.

Our Drincke was warm Rack outt of a straunge bottle, For on the one side it had a bigge hole wherin they putt kindled coales with a little grate for the ashes to fall Downe in to another place, the licor going round aboutt all within the said bottle. This allsoe serves somtymes to warme their Chaa aforementioned, which they allwaies Drincke hotte as the Turckes Doe Coffea, and I thinck used For the same, partly to passe away the tyme, butt Cheiffly For their stomacks sake, it beeing accompted very wholesome.

Peter Mundy

The Travels of Peter Mundy in Europe
and Asia 1608–1667, vol. iii (1919)

Rack] spirituous liquor

MRS HUTCHINSON'S MARRIAGE TO COLONEL JOHN HUTCHINSON

(1638)

THE women, with witty spite, represented all her faults to him, which chiefly terminated in the negligence of her dress and habit, and all womanish ornaments, giving herself wholly up to study and writing. Mr. Hutchinson, who had a very sharp and pleasant wit, retorted all their malice with such just reproofs of their idleness and vanity, as made them hate her, who, without affecting it, had so engaged such a person in her protection, as they with all their arts could not catch. He, in the meanwhile prosecuted his love with so much discretion, duty, and honour, that at the length, through many difficulties he accomplished his design. I shall pass by all the little amorous relations, which, if I would take the pains to relate, would make a true history of a more handsome management of love than the best romances describe; but these are to be forgotten as the vanities of youth, not worthy of mention among the greater transactions of his life. There is this only to be recorded, that never was there a passion more ardent and less idolatrous; he loved her better than his life, with inexpressible tenderness and kindness, had a most high obliging esteem of her, yet still considered honour, religion, and duty above her, nor ever suffered the intrusion of such a dotage as should blind him from marking her imperfections; these he looked upon with such an indulgent eye as did not abate his love and esteem of her, while it augmented his care to blot out all those spots which might make her appear less worthy of that respect he paid her; and thus indeed he soon made her more equal to him than he found her; for she was a very faithful mirror, reflecting truly, though but dimly, his own glories upon him, so long as he was present; but she, that was nothing before his inspection gave her a fair figure, when he was removed, was only filled with a dark mist, and never could again take in any delightful object, nor return any shining representation. The greatest excellency she had was the power of apprehending and the virtue of loving his; so as his shadow she waited on him everywhere, till he was taken into that region of light which admits of none, and then she vanished into nothing. It was not her face he loved, her honour and her virtue were his mistresses; and these (like Pygmalion's) images of his own making, for he polished and gave form to what he found with all the roughnesses of the quarry about it; but meeting with a compliant subject for his own wise government, he found as much satisfaction as he gave, and never had occasion to number his marriage among his infelicities. That day that the friends on both sides met to conclude the marriage, she fell sick of the small-pox, which was many ways a great trial upon him. First, her life was almost in desperate hazard, and then the disease, for the present, made her the most deformed person that could be seen, for a great while after she recovered; yet he was nothing troubled at it, but married her as soon as she was able to quit the chamber, when the priest and all that saw her were affrighted to look on her; but God recompensed his justice and constancy by restoring her, though she was longer than ordinary before she recovered, as well as before.

Lucy Hutchinson

Memoirs of Colonel Hutchinson (1806). Text from
Firth's edition (1906). Written 1664–71

THE KENTISH SQUIRE AND THE WITCH
(1641)

BROTHER BARGRAVE,

The bearer hereof, by name Goodwife Gilnot, either maliciously or ignorantly, or both maliciously and ignorantly, accused to bee a witch, and having thereby sustained losse of her good name, and by reason thereof being much troubled and perplexed in minde, doth become your humble petitioner that the calumnies layd against her may either be fully proved or the authors of them may receave condigne punishment. I can no way blame the woman for being troubled at the losse of her good name, for all her riches are not to be compared unto it; if she be esteemed such a kind of creature everie body will be afraid of her and noe body set her aworke, insomuch as truely shee will bee utterlie undone.

The allegations agt. this woman are that shee hath bewitched one Brake, who being ill in bed beleiveth her to bee the cause thereof.

2. The said Brake hath lost divers sheepe and shee is accused to be the cause that they have suffered this sheep-wrake.

To answer the first of these allegations, I say hee is in a consumption, the sayd Brake, and will not follow our advise to be at the charge to go to a phisition who by God's help may cure him. To the second I answer, I myselfe have lost divers sheepe and cattell this yeere, and soe have my neighbours likewise, who are not soe simple to beleve they were bewitched, nor soe malitious as to accept anybody for bewitching them.

Thirdly, that she hath a wart or Teat uppon her body wherewith shee giveth her familier sucke.

I answer to the third, I believe of not a marke uppon her body but what all women have as well as shee, or none injurie if they had it not. She hath a small wart uppon her brest, which you may see and you please, and believe it there is none so familier with her as to receive any sustenance from thence.

But such is the blindness of men in these latter times that, as St. Paul preached, they depart from the faith and give heed to spirits of error and doctrines of devills, nay speake lies; and such depe roote hath the fables of witchcrafte taken hold in the heart of this and other silly men, now and here, that they will not with patience endure the hand and correction of God, for if any adversity, sicknes, losse of corne and catle, doe happen to their prosperity, they accuse some neighbour or other for a witch; as if there were no God in Israell that ordereth all things according to his good pleasure, punishing both iust and uniust with losses and afflictions according as hee thinketh good, but that certaine creatures here in earth, called witches, must needes be the authors of men's miseries, as though they themselves were innocents and had deserved no such punishments . . .

Sir, my earnest request unto you is that you will not lightly beeleve such false and malitious reports as you heare, or may heare, alledged against this woman, whom I beeleive to bee religiously disposed. Certen I am shee hath undergone a great deale of labour to bring up her charge of children, and hath taken noe small care to have them instructed up in the feare of God, and therefore it is the more pittie to have her Labour under soe great a scandall. And for soe much as the neighbors healp them selves together, and the poore woman's cry, though it reach to heaven, is scarce heard heere uppon earth, I thought I was bound in conscience to speake in her behalfe . . .

Your very lo: Bro:

H.O.

Sep. 23 1641

Henry Oxinden
The Oxinden Letters 1607–1642 (1933)

Horsemanship

(1643)

To make a horse fit for the wars, and embolden him against all terrors, these inventions are useful: to beat a drum out of the stable first, and then give him his provender: then beat a drum in the stable by degrees, and then give him his provender upon the drum. When he is acquainted herewith sufficiently, you must shoot off a pistol out of the stable, before he hath his provender: then you may shoot off a pistol in the stable, and so by degrees bring it as near to him as you can till he be acquainted with the pistol, likewise remembering still after every shot to give him more provender. You must also cause his groom to put on bright armour, and so to rub his heels and dress him. You must also present a sword before him in the said armour, and when you have done, give him still some more provender. Lastly, his rider must bring his horse forth into the open field, where a bright armour must be fastened upon a stake, and set forth in the likeness of an armed man as much as possible; which being done, the rider must put his horse on until he make him not only approach the said image, but throw it down: which being done, you must be sure to give him some provender, that he may be encouraged to do the like against an adversary in battle. It will be good also that two men do hold up a cloak betwixt them in the field, and then the rider to put the horse to it until he leap over, which cloak also they may raise as they see occasion, when the horse is able to leap so high. You shall do well also to use your horse to swimming; which you may do, either by trailing him after you at the tail of a boat, in a good river, holding him by the head at the length of the bridle, or by putting a good swimmer in a linen waistcoat and breeches upon him.

It will be fit for a gentleman also to learn to swim, unless he be given cramps and convulsions; howbeit, I must confess, in my own particular, that I cannot swim; for, as I was once in danger of drowning, my mother, upon her blessing, charged me never to learn swimming, telling me further, that she had heard of more drowned than saved by it; which reason, though it did not prevail with me, yet her commandment did. It will be good also for a gentleman to learn to leap, wrestle, and vault on horseback; they being all of them qualities of great use. I do much approve likewise of shooting in the long-bow, as being both an healthful exercise and useful for the wars, notwithstanding all that our firemen speak against it; for, being an hundred archers against so many musqueteers, I say if the archer comes within his distance, he will not only make two shoots, but two hits for one.

The exercises I do not approve of are riding of running horses, there being much cheating in that kind; neither do I see why a brave man should delight in a creature whose chief use is to help him to run away. I do not much like of hunting horses, that exercise taking up more time than can be spared from a man studious to get knowledge; it is enough, therefore, to know the sport, if there be any in it, without making it an ordinary practice; and, indeed, of the two, hawking is the better, because less time is spent in it. And upon these terms also I can allow a little bowling; so that the company be choice and good.

The exercises I wholly condemn, are dicing and carding, especially if you play for any great sum of money, or spend any time in them; or use to come to meetings in dicing-houses where cheaters meet and cozen young gentlemen of all their money.

Edward, Lord Herbert of Cherbury

Autobiography (1764). Text from Lee's edition (1886). Written c. 1643

At Marston Moor

(1644)

To Colonel Valentine Walton.

DEAR SIR,

It's our duty to sympathise in all mercies; and to praise the Lord together in chastisements or trials, that so we may sorrow together.

Truly England and the Church of God hath had a great favour from the Lord, in this great Victory given unto us, such as the like never was since this War began. It had all the evidences of an absolute Victory obtained by the Lord's blessing upon the Godly Party principally. We never charged but we routed the enemy. The Left Wing which I commanded, being our own horse, saving a few Scots in our rear, beat all the Prince's horse. God made them as stubble to our swords. We charged their regiments of foot with our horse, and routed all we charged. The particulars I cannot relate now; but I believe, of Twenty-thousand the Prince hath not Four-thousand left. Give glory, all the glory, to God. –

Sir, God hath taken away your eldest Son by a cannon-shot. It brake his leg. We were necessitated to have it cut off, whereof he died.

Sir, you know my own trials this way; but the Lord supported me with this, That the Lord took him into the happiness we all pant for and live for. There is your precious child full of glory, never to know sin nor sorrow any more. He was a gallant young man, exceedingly gracious. God give you His comfort. Before his death he was so full of comfort that to Frank Russel and myself he could not express it, 'It was so great above his pain.' This he said to us. Indeed it was admirable. A little after, he said, One thing that lay upon his spirit. I asked him, What that was? He told me that it was,

That God had not suffered him to be any more the executioner of His enemies. At his fall, his horse being killed with the bullet, and as I am informed three horses more, I am told he bid them, Open to the right and left, that he might see the rogues run. Truly he was exceedingly beloved in the Army, of all that knew him. But few knew him; for he was a precious young man, fit for God. You have cause to bless the Lord. He is a glorious Saint in Heaven; wherein you ought exceedingly to rejoice. Let this drink up your sorrow; seeing these are not feigned words to comfort you, but the thing is so real and undoubted a truth. You may do all things by the strength of Christ. Seek that, and you shall easily bear your trial. Let this public mercy to the Church of God make you forget your private sorrow. The Lord be your strength; so prays

Your truly faithful and loving brother,

OLIVER CROMWELL

[*July 5th*, 1644]

My love to your Daughter, and to my Cousin Perceval, Sister Desborow, and all friends with you.

Oliver Cromwell's Letters and Speeches (1845), ed. T. Carlyle
Text from the enlarged third edition (1850)

SPANISH MANNERS

(1645)

THE *Spaniard* is generally given to gaming, and that in excesse; he will say his prayers before, and if he win, he will thank God for his good fortune after; Their common game at cards (for they very seldom play at dice) is *Primera*, at which the King never shows his game, but throws his cards with their faces down on the table: He is Merchant of all the cards and dice thro' all the Kingdom, he hath them made for a penny a pair, and he retails them for twelvepence; so that 'tis thought he hath 30000l a year by this trick at cards. The *Spaniard* is very devout in his way, for I have seen him kneel in the very dirt when the *Ave Mary* bel rings; and some if they spy two straws or sticks lie crossewise in the street, they will take them up and kisse them, and lay them down again. He walks as if he marcht and seldome looks on the ground, as if he contemnd it. I was told of a *Spaniard,* who having got a fall by a stumble and broke his nose, rose up, and in a disdainfull manner said, *Voto a tal esto es caminar por la tierra;* This is to walk upon earth. The *Labradors* and the Countrey Swains here are sturdy and rationall Men, nothing so simple or servile as the *French Peasan who is born in chains.* Tis true, the *Spaniard* is not so conversable as other Nations; (unless he hath traveld), else he is like *Mars* among the Planets, impatient of Conjunction: nor is he so free in his gifts and rewards; as the last Summer it happned that Count *Gondamar,* with Sir *Francis Cotington,* went to see a curious House of the Constable of *Castiles,* which had bin newly built here; the keeper of the house was very officious to shew him every room with the garden, grotha's, and aqueducts, and presented him with som Fruit; *Gondomar* having bin a long time in the House, coming out, put many Complements of thanks upon the man, and so was going away, Sir *Francis* whisperd him in the eare and askd him whether he would give the man any thing that took such pains: Oh, quoth *Gondomar,* well remembred; *Don Francisco,* have you ever a double pistole about you? if you have, you may give it him, *and then you pay him after the* English *manner; I have paid him already after the* Spanish . . .

Touching their women, nature hath made a more visible

Labradors] labourers   *grotha's*] grottoes

distinction 'twixt the two sexes here, then else where; for the men for the most part are swarthy and rough, but the women are made of a far finer mould, they are commonly little; And whereas there is a saying that makes a compleat woman, let her be *English* to the neck, *French* to the wast, and *Dutch* below; I may adde for hands and feet let her be *Spanish*, for they have the least of any. They have another saying, a *Frenchwoman* in a dance, a *Dutchwoman* in the kitchin, an *Italian* in a window, an *Englishwoman* at board, and the *Spanish* a bed. When they are maried they have a priviledge to wear high shooes, and to paint, which is generally practised here and the Queen useth it her self. They are coy enough, but not so froward as our *English*, – for if a Lady goe along the street, (and all women going here vaild, and their habit so generally like, one can hardly distinguish a Countesse from a coblers Wife), if one should cast out an odde ill sounding word, and ask her a favor, she will not take it ill, but put it off, and answer you with some witty retort. After 30. they are commonly past childbearing, and I have seen women in *England* look as youthful at 50. as some here at 25. Money will do miracles here in purchasing the favor of Ladies, or anything els, though this be the Countrey of money, for it furnisheth well-near all the world besides, yea their very enemies, as the *Turk* and *Hollander*; in so much that one may say, the *Coyn* of *Spain* is as *Catholic*, as her *King*. Yet tho' he be the greatest King of gold and silver Mines in the world, (I think) yet the common currant Coyn here is copper, – and herein I beleeve the *Hollander* hath done him more mischief by counterfeiting his copper coins, then by their arms, bringing it in by strange surreptitious wayes, as in hollow sows of tin and lead, hollow masts, in pitcht buckets under water and other wayes. But I fear to be injurious to this great King to speak of him in so narrow a compasse, a great King indeed, though the *French* in a slighting way compare his Monarchy to a *Beggar's Cloak made up of Patches*, they are Patches indeed, but such as he hath not the like: the *East Indies* is a patch embroyderd with Pearl, Rubies, and Diamonds: *Peru* is a patch embroyderd with massy gold, *Mexico* with silver, *Naples* & *Milan* are patches of cloth of Tissue,—and if these patches were in one peece, what would become of his Cloak embroyderd with Flower deluces?

James Howell

Epistolæ Ho-Elianæ. Familiar Letters
Domestic and Forren . . . (1645)

THE CHARACTER OF OLIVER CROMWELL

(1599–1658)

HE was one of those Men, *quos vituperare ne inimici quidem possunt, nisi ut simul laudent*; . . . for he could never have done half that mischief without great parts of Courage, Industry, and Judgement. He must have had a wonderful understanding in the Natures and Humours of Men, and as great a dexterity in applying them; who, from a private and obscure birth (though of a good family) without Interest or Estate, Alliance or Friendship, could raise himself to such a height, and compound and knead such opposite and contradictory tempers, humours, and interests into a consistence, that contributed to His designs, and to their own destruction; whilst himself grew insensibly powerful enough to cut off those by whom he had climbed, in the instant that they projected to demolish their own building. What was said of *Cinna* may very justly be said of Him, *ausum eum, quae nemo auderet bonus: perfecisse, quae a nullo, nisi fortissimo perfici possunt*. . . . Without doubt, no Man with more wickedness ever attempted any thing, or brought to pass what he desired more wickedly, more in the face and contempt of Religion, and moral Honesty; yet wickedness as great as his could never have accomplish'd those designs, without the assistance of a great Spirit, an admirable circumspection, and sagacity, and a most magnanimous resolution.

When he appeared first in the Parliament, he seem'd to have a Person in no degree gracious, no ornament of discourse, none of those Talents which use to conciliate the Affections of the Stander by: yet as he grew into Place and Authority, his parts seem'd to be raised, as if he had conceal'd Faculties, till he had occasion to use them; and when he was to act the part of a great Man, he did it without any indecency, notwithstanding the want of Custom.

After he was confirm'd and invested Protector by the humble *Petition and Advice*, he consulted with very few upon any Action of importance, nor communicated any enterprise he resolved upon, with more than those who were to have principal parts in the execution of it; nor with them sooner than was absolutely necessary. What he once resolved, in which he was not rash, he would not be disswaded from, nor endure any contradiction of his power and authority; but extorted obedience from them who were not willing to yield it...

[He] was not so far a Man of blood, as to follow *Machiavel's* method; which prescribes upon a total alteration of Government, as a thing absolutely necessary, to cut off all the heads of those, and extirpate their Families, who are Friends to the old one. It was confidently reported that, in the Council of Officers, it was more than once proposed, 'that there might be a general Massacre of all the Royal Party, as the only expedient to secure the Government', but that *Cromwell* would never consent to it; it may be, out of too much contempt of his Enemies. In a word, as he was guilty of many Crimes against which Damnation is denounced, and for which Hell-fire is prepared, so he had some good Qualities which

have caused the Memory of some Men in all Ages to be celebrated; and he will be look'd upon by Posterity as a brave
wicked Man.

Edward Hyde, Earl of Clarendon

The History of the Rebellion and Civil Wars, vol. iii (1704)
Text from the edition of 1706. Written 1646-71

THE CHARACTER OF HENRY HASTINGS

(1551-1650)

MR HASTINGS, by his quality, being the son, brother, and
uncle to the Earls of Huntingdon, and his way of living, had
the first place amongst us. He was peradventure an original
in our age, or rather the copy of our nobility in ancient days
in hunting and not warlike times: he was low, very strong
and very active, of a reddish flaxen hair, his clothes always
green cloth, and never all worth when new five pounds. His
house was perfectly of the old fashion, in the midst of a large
park well stocked with deer, and near the house rabbits to
serve his kitchen, many fish-ponds, and great store of wood
and timber; a bowling-green in it, long but narrow, full of
high ridges, it being never levelled since it was ploughed;
they used round sand bowls, and it had a banqueting house
like a stand, a large one built in a tree. He kept all manner
of sport hounds that ran buck, fox, hare, otter, and badger,
and hawks long and short winged; he had all sorts of nets for
fishing: he had a walk in the New Forest and the manor of
Christ Church. This last supplied him with red deer, sea and
river fish; and indeed all his neighbours' grounds and royal-
ties were free to him, who bestowed all his time in such sports,
but what he borrowed to caress his neighbours' wives and
daughters, there being not a woman in all his walks of the
degree of a yeoman's wife or under, and under the age of

forty, but it was extremely her fault if he were not intimately acquainted with her. This made him very popular, always speaking kindly to the husband, brother, or father, who was to boot very welcome to his house, whenever he came; there he found beef pudding and small beer in great plenty, a house not so neatly kept as to shame him or his dirty shoes, the great hall strewed with marrow-bones, full of hawks' perches, hounds, spaniels, and terriers, the upper sides of the hall hung with the fox-skins of this and the last year's skinning, here and there a polecat intermixed, guns and keepers' and huntsmen's poles in abundance. The parlour was a large long room as properly furnished; on a great hearth paved with brick lay some terriers and the choicest hounds and spaniels; seldom but two of the great chairs had litters of young cats in them which were not to be disturbed, he having always three or four attending him at dinner, and a little white round stick of fourteen inches long lying by his trencher that he might defend such meat as he had no mind to part with to them. The windows, which were very large, served for places to lay his arrows, crossbows, stonebows, and other such like accoutrements; the corners of the room full of the best chose hunting and hawking poles; an oyster-table at the lower end, which was of constant use twice a day all the year round, for he never failed to eat oysters before dinner and supper through all seasons. The neighbouring town of Poole supplied him with them. The upper part of this room had two small tables and a desk, on the one side of which was a church Bible, on the other the Book of Martyrs; on the tables were hawks' hoods, bells, and such like, two or three old green hats with their crowns thrust in so as to hold ten or a dozen eggs, which were of a pheasant kind of poultry he took much care of and fed himself; tables, dice, cards and boxes were not wanting. In the hole of the desk were store of tobacco-pipes that had been used. On one side of this end of the room was the door of a closet, wherein stood the strong beer and the wine, which never came thence but in single glasses, that being the rule of the house exactly observed, for he never exceeded in drink or permitted it. On the other side was a door into an old chapel not used for devotion; the pulpit, as the safest place, was never wanting of a cold chine of beef, pasty of venison, gammon of bacon, or great apple-pie, with thick crust extremely baked. His table cost him not much, though it was very good to eat at, his sports supplying all but beef and mutton, except Friday, when he had the best sea-fish as well as other fish he could get, and was the day that his neighbours of best quality most visited him. He never wanted a London pudding, and always sung it in with 'my part lies therein-a.' He drank a glass of wine or two at meals, very often syrup of gilliflower in his sack, and had always a tun glass without feet stood by him holding a pint of small beer, which he often stirred with a great sprig of rosemary. He was well-natured, but soon angry, calling his servants bastard and cuckoldy knaves, in one of which he often spoke truth to his own knowledge, and sometimes in both, though of the same man. He lived to a hundred, never lost his eyesight, but always writ and read without spectacles, and got to horse without help. Until past fourscore he rode to the death of a stag as well as any.

Anthony Ashley Cooper, first Earl of Shaftesbury

'Fragment of Autobiography' [this portion first printed 1754]. Text from *Memoirs of . . . Shaftesbury*, ed. W. D. Christie (1859) Written ?c.1680

tun glass] a barrel-shaped drinking-glass (?)

On the Netherlands

(1648)

THEY are a general Sea-land: the great Bog of *Europe*. There is not such another Marsh in the world, that's flat. They are an universal Quagmire; Epitomiz'd, *A green Cheese in pickle*. There is in them an Æquilibrium of mud and water. A strong Earth-quake would shake them to a *Chaos*, from which the successive force of the Sun, rather than Creation, hath a little emended them. They are the Ingredients of a Black-pudding, and want onely stirring together: Marry, 'tis best making on't a dry Summer, else you will have more bloud than grist; and then have you no way to make it serve for any thing, but to spread it under *Zona Torrida*, and so dry it for Turfs.

... the Vessels of the house [are] marshalled about the room like Watchmen: All as neat as if you were in a Citizens wives Cabinet; for unless it be themselves, they let none of Gods creatures lose any thing of their native beauty.

Their Houses, especially in their Cities are the best eye-beauties of their Countrey: for cost and sight they far exceed our *English*, but they want their magnificence. Their Lining is yet more rich than their out-side, not in Hangings but Pictures, which even the poorest are furnisht with: Not a Cobler but has his toyes for ornament. Were the knacks of all their houses set together, there would not be such another *Bartholomew-Fair* in Europe.

Their Artists for these are as rare as thought, for they can paint you a fat Hen in her feathers. . . .

You would think being with them you were in old *Israel*, for you find not a beggar among them. Nor are they mindful of their own alone but strangers also partake of their Care and Bounty. If they will depart, they have money for their Convoy. If they stay, they have work provided. If unable, they find an Hospitall. Their Providence extends even from the Prince to the catching of flies....

In all their Manufactures they hold a truth and constancy: for they are as fruits from Trees, the same every year that they are at first; Not Apples one year and Crabs the next; and so for ever after. In the sale of these they are also at a word, they will gain rather than exact, and have not that way whereby our Citizens abuse the wise, and cozen the ignorant; and by their infinite over-asking for commodities, proclaim to the world that they would cheat all if it were in their power.

Yet they are in some sort Gods, for they set bounds to the Sea, and when they list let it pass them. Even their dwelling is a miracle; They live lower than the fishes in the very lap of the floods, and incircled in their watry Arms. They are the *Israelites* passing through the Red-Sea. The waters wall them in, and if they set ope their sluces shall drown up their enemies.

Owen Felltham

A Brief Character of the Low-Countries (1648)
Text from *Resolves* (eighth edition, 1661)

THE CHARACTER OF THE FRENCH

(1652)

THE *French Children* are the fairest letter that *Nature*, I think, can shew through all the humane *Alphabet*; but though they be *Angels* in the *cradle*, yet they are more like *Divels* in the *saddle*: age generally shewing, that what she so soon bestowes, she takes as fast away; for the *French* (after twenty) presently strike forty in their faces, and especially amongst their *Women*, who are then extremely decayed, when ours, if not *beautifull*, are yet very *tolerable* at those years; which, whether it proceeds from the *siccity* of the air, *drinking water, ill diet*, or other *accident*, I dare not easily determine; and yet I am the rather inclined to think, something of that nature it must needs be, when we finde the *women* of *Quality* for the most part as exquisite Beauties as any the whole world produces, without disparaging *our Ladies* at home, whom I would be unwilling this *Paragraph* should in the least degree offend....

It is a true observation of one, that a *French man* appears a *child* at all ages; but in practice and negotiation you shall finde him a *man*. It is the *Field* and the *Court* which the *Gentry* affect as the best of Education; and thence I am inclined to beleeve, they contract amongst them that *indifferency* of beleeving and living, in which they are generally more open and free then even the *Italians*; albeit yet not in all points so *enormous* as the depraved youth of *England*, whose prodigious *disbaucheries* and late unheard of extravagancies, far surpasse the madnesse of all other *civilized Nations* whatsoever. *Gaming* also they frequent, but are in no one vice so abandoned, as to the exhausting their *Estates*, especially in point of *drink* and *Tobacco*; which, though it have of late got some footing upon the more *vile sort*, and infected some *Northern parts* of the *Kingdom*; yet few persons of Quality use either in *excesse*: but what they do not in *drink*, they pay in *bread*, and are strange devourers of *Corn*; they adore a *good pottage* (whatever the rest of the *Repast* be) as the *Egyptians* did *garlick*: nor will a true *Monsieur* be brought at any rate to taste a glasse of wine, *sans premier manger*; which although they neither do so much, nor sit so long at it, yet they use to *collation* more often, the most temperate of them.

The *passions* of the people are suddenly imported and puffed up with a *Victory*, and as soon dejected with the least repulse or loss. They are prodigall, and splendid in *externals*, but seldome undoe themselves in *house-keeping and hospitality*: The best sort eat like *Princes*, and far exceed our Tables; the *common*, worse then *dogs*: generally, so they flourish and appear for a *month or two* in the summer, they will fare hard enough the rest of the yeer besides; and such as minde onely their profit, have little *charity*, where they see no evident *Interest*. They are exceedingly *courteous*, and have generally their *tongues well hung*; which promptitude of theirs, as it becomes them well in *encounter*, so they are for the most part of *joviall conversation*, and far from that constrained addresse which is naturall to our *sullen Nation*, who never think our selves acquainted, till we treate one another with *Jack and Tom*; familiarities, which, as we finde no where else in use, so they commonly terminate in rude and vain Associations.

John Evelyn
The State of France . . . (1652)

A Riot at Ulverston

(1652)

Soe off a sudden all ye people in ye steeplehouse was in an outrage & an uproare: that they fell upon mee in ye steeplehouse before his face: & knockt mee doune & kikt mee & trampeld upon mee before his face: & people tumbled over there seates for feare: & att last hee[1] came & tooke mee from amongst ye people again: & led mee out of ye steeplehouse & putt mee Into ye hands of ye Constables & other officers hands & bid them whippe mee & putt mee out of ye tounde & then they led mee about a quarter of a mile some takeinge holde by my collar & some by ye armes & shoulders & shooke & dragged mee & some gott hedge stakes: & holme bushes & other staffs: & many freindely people that was come to the

1. John Sawrey, a magistrate.

markett: & some came Into ye steeplehouse to heare mee: many of them they knockt doune & broake there heads alsoe & ye bloode rann doune severall people soe as I never saw ye like In my life: as I lookt att them when they was dragginge mee alonge. . . .

And when they had ledd mee to ye common & a multitude of people followinge: there they fell upon mee with there staffes & hedgestakes & ye constables & officers gave mee some blowes over my backe with there willowe rodds & soe thrust mee amongst ye rude multitude: & they then fell upn mee as aforesaid with there stakes & clubbs & beate mee on my heade & armes & shoulders till they had mased mee & att last I fell doune upon ye wett common: & when I recovered my selfe again & saw my selfe lyinge on a watery common & all ye people standinge about mee I lay a litle still & ye power of ye Lord sprange through mee & ye eternall refreshinges refresht mee that I stoode uppe againe in ye eternall power of God & stretched out my armes amongst them all & saide againe with a loude voice strike againe heere is my armes my heade & my cheekes: & there was a mason a rude fellow a professor hee gave me a blowe with all his might Just a toppe of my hande as it was stretched out with his walkinge rule staffe: & my hande & arme was soe nummed & bruised that I coulde not draw itt in unto me againe: soe ye people cryed out hee hath spoiled his hande for ever haveinge any use of it more & I looket att it in ye love of God & I was in ye love of God to them all that had persecuted me.

And after a while ye Lords power sprange through mee againe & through my hande & arme that in a minute I recovered my hande & arme & strength in ye face & sight of them all.

George Fox

Journal (1694). Text from MSS as first
printed 1911. Written 1673–7

IF WANT OF KINDNESS WERE THE ONLY CRIME . . .

Sr   *Sept. 1653*

if want of kindenesse were the only Crime I exempted from
pardon, twas not that I had the least aprehension you could
bee Guilty of it, but to show you (by Excepting only an impossible thing) that I Excepted nothing; Noe in Earnest, I can
fancy noe such thing of you; or if I could, the quarrell would
bee to my self, I should never forgive my owne ffolly that
led mee to choose a friend that could bee false; but i'le leave
this (wᶜʰ is not much to the purpose) and tell you how with
my usuall impatience I Expected your letter, and how colde it
went to my heart to see it soe short a one, twas soe great a
paine to mee that I am resolved you shall not feell it nor can
I in Justice, punnish you for a fault unwillingly committed;
if I were your Enemy, I could not use you ill, when I saw
fortune doe it too, and in gallantry & good nature both I
should think my self rather Obliged to prottect you from her
injuryes (if it lay in my power) then double them upon you;
these things considerd I beleeve this letter will bee longer then
ordinary; kinder, I think it cannot bee, I alway's speak my
heart to you, and that is soe much your friend it never fur-
nishes mee with any thing to your disadvantage; I am glad
you are an admirer of Telesile as well as I, in my opinion tis
a fine Lady, but I know you will pitty poore Amestris strangly
when you have read her Storry. i'le swear I cryed for her when I
read it first though shee were but an imaginary person, and sure
if any thing of that kinde can deserve it her misfortunes may.

God forgive mee I was as neer Laughing Yesterday where
I should not; would you beleeve that I had the grace to goe
heare a sermon upon a week day, in Earnest tis true, and Mr
Marshall[1] was the Man that preached, but never any body was

---

1. Puritan divine, one of the 'Smectymnuus' group, d. 1655.

soe defeated, hee is soe famed that I Expected rare things from him and seriously I listned to him at first with as much reverence and attention as if hee had bin S^{nt} Paul. and what doe you think hee told us? why that if there were noe kings no Queens, noe Lord's no Lady's noe Gentlemen nor Gentlewomen, in the world, twould bee noe losse at all to God Almighty. this wee had over some forty times wch made mee remember it whither I would or not, the rest was much at this rate, Enterlarded with the prittyest od phrases that I had the most adoe to look soberly enough for the place I was in that ever I had in my life; hee do's not preach soe alway's sure; if hee do's I cannot beleeve his Sermon's will doe much toward's the bringing any body to heaven, more then by Exerciseing there Patience; Yet i'le say that for him, hee stood stoutly for Tyth's though in my opinion few deserved them lesse then hee, and it may bee hee would bee better without them. yet you are not Convinced you say that to bee miserable is the way to bee good. to some Natures I think it is not, but there are many of soe carelesse & vaine a Temper that the least breath of good fortune swell's them with soe much Pride, that if they were not putt in minde somtimes by a sound Crosse or two, that they are Mortall, they would hardly think it posible, and though tis a signe of a servile Nature when feare produces more of reverence in us then love, yet there is more danger of forgetting on's self in a prosperous fortune then in the contrary, and affliction may bee the surest (though not the pleasantest) Guide to heaven; what think you might not I preach with Mr Marshall for a wager? but you could fancy a perfect happinesse heer you say. that is not much, many People doe soe, but I never heard of any body that had it more then in fancy, soe that twill not bee Strange if you should misse on't. one may bee happy to a good degree I think in a faithfull friend, a Moderate fortune and a retired life, farther then this I know nothing to wish, but if there bee any thing beyond it I wish it you.

You did not tell mee what carryed you out of Towne in such hast, I hope the occasion was good; you must account to me for all that I lost by it, I shall Expect a whole Pacquett next week. O mee I have forgott this once or twice to tell you that if it bee noe inconvenience to you I could wish you would change the place of dirrection for my letters. certainly that Jones know's my Name. I bespoke a sadle of him once, and though it bee a good while agon, yet I was soe often with him aboute it, haveing much adoe to make him understand how I would have it, it being of a ffashion hee had never seen though since it bee common, that I am confident hee has not forgott mee, besydes that upon it hee gott my Brothers Custom and I cannot tell whither hee do's not use the shop still.

Jane[1] presents her humble service to you and has sent you somthing in a boxe, tis hard to imagin what shee can finde heer to present you withall, and I am much in doubt whither you will not pay to dear for it if you discharge the Carriage, tis a pritty freedom she takes but you may thank your selfe, shee thinks because you call her ffellow Servant she may use you accordingly, I bred her better, but you have spoyled her.

Is it true that my Lord Whitlock[2] goes Ambassador where my Lord L. should have gon? I know not how hee may apear in a Swedish Court, but hee was never meant for a Courtier at home I beleeve. Yet tis a gracious Prince, hee is often in this Country and always do's us the favour to send for his fruit hither, hee was makeing a Purchase of one of the best houses in the County, I know not whither hee go's on with it, but tis such a one as will not become any thing lesse then a lord, and there is a talke as if the Chancery were goeing downe, if soe his title goes with it I think; twill bee sad news for my Lord Keebles son, hee will have nothing left to say when my

1. Dorothy Osborne's companion.
2. Bulstrode Whitelock (1605–1675), recently one of the Commissioners for the Great Seal.

Lord my father is taken from him; were it not better that I had nothing to say neither, then that I should entertaine you with such sencelesse things? I hope I am halfe asleep, nothing Else can Excuse mee, if I were quite asleep I should say fine things to you, I often dream I doe, but perhaps if I could remember them they are noe wiser then my wakeing discourses, good night.

Dorothy Osborne

The Letters of Dorothy Osborne to William Temple
(first complete publication, 1888). Text from
Moore Smith's edition (Oxford, 1928)

THE DEATH OF RICHARD EVELYN

(1658)

1658. 27 Jan. After six fits of an ague died my son *Richard*, 5 years and 3 dayes old onely, but at that tender age a prodigy for witt and understanding; for beauty of body a very angel; for endowment of mind of incredible and rare hopes. To give onely a little taste of some of them, and thereby glory to God: at 2 years and halfe old he could perfectly reade y^e *English*, *Latin*, *French*, or *Gottic* letters, pronouncing the 3 first languages exactly. He had before the 5th yeare, or in that yeare, not onely skill to reade most written hands, but to decline all the nouns, conjugate the verbs regular, and most of ye irregular; learn'd out *Puerilis*, got by heart almost ye entire vocabularie of *Latine* and *French* primitives and words, could make congruous syntax, turne *English* into *Latin*, and *vice versâ*, construe and prove what he read, and did the government and use of relatives, verbs, substantives, elipses, and many figures and tropes, and made a considerable progress in *Comenius's Janua*; began himselfe to write legibly, and had a strong passion for *Greeke*. The number of verses he could recite was

42

prodigious, and what he remember'd of the parts of playes, which he would also act; and when seeing a *Plautus* in one's hand, he ask'd what booke it was, and being told it was comedy, and too difficult for him, he wept for sorrow. Strange was his apt and ingenious application of fables and morals, for he had read *Æsop*; he had a wonderful disposition to mathematics, having by heart divers propositions of *Euclid* that were read to him in play, and he would make lines and demonstrate them. As to his piety, astonishing were his applications of Scripture upon occasion, and his sense of God; he had learn'd all his Catechisme early, and understood yᵉ historical part of yᵉ Bible and New Testament to a wonder, how *Christ* came to redeeme mankind, and how, comprehending these necessarys himselfe, his godfathers were discharg'd of their promise. These and the like illuminations far exceeding his age and experience, considering the prettinesse of his addresse and behaviour, cannot but leave impressions in me at the memory of him. When one told him how many dayes a Quaker had fasted, he replied that was no wonder, for *Christ* had said man should not live by bread alone, but by yᵉ Word of God. He would of himselfe select yᵉ most pathetic psalms, and chapters out of *Job*, to reade to his mayde during his sicknesse, telling her when she pitied him that all God's children must suffer affliction. He declaim'd against yᵉ vanities of yᵉ world before he had seene any. Often he would desire those who came to see him to pray by him, and a yeare before he fell sick, to kneel and pray with him alone in some corner. How thankfully would he receive admonition! how soon be reconciled! how indifferent, yet continualy cherefull! He would give grave advice to his brother *John*, beare with his impertinencies, and say he was but a child. If he had heard of or saw any new thing he was unquiet till he was told how it was made; he brought to us all such difficulties as he found in books, to be expounded. He had learn'd by heart divers

sentences in *Latin* and *Greeke*, which on occasion he would produce even to wonder. He was all life, all prettinesse, far from
morose, sullen, or childish in any thing he said or did. The
last time he had ben at church (wch was at *Greenwich*), I ask'd
him, according to costome, what he remembred of ye sermon;
two good things, father, said he, *bonum gratiæ* and *bonum
gloriæ*, with a just account of what ye preacher said. The day
before he died he cal'd to me, and in a more serious manner
than usual told me that for all I loved him so dearly I should
give my house, land, and all my fine things, to his brother
Jack, he should have none of them; and next morning, when
he found himself ill, and that I persuaded him to keepe his
hands in bed, he demanded whether he might pray to God
with his hands un-joyn'd; and a little while after, whilst in
great agonie, whether he should not offend God by using his
holy name so often calling for ease. What shall I say of his
frequent pathetical ejaculations utter'd of himself; Sweete
Jesus save me, deliver me, pardon my sinns, let thine angels
receive me! So early knowledge, so much piety and perfection! But thus God having dress'd up a Saint fit for himselfe,
would not longer permit him with us, unworthy of ye future
fruites of this incomparable hopefull blossome. Such a child I
never saw! for such a child I blesse God in whose bosome he
is! May I and mine become as this little child which now
follows the child *Jesus* that Lamb of God in a white robe
whithersoever He goes; Even so, Lord *Jesus, fiat voluntas tua*!
Thou gavest him to us, Thou hast taken him from us, blessed
be ye name of ye Lord! that I had any thing acceptable to Thee
was from thy grace alone, since from me he had nothing but
sin, but that Thou hast pardon'd! blessed be my God for ever,
amen!

In my opinion he was suffocated by ye women and maids
that tended him, and cover'd him too hot with blankets as he
lay in a cradle, near an excessive hot fire in a close room. I

suffer'd him to be open'd, when they found that he was what is vulgarly call'd liver-grown. I had his body coffin'd in lead and reposited in the church of *Deptford* accompanied with divers of my relations and neighbours, among whom I distributed rings with this motto, *Deus abstulit*; intending, God willing, to have him transported with my own body to be interr'd in our dormitory in *Wotton* church, in my dear native county *Surrey*, and to lay my bones and mingle my dust with my fathers, if God be gracious to me and make me as fit for Him as this blessed child was. The Lord *Jesus* sanctify this and all other my afflictions, amen!

15 Feb. The afflicting hand of God being upon us, it pleas'd Him also to take away from us this morning my youngest sonn, *George*, now 7 weekes languishing at nurse, breeding teeth, and ending in a dropsie. God's holy will be done! He was buried at *Deptford* church yᵉ 17th.

This had been yᵉ severest winter that any man alive had known in *England*. The crowes feete were frozen to their prey. Islands of ice inclos'd both fish and fowl frozen, and some persons in their boates.

John Evelyn
*Memoirs Illustrative of the Life and Writings
of John Evelyn, Esq., F.R.S.* (1818)

On Marrying a Beauty

(1658)

If none of my perswasions, nor others wofull Experience, daily met with in the world, can deterre you from yoking your self to anothers desires, make not a *celebrated beauty* the object of your choice; unless you are ambitious of rendring your house as populous as a Confectioners Shop; to which the gaudy Wasps, no less than the liquorish Flies, make it their businesse to resort, in hope of obtaining a lick at your Honey-pot: which though bound up with the strongest obligations or resolutions, and sealed by never so many protestations, yet feminine vessels are obnoxious to so many frailities, as they can hardly bear without breaking, the Pride and Content, they naturally take in seeing themselves adored; Neither can you, according to the *loose custome of England* decently restraine Her from this Concourse, without making demonstration of Jealousy towards her (by which you confess your self a *Cuckold* in your own imagination already) or Incivility to such as come to visit you; though it may be strongly presumed, Your sake hath the least share in this Ceremony; however tied in Manners to attend with patience, till his *Worship*, perhaps his *Lordship*, had pumped his wit dry, having no more Complements left but to take leave: Thus, with his Invention rebated, but not his Lust, he returns home; where the old preserver of baudery, his Kinswoman, perceiving, by his dejected countenance, that he came short of his desires, and wanting a new gowne, imbarks her self for the imployment; and to put the honester face upon so ugly a designe, she contracts a straight alliance with your (yet possibly unconquered) Bedfellow, and under pretence of a Gossiping, or perhaps a voyage to some Religious Exercise, hurries her away in his *Honour's* Coach to a Meeting house, where though she be taken by Storme, is fairely sent home with Bag and Baggage, being only plundered of what you are not likely to misse; And finding it unsafe to complaine, returns again upon her parole, or so often as her new Governor pleaseth to summon her, sheltering the Fault under Custome, your unavoidable Fate, or perhaps Providence (which for their excuse, some are wicked enough to pleade) till her Forehead be as much hardened with Impudence, as yours is by Reproaches, &c. And yet he is the happier owner, who hath a Wife wise enough to conceale the reall Hornes of her Husband, then she, that being innocent, doth by her light carriage make the base symptomes appear in the world's opinion: Oh remember this, when you are about to forget the Pleasure and Safety, only to be found in a *Single Life*.

Francis Osborn

Advice to a Son (1658). Text from
the sixth edition of 1658

LONDON SMOKE

(1661)

... THE immoderate use of, and indulgence to *Sea-coale* alone in the City of *London*, exposes it to one of the fowlest inconveniences and reproches, that can possibly befall so noble, and otherwise incomparable City: and that, not from the *Culinary* fires, which for being weak, and lesse often fed below, is with such ease dispell'd and scatter'd above, as it is hardly at all discernible, but from some few particular Tunnells and Issues, belonging only to *Brewers*, *Diers*, *Lime-burners*, *Salt*, and *Sope-boylers*, and some other private Trades, *One* of whose *Spiracles* alone, does manifestly infect the *Aer* more then all the Chimnies of *London* put together besides. And that this is not the least *Hyperbolie*, let the best of Judges decide it, which I take to be our senses: Whilst these are belching it forth their sooty jaws, the City of *London* resembles the face rather of *Mount Ætna*, the *Court of Vulcan*, *Stromboli* or the Suburbs of *Hell*, then an Assembly of Rational Creatures, and the Imperial seat of our incomparable *Monarch*. For when in all other places the *Aer* is most Serene and Pure, it is here Ecclipsed with such a cloud of Sulphure, as the Sun it self, which gives day to all the World besides, is hardly able to penetrate and impart it here; and the weary *Traveller*, at many miles distance, sooner smells, then sees the City to which he repairs. This is that pernicious Smoake which sullyes all her Glory, superinducing a sooty Crust or furr upon all that it lights, spoyling the move-ables, tarnishing the Plate, Gildings, and Furniture, and cor-roding the very Iron-bars and hardest stones with those piercing and acrimonious Spirits which accompany its Sul-phure; and executing more in one year, then expos'd to the pure *Aer* of the country it could effect in some hundreds . . .

It is this horrid smoake which obscures our Churches, and makes our Palaces look old, which fouls our clothes, and corrupts the Waters, so as the very Rain, and refreshing Dews which fall in the several Seasons, precipitate this impure vapour, which, with its black and tenacious quality, spots and contaminates whatsoever is expos'd to it.

— Calidoque involvitur undique fumo.

It is this which scatters and strews about those black and smutty *Atomes* upon all things where it comes, insinuating it self into our very secret *Cabinets*, and most precious *Reposi-tories:* Finally, it is this which diffuses and spreads a Yellow-nesse upon our choycest Pictures and Hangings: which does this mischief at home; is *Avernus* to *Fowl*, and kills our *Bees* and *Flowers* abroad, suffering nothing in our Gardens to bud, display themselves, or ripen; so as our *Anemonies*, and many other choycest Flowers, will by no industry be made to blow in *London*, or the Precincts of it, unlesse they be raised on a *Hot-bed*, and govern'd with extraordinary Artifice to acceller-ate their springing, imparting a bitter and ungrateful Tast to those few wretched *Fruits*, which never arriving to their desired maturity, seem, like the *Apples* of *Sodome*, to fall even to dust, when they are but touched.

John Evelyn

*Fumifugium: or the Inconveniencie of the Aer
and Smoak of London Dissipated* . . . (1661)

FOODS AND DRINKS

(1662)

CHESHIRE CHEESE

Poor men do eat it for *hunger*, Rich for *digestion*. It seems that the *Ancient British* had no skill in the making thereof, till *taught* by the *Romans*, and now the *Romans* may even *learn* of us more exactness therein. This County doth afford the best for quantity and quality, and yet their *Cows* are not (as in other Shires) housed in the Winter, so that it may seem strange that the hardiest *Kine* should yield the *tenderest cheese*. Some Esayed in vain to make the like in other places, though hence they fetch'd both their *Kine* and *Dary-maids*. It seems they should have fetch'd their *ground* too, (wherein surely some *Occult excellency* in this kind), or else so good *Cheese* will not be made. I hear not the like commendation of the *Butter* in this County, and perchance these two Commodities, are like Stars of a different Horizon, so that the *Elevation* of the one to *Eminency* is the *Depression* of the other.

*

CORNISH PILCHARDS

Plenty hereof are taken in these parts, persecuted to the shore by their enemies, the *Tunny* and *Hake*, till in pursuance of their private revenge, they all become a prey to the Fisherman. The *Pilchard* may seem contemptible in it self, being so small, though the wit of the vulgar here will tell you, they have seen *many pilchards* an *ell-long*, understand it laid at length, head and tail together. Their numbers are incredible, imploying a power of poor people, in Polling, (that is, Beheading,) Gutting, Splitting, Powdering and Drying them, and then (by the name of *Fumadoes*,) with Oyle and a Lemon, they are meat for the mightiest *Don* in *Spain*. I wish, not only their nets, but fish may hold, suspecting their daily decay, their shoals usually shifting coasts, and verging more westward to *Ireland*. Other fish here be which turn to good account, all welcome to Fishermens hooks, save the *Star-fish*, esteemed contagious.

*

DERBYSHIRE ALE

Ceres being our English *Bacchus*, this was our Ancestors common drink, many imputing the strength of their *Infantry* (in drawing so stiff a Bow) to their constant (but moderate) drinking thereof. Yea, now the English begin to turn to *Ale* (may they in due time regain their former vigorousness:) and whereas in our remembrance, *Ale* went out when *Swallows* came in, seldom appearing after *Easter*; it now hopeth (having climed up *May Hill*) to continue its course all the year. Yet have we lost the *Preservative*, what ever it was, which (before *Hops* was found out) made it last so long in our Land some *two hundred years* since, for half a year at the least after the brewing thereof; otherwise of necessity they must brew every day, yea pour it out of the *Kive* into the *Cup*, if the prodigious English Hospitality in former ages be considered, with the multitude of *menial Servants* and strangers entertained. Never was the Wine of *Sarepta* better known to the *Syrians*, that of *Chios* to the *Grecians*, of *Phalernum* to the *Latines*, than the *Canary* of *Derby* is to the *English* thereabout.

*

NORFOLK RABBITS

These are an Army of natural *Pioners*, whence men have learned *cuniculos agere*, the Art of undermining. They thrive best on barren ground, and grow fattest in the hardest frosts. Their flesh is fine and wholesome. If Scotish-men tax our language as improper, and smile at our *wing of a Rabbit*, let us laugh at their *shoulder of a Capon*.

Their skins were formerly much used, when furs were in fashion; till of late our Citizens, of *Romans* are turned *Grecians* have laid down their grave gowns, and took up their light cloaks; men generally disliking all habits, though emblemes of honour, if also badges of age.

Their *rich* or *silver-hair-skins*, formerly so dear, are now levelled in prices with other colours, yea, are lower then black in estimation, because their wool is most used in making of hats, commonly (for the more credit) called *Half-Beavers*, though many of them hardly amount to the proportion of *Semi-Demi-Castors*.

*

SUFFOLK BUTTER

For Quantity and Quality this County doth excel, and venteth it at *London*, and elsewhere. The *Child* not yet *come to*, and the *old Man* who is *past* the use of *Teeth* eateth no *softer*, the poor Man no *cheaper* (in this Shire), the Rich no *wholesomer* food, I mean in the morning. It was half our Saviour's *Bill of Fare* in his Infancy, *Butter and Hony shall he eat*.

It is of a *Cordial*, or, if I may say, *Antidotal* Nature. The story is well known of a Wife which desiring to be a Widow, incorporated Poison in the Butter, whereon her Husband had his principal repast. The poor man finding himself strangely affected, repaired to a Physician, who by some Symptomes suspecting poison, demanded of his Patient which was his chiefest Diet. The sick man told him, that he fed most constantly on *Butter*. *Eat Butter still* (return'd the Physician) *which hitherto hath saved your Life*, for it corrected the poison, that neither the *malignity thereof*, nor the *malice of the Wife*, could have their full operation.

Thomas Fuller
The History of the Worthies of England (1662)

The Fire of London

[September 2nd, 1666] ... River full of lighters and boats taking in goods, and good goods swimming in the water, and only I observed that hardly one lighter or boat in three that had the goods of a house in, but there was a pair of Virginalls in it ... walked to my boat; and there upon the water again, and to the fire up and down, it still encreasing, and the wind great. So near the fire as we could for smoke; and all over the Thames, with one's face in the wind, you were almost burned with a shower of fire-drops. This is very true; so as houses were burned by these drops and flakes of fire, three or four, nay, five or six houses, one from another. When we could endure no more upon the water, we to a little ale-house on the Bankside, over against the Three Cranes, and there staid till it was dark almost, and saw the fire grow; and, as it grew darker, appeared more and more, and in corners and upon steeples, and between churches and houses, as far as we could see up the hill of the City, in a most horrid malicious bloody flame, not like the fine flame of an ordinary fire ... We staid till, it being darkish, we saw the fire as only one entire arch of fire from this to the other side of the bridge, and in a bow up the hill for an arch above a mile long: it made me weep to see it. The churches, houses, and all on fire and flaming at once; and a horrid noise the flames made, and the cracking of houses at their ruine. So home with a sad heart, and there find every body discoursing and lamenting the fire.

Samuel Pepys

Diary (1825). Text from Wheatley's
edition (London, 1893–9)

A Prize-Fight

[MAY 27th, 1667] . . . So to my chamber, and there did some little business, and then abroad, and stopped at the Beargarden-stairs, there to see a prize fought. But the house so full there was no getting in there, so forced to go through an alehouse into the pit, where the bears are baited; and upon a stool did see them fight, which they did very furiously, a butcher and a waterman. The former had the better all along, till by and by the latter dropped his sword out of his hand, and the butcher, whether not seeing his sword dropped I know not, but did give him a cut over the wrist, so as he was disabled to fight any longer. But, Lord! to see how in a minute the whole stage was full of watermen to revenge the foul play, and the butchers to defend their fellow, though most blamed him; and there they all fell to it knocking down and cutting many on each side. It was pleasant to see, but that I stood in the pit, and feared that in the tumult I might get some hurt. At last the rabble broke up, and so I away to White Hall and so to St. James's.

Samuel Pepys
Diary (1825). Text from Wheatley's
edition (London, 1893–9)

A Country Excursion: Epsom and the Downs

[JULY 14th, 1667.] Up, and my wife, a little before four, and to make us ready; and by and by Mrs. Turner come to us, by agreement, and she and I staid talking below, while my wife dressed herself, which vexed me that she was so long about it keeping us till past five o'clock before she was ready. She ready; and, taking some bottles of wine, and beer, and some cold fowle with us into the coach, we took coach and four horses, which I had provided last night, and so away . . . I carried them to see my cozen Pepys's house, and 'light, and walked round about it, and they like it, as indeed it deserves, very well, and is a pretty place; and then I walked them to the wood hard by, and there got them in the thickets till they had lost themselves, and I could not find the way into any of the walks in the wood, which indeed are very pleasant, if I could have found them. At last got out of the wood again; and I, by leaping down the little bank, coming out of the wood, did sprain my right foot, which brought me great present pain, but presently, with walking, it went away for the present, and so the women and W. Hewer and I walked upon the Downes, where a flock of sheep was; and the most pleasant and innocent sight that ever I saw in my life – we find a shepherd and his little boy reading, far from any houses or sight of people, the Bible to him; so I made the boy read to me, which he did, with the forced tone that children do usually read, that was mighty pretty, and then I did give him something, and went to the father, and talked with him; and I find he had been a servant of my cozen Pepys's house, and told me what was become of their old servants. He did content himself mightily in my liking his boy's reading, and did bless God for him, the most like one of the old patriarchs that ever I saw in my life, and it brought those thoughts of the old age of the world in my mind for two or three days after. We took notice of his woolen knit stockings of two colours mixed, and of his shoes shod with iron shoes, both at the toe and heels, and with great nails in the soles of his feet, which was mighty pretty: and, taking notice of them, "Why," says the poor man, "the downes, you see, are full of stones, and we are faine to shoe ourselves thus; and these," says he, "will make the stones fly till they sing before me." I did give the poor man something, for which he was mighty thankful, and I tried to cast stones with his horne crooke. He values his dog mightily, that would turn a sheep any way which he would have him, when he goes to fold them: told me there was about eighteen scoare sheep in his flock, and that he hath four shillings a week the year round for keeping of them: so we posted thence with mighty pleasure in the discourse we had with this poor man, and Mrs. Turner, in the common fields here, did gather one of the prettiest nosegays that ever I saw in my life. So to our coach, and through Mr. Minnes's wood, and looked upon Mr. Evelyn's house; and so over the common, and through Epsum towne to our inne, in the way stopping a poor woman with her milk-pail, and in one of my gilt tumblers did drink our bellyfulls of milk, better than any creame; and so to our inne, and there had a dish of creame, but it was sour, and so had no pleasure in it; and so paid our reckoning, and took coach, it being about seven at night, and passed and saw the people walking with their wives and children to take the ayre, and we set out for home, the sun by and by going down, and we in the cool of the evening all the way with much pleasure home, talking and pleasing ourselves with the pleasure of this day's work, Mrs. Turner mightily pleased with my resolution, which, I tell her, is never to keep a country-house, but to keep a coach, and with my wife on the Saturday to go sometimes for a day to this place, and then quit to another place; and there is more variety and as little charge, and no trouble, as there is in a country-house. Anon it grew dark, and as it grew dark we had the pleasure to see several glow-wormes, which was mighty pretty, but my foot begins more and more to pain me, which Mrs. Turner, by keeping her warm hand upon it, did much ease; but so that when we come home, which was just at eleven at night, I was not able to walk from the lane's end to my house without being helped, which did trouble me, and therefore to bed presently, but, thanks be to God, found I had not been missed, nor any business happened in my absence. So to bed, and there

had a cere-cloth laid to my foot and leg alone, but in great
pain all night long.

Samuel Pepys
Diary (1825). Text from Wheatley's
edition (London, 1893–9)

THE BOOKSELLER IN HELL

(1667)

I PASS'D forward then into a little *Dark Alley*, where it made
me start to hear one call me by my Name, and with much
ado I perceiv'd a fellow there all wrapt up in *Smoke* and *Flame*.
Alas! Sir says he; *Have you forgotten your old Book-seller in
Popes-Head-Alley?* I cry thee mercy, good *Livewell*, quoth I,
What? *art thou here? Yes, yes, Sir* (says he) *'tis e'en too true.* I
never dreamt it would have come to this. He thought I must
needs pity him, when I knew him: but truly I reflected rather
upon the Justice of his Punishment. For in a word, his Shop
was the very Mint of *Heresie, Schism*, and *Sedition*. I put on a
Face of *Compassion* however, to give him a little Ease, which
he took hold of, and vented his Complaint. *Well Sir* (sayes
He) *I would my father had made me a Hangman, when he made
me a Stationer;* for we are call'd to Accompt for Other Men's
Works, as well as for our Own. And one thing that's cast in
our Dish, is the selling of *Translations*, so *Dog-Cheap*, that
every *Sot* knows now as much as would formerly have made
a Passable Doctor, and every *Nasty Groom*, and *Roguy Lac-
quay* is grown as familiar with *Homer, Virgil, Ovid*, as if 'twere
*Robin the Devil; The Seven Champions; or a piece of George
Withers.* He would have talkt on, if a Devil had not stopt his
Mouth with a *Whiffe* from a rowle of his own Papers, and
Choak't him with the smoak on't. The Pestilent Fume would
have dispatch't me too, if I had not got presently out of the

reach on't. But I went on my way, saying, this to myself; If the *Book-seller* be thus Criminal, what will become of the *Author*!

Sir Roger L'Estrange
The Visions of Don Francisco de Quevedo
Villegas ... made English by R.L. (1667)
Text from the fifth edition of 1673

SIR KENELM DIGBY

(1603–65)

HE was such a goodly handsome person, gigantique and great voice, and had so gracefull elocution and noble addresse, etc. that had he been drop't out of the clowdes in any part of the worlde, he would have made himselfe respected... He was envoyé from Henrietta Maria (then Queen-mother) to Pope Innocent X where at first he was mightily admired; but after some time he grew high, and hectored with his holinesse, and gave him the lye. The pope sayd he was mad.

He was well versed in all kinds of learning. And he had also this vertue, that no man *knew better how to abound, and to be abased*, and either was indifferent to him. No man became grandeur better; sometimes again he would live only with a lackey, and horse with a foote-cloath.

He was very generous, and liberall to deserving persons. When Abraham Cowley was but 13 yeares old, he dedicated to him a comedy, called *Love's Riddle*, and concludes in his epistle – 'The Birch that whip't him then would prove a Bay.' Sir K. was very kind to him...

A^{nno} — (quaere the countess of Thanet) much against his mother's, etc., consent, he maried that celebrated beautie and courtezane, Mrs. Venetia Stanley, whom Richard earle of Dorset kept as his concubine, had children by her, and setled on her an annuity of 500*li*. per annum; which after Sir K. D.

maried was unpayd by the earle; and for which annuity Sir
Kenelme sued the earle, after mariage, and recovered it. He
would say that a handsome lusty man that was discreet might
make a vertuose wife out of a brothell-house. This lady carried herselfe blamelessly, yet (they say) he was jealous of her.
She dyed suddenly, and hard-hearted woemen would censure
him severely.

After her death, to avoyd envy and scandall, he retired in
to Gresham Colledge at London, where he diverted himselfe
with his chymistry, and the professors' good conversation.
He wore there a long mourning cloake, a high crowned hatt,
his beard unshorne, look't like a hermite, as signes of sorrowe
for his beloved wife, to whose memory he erected a sumptu-
ouse monument, now quite destroyed by the great conflag-
ration. He stayed at the colledge two or 3 yeares.

John Aubrey
Brief Lives (1813). Text from Clark's edition
(Oxford, 1897). Written 1669–96

THE DISCIPLES OF MR HOBBES

O, BY all means, says a fourth, Mr. *Hobbs* must needs be in
the right: I'll pawn half my Estate upon it, that he is: He shall
dispute with all the *Ecclesiasticals* for a hundred pounds of my
money. For he perceives now where the *pinch* of the business
lies: for he has *worn* him above this half year in his *pocket, day*
and *night*: and have above twenty places of *moment* turn'd
down: some before, and some after the Candle was out. O,
says he, how ignorant, and deadly cold am I, if by chance
I leave him at home: he is a great deal more comfortable and
warm than a *squirrel* in the sleeve. But if you happen upon
one, that has worn the *Philosopher* so long; that two or three

of his Phrases are got through his *pocket*, and at last have insinuated themselves into his temper: he proves presently a *Chair-man* in all companies: and if he looks but upon a *Clergyman*, he is as great a *Prince*, as ever *Mr. Hobbs* gave power to. Then, come Sir, says he, Come now for your *Immaterial substances*: have you ever a one about you, Sir? I hear that you are much acquainted with them: you live by the *Spirit*, Sir; it is a wonder that you should not have one in your pocket: I have got *honest Material Mr. Hobbs* in mine. I could shew you for a need, Sir, *Spirit of Wine*, *Spirit of Salt*, or *Spirit of Harts-horn*: but I have enquired, and never could get, or see any *Spirit of Substance*. *Spirit of Substance*! that's fine indeed. What, *Essence of Essence*? pretty I profess. Indeed we have had a very curious time of it, a company of very seeing *Priests*, and searching *Philosophers*: that should go on, and on, and teach one another such plain, palpable, and manifest contradictions. Ask them, how such an Effect come to pass: it is done, say they, by an incorporeal Substance. Wonderfully acute indeed! that is, by *no body*: or by a *no body body*: or by a *no thing thing*. It was very well for this *Nation*, that *Mr. Hobbs* was born at last; and *half a dozen of us* of willingness, and parts, to understand him; otherwise the *world* had continued in a brave blind condition . . . And whereas heretofore it was a work of many years study, and seriousness: that could entitle one but to be suspected of *Atheism*: now he that has but seen *Mr. Hobb's Book*, and can make but a *Mouse-trap*, is as fully priviledg'd, as if he could *pluck up the Earth by the roots*, or *make a man*.

John Eachard

Some Observations upon the Answer to . . .
the Contempt of the Clergy (1671)

The Character of Mr Bayes,[1] an Ambitious Clergyman

(1672)

He follow'd the Town life, haunted the best companies; and, to polish himself from any Pedantick roughness, he read and saw the Playes, with much care and more proficiency than most of the Auditory. But all this while he forgot not the main chance, but hearing of a vacancy with a Noble man, he clapp'd in, and easily obtained to be his Chaplain. From that day you may take the date of his Preferments and his Ruine. For having soon wrought himself dexterously into his Patrons favour, by short Graces and Sermons, and a mimical way of drolling upon the *Puritans*, which he knew would take both at Chappel and Table; he gained a great Authority likewise among all the domesticks. They all listened to him as an Oracle: and they allow'd him by common consent, to have not only all the *Divinity*, but more wit too than all the rest of the family put together. This thing alone elevated him exceedingly in his own conceit, and raised his *Hypocondria* into the Region of the Brain: that his head swell'd like any Bladder with wind and vapour. But after he was stretch'd to such an height in his own fancy, that he could not look down from top to toe but his Eyes dazled at the Precipice of his Stature; there fell out, or in, another natural chance which push'd him headlong. For being of an amorous complexion, and finding himself (as I told you) the *Cock-Divine* and the *Cock-Wit* of the Family, he took the priviledge to walk among the Hens: and thought it was not impolitick to establish his new-acquired Reputation upon the Gentlewomens side. And they that perceived he was a Rising-Man, and of pleasant Conversation, dividing his Day among

1. Marvell's name for his adversary Samuel Parker, F.R.S. (1640–1688), later Bishop of Oxford, an opponent of religious toleration.

them into Canonical hours, of reading now the Common-Prayer, and now the Romances; were very much taken with him. The Sympathy of Silk began to stir and attract the Tippet to the Pettycoat and the Petticoat toward the Tippet. The innocent Ladies found a strange unquietness in their minds, and could not distinguish whether it were Love or Devotion. Neither was he wanting on his part to carry on the Work; but shifted himself every day with a clean Surplice, and, as oft as he had occasion to bow, he directed his Reverence towards the Gentlewomens Pew. Till, having before had enough of the Libertine, and undertaken his Calling only for Preferment; he was transported now with the Sanctity of his Office, even to extasy: and like the Bishop over *Maudlin Colledge* Altar, or like *Maudlin de la Croix*, he was seen in his Prayers to be lifted up sometimes in the Air, and once particularly so high that he crack'd his Scul against the Chappel Ceiling. I do not hear for all this that he had ever practised upon the Honour of the Ladies, but that he preserved alwayes the Civility of a *Platonick Knight-Errant*. For all this Courtship had no other operation than to make him stil more in love with himself: and if he frequented their company, it was only to speculate his own Baby in their Eyes. But being thus, without Competitor or Rival, the Darling of both Sexes in the Family and his own Minion; he grew beyond all measure elated, and that crack of his Scull, as in broken Looking-Glasses, multipli'd him in self-conceit and imagination.

Having fixed his Center in this Nobleman's House, he thought he could now move and govern the whole Earth with the same facility. Nothing now would serve him but he must be a madman in print, and write a Book of *Ecclesiastical Policy*. There he distributes all the *Territories of Conscience* into the Princes Province, and makes the *Hierarchy* to be but Bishops of the Air: and talks at such an extravagant rate in things of higher concernment, that the Reader will avow that in the whole discourse he had not one *lucid interval*. This Book he was so bent upon, that he sate up late at nights, and wanting sleep, and drinking sometimes Wine to animate his Fancy, it increas'd his Distemper. Beside that too he had the misfortune to have two Friends, who being also out of their wits, and of the same though something a calmer phrensy, spurr'd him on perpetually with commendation. But when his Book was once come out, and he saw himself an Author; that some of the Galants of the Town layd by the new Tune and the *Tay, tay, tarry*, to quote some of his impertinencies; that his Title page was posted and pasted up at every avenue next under the Play for that afternoon at the Kings or the Dukes House: the Vain-Glory of this totally confounded him. He lost all the little remains of his understanding, and his *Cerebellum* was so dryed up that there was more brains in a Walnut and both their Shells were alike thin and brittle. The King of *France* that lost his wits, had not near so many unlucky circumstances to occasion it: and in the last of all there is some Similitude. For, as a negligent Page that rode behind and carried the Kings Lance, let it fall on his head, the King being in Armour, and the day hot, which so disordered him that he never recovered it: so this Gentleman, in the Dog-dayes, stragling by *Temple-bar*, in a massy Cassock and Surcingle, and taking the opportunity at once to piss and admire the Title-page of his Book; a tall Servant of his, one *J.O.*[1] that was not so careful as he should be, or whether he did it of purpose, lets another Book of four hundred leaves fall upon his head; which meeting with the former fracture in his *Cranium*, and all the concurrent Accidents already mentioned, has utterly undone him.

Andrew Marvell

The Rehearsal Transpros'd . . . (1672)

1. John Owen, Independent divine, who joined in the controversy against Parker.

DICE AT THE ORDINARY

(1674)

THE day being shut in, you may properly compare this place to those Countries which lye far in the North, where it is as clear at midnight as at noonday: And though it is a house of Sin, yet you cannot call it a house of Darkness, for the Candles never go out till morning, unless the sudden fury of a losing Gamester make them extinct.

This is the time (when ravenous beasts usually seek their prey) wherein comes shoals of *Huffs*, *Hectors*, *Setters*, *Gilts*, *Pads*, *Biters*, *Divers*, *Lifters*, *Filers*, *Budgies*, *Droppers*, *Crossbyters*, &c., and these may all pass under the general and common appellation of *Rooks*. And in this particular, an *Ordinary* serves as a *Nursery* for *Tyburn*; for if any one will put himself to the trouble of observation, he shall find, that there is seldom a year wherein there are not some of this Gang hang as *pretious Jewels* in the ear of *Tyburn*: Look back and you will find a great many gone already, God knows how many are to follow.

These Rooks are in continual motion, walking from one Table to another, till they can discover some unexperienc'd young Gentleman, Casheer or Apprentice, that is come to this *School of Virtue*, being unskill'd in the quibbles and devices there practised; these they call *Lambs*, or *Colls*: Then do the *Rooks* (more properly called *Wolves*) strive who shall fasten on him first, following him close, and engaging him in some advantageous Bets, and at length worries him, that is, gets all his money, and then the Rooks (Rogues I should have said) laugh and grin, saying, *the Lamb is bitten*.

Some of these *Rooks* will be very importunate to borrow money of you without any intention to pay you; or to go with you seven to twelve half a Crown or more, whereby without a very great chance (ten to one or more) he is sure to win: If you are sensible hereof, and refuse his proposition, they will take it so ill, that if you have not an especial care they will pick your pocket, nim your gold or silver buttons off your Cloak or Coat; or it may be draw your silver-hilted Sword out of your belt without discovery, especially if you are eager upon your Cast, which is done thus; the silver buttons are strung, or run upon Cats guts fastned at the upper and nether end; now by ripping both ends very ingeniously (as they call it) give it the gentile pull, and so rub off with the buttons; and if your cloak be loose 'tis ten to one they have it.

But that which will most provoke (in my opinion) any mans rage to just satisfaction, is their throwing many times at a good sum with a *dry fist* (as they call it) that is; if they *nick* you, 'tis theirs; if they lose, they owe you so much with many other quillets: some I have known so abominably impudent, that they would snatch up the Stakes, and thereupon instantly draw, saying, if you will have your money you must fight for it; for he is a Gentleman and will not want: however, if you will be patient, he will pay you another time; if you are so tame to take this, go no more to the Ordinary; for then the whole Gang will be ever and anon watching an opportunity to make a *Mouth* of you in the like nature. If you nick them, 'tis odds, if they wait not your coming out at night and beat you: I could produce you an hundred examples in this kind, but they will rarely adventure on the attempt unless they are backt with some *Bully-Huffs*, and *Bully-Rocks*, with others whose fortunes are as desperate as their own. We need no other testimony to confirm the danger of associating with these Anthropo-phagi or Man-Eaters, than *Lincolns*-Inn-Fields whilst *Speerings Ordinary* was kept in Bell-yard, and that you need not want a pair of Witnesses for the proof thereof, take in also *Covent-Garden*.

Neither is the House it self to be exempted, every night almost some one or other, who either heated with Wine, or made cholerick with the loss of his Money, raises a quarrel, swords are drawn, box and candlesticks thrown at one anothers head, Tables overthrown, and all the House in such a Garboyl, that it is the perfect Type of Hell.

Charles Cotton
The Compleat Gamester ... (1674)

A Chaplain's Double-Dealing

(1678)

[*Mr Nichols, chaplain to Sir Charles and Lady Howard at Naworth Castle, Cumberland, where Anne Murray (later Lady Halkett) is a guest, has caused trouble between the friends by falsely suggesting that Anne imagines that Sir Charles is in love with her and that his lady is jealous of her in consequence.*]

"MADAM, (said I,) I must acknowledge I did beleeve him my freind, and so excellent a man that I thought, as all in your familly did, that itt was a blesing to have him in yᵉ howse. Butt now so much the greater is my misfortune to have him for my accuser, who is so much respected by all, and whose very profesion would inforce beleefe. I love nott retaliation, and to returne ill for ill, butt since I have no other way to asert my owne inocency I must freely declare hee was himselfe the only person that took paines to perswade mee you were jelouse of mee; and when I resolved to vindicate my selfe from whatever might seem to give occation for itt, hee diswaded mee, and said you had too much pride to owne itt, and that you would butt laugh att mee, and 'twould expose mee to your scorne; and what hee related as my words were his owne, wᶜʰ when at any time I contredicted, hee would say itt was

my partiality made mee defend you, and nott my reason.
This, madam, is so great a truth that I will owne itt before
him whenever you find it convenientt. But pray, madam,
(said I,) when hee told you all these things to my disadvantage,
did itt not lesen your beleefe of itt comming from a person
who proffesed to have so great respect for mee, and yett per-
forming acts so contrary to itt? Did nott this plead for mee in
your thoughts, that hee who could disemble might bee unjust, and I inocentt?" "I confese (said my Lady,) itt did prevaile much on your side, and one day when hee was railing
against you I said to him, How comes you are so civill to her,
and profese so great a esteeme of her, if you have so ill an
opinion of her?" "I an esteeme of her? (replied hee,) I could
nott butt bee civill to her because I saw S^r Ch. and your La.
respect her; butt God is my wittnese I never looked upon her
butt as one of the ayreiest things that ever I saw, and admired
what itt was your La. and S^r Ch. saw in her to bee so kind to
her." I smiled and said, "I wish I could as easily confirme hee
was the author of what hee related of mee, as I can, under his
owne hand, that hee had better thoughts of mee then so ayry
a thing as hee then represented mee." Shee was desirous to
see ye letter; wch I shewed her, with the copy of my owne to
wch his was an answeare . . . As soon as my Lady H read the
letter, shee said, "I am afraid this man hath deceaved us all, and
will prove a villaine." While wee were at this discourse S^r Ch.
knoct att the doore; wee lett him in, and he smiling said,
"I hope you understand one another." Wee gave him some
short accountt of what had beene betwixt us, wch hee said did
confirme what hee had beene of opinion of a pritty while;
"butt (sayed hee,) I will injoyne you both, what ever paseth
betwixt you when you are alone, lett noe person know butt
that you are still att the same distance you were before, till
my returne; for I am imediately informed of some mose-
troopers that are plundering in the country, and I and all my

men are going to try if wee can take them; therfore you must pray for mee, since I cannot goe with you now to the chapell." Wee both promised to follow his injunctions, and parted.

Anne, Lady Halkett
Autobiography (1875). Written 1678

HOBBES

(1588–1678)

His complexion. In his youth he was unhealthy, and of an ill complexion (yellowish).

His[1] lord, who was a waster, sent him up and downe to borrow money, and to gett gentlemen to be bound for him, being ashamed to speake him selfe: he tooke colds, being wett in his feet (then were no hackney coaches to stand in the streetes), and trod both his shoes aside the same way. Notwithstanding he was well-beloved: they lov'd his company for his pleasant facetiousnes and good-nature.

From forty, or better, he grew healthier, and then he had a fresh, ruddy, complexion. He was *sanguineo-melancholicus*; which the physiologers say is the most ingeniose complexion. He would say that 'there might be good witts of all complexions; but good-natured, impossible'.

Head. In his old age he was very bald (which claymed a veneration); yet within dore, he used to study, and sitt, bare-headed, and sayd he never tooke cold in his head, but that the greatest trouble was to keepe-off the flies from pitching on the baldnes. His head was — inches in compasse (I have the measure), and of a mallet-forme (approved by the physiologers).

1. This only *inter nos* [Aubrey's note].

Skin. His skin was soft and of that kind which my Lord Chancellor Bacon in his *History of Life and Death* calles a goose-skin, i.e. of a wide texture:–

Crassa cutis, crassum cerebrum, crassum ingenium.

Face not very great; ample forehead; whiskers yellowish-redish, which naturally turned up – which is a signe of a brisque wit, e.g. James Howell, Henry Jacob of Merton College.

[*Beard.*] Belowe he was shaved close, except a little tip under his lip. Not but that nature could have afforded a venerable beard (Sapientum pascere barbam – Horat. Satyr. lib.2), but being naturally of a cheerfull and pleasant humour, he affected not at all austerity and gravity to looke severe . . . He desired not the reputation of his wisdome to be taken from the cutt of his beard, but from his reason –

Barba non facit philosophum. 'Il consiste tout en la pointe de sa barbe et en ses deux moustaches; et, par consequence, pour le diffaire il ne faut que trois coups de ciseau.' – Balzac *Lettres*, tom. 2, p. 242.

Eie. He had a good eie, and that of a hazell colour, which was full of life and spirit, even to the last. When he was earnest in discourse, there shone (as it were) a bright live-coale within it. He had two kind of looks: – when he laugh't, was witty, and in a merry humour, one could scarce see his eies; by and by when he was serious and positive, he open'd his eies round (i.e. his eielids). He had midling eies, not very big, nor very little (from Sir W[illiam] P[etty]).

Stature. He was sixe foote high, and something better (quaere James Wh[eldon]), and went indifferently erect, or rather, considering his great age, very erect.

Sight; witt. His sight and witt continued to the last. He had a curious sharp sight, as he had a sharpe witt, which was also so sure and steady (and contrary to that men call bro[a]d-witednes) that I have heard him oftentimes say that in multiplying and dividing he never mistooke a figure: and so in other things.

John Aubrey

Brief Lives (1813). Text from Clark's edition
(Oxford, 1897). This life was written 1679–80

THE SECOND BOTTLE

(1679)

To Henry Saville.

Oh! *That second Bottle* (Harry!) *is the sincerest, wisest, and most impartial downright Friend we have*; tells us Truth of *our selves*, and forces us to speak Truths of *others*; banishes *Flattery* from our *Tongues*, and *Distrust* from our *Hearts*; sets us above the *mean policy of Court-Prudence*, which makes us lie to one another *all Day*, for fear of being *Betray'd* by each other *at Night*. And (before *God*) I believe the *errantest Villain breathing is honest as long as that Bottle lives*, and few of *that Tribe* dare venture upon him, at least among the *Courtiers* and *Statesmen*. I have seriously consider'd one Thing, That of the three Businesses of this Age, *Women, Politicks and Drinking*, the *last* is the only Exercise at which you and I have not prov'd our selves *errant Fumblers*: If you have the *Vanity* to think *otherwise*; when we meet, let us appeal to Friends of *both sexes*, and as they shall determine, live and die *their Drunkards*, or *entire Lovers*. For, as we mince the Matter, it is hard to say which is the most *tiresom Creature, Loving Drunkard*, or the *Drunken Lover*.

Bath, June 22, [?1679].

John Wilmot, Earl of Rochester
Familiar Letters by Lord Rochester and Others (1697)

CHARLES II AND THE EARL OF CLARENDON

... HE[1] was affable and easy, and loved to be made so by all about him. The great art of keeping him long was, the being easy, and the making every thing easy to him. He had made such observations on the *French* government, that he thought a King who might be checkt, or have his Ministers called to an account by a Parliament, was but a King in name. He had a great compass of knowledge, tho' he was never capable of much application or study. He understood the Mechanicks and Physick; and was a good Chymist, and much set on several preparations of Mercury, chiefly the fixing it. He understood navigation well: But above all he knew the architecture of ships so perfectly, that in that respect he was exact rather more than became a Prince. His apprehension was quick, and his memory good. He was an everlasting talker. He told his stories with a good grace: But they came in his way too often. He had a very ill opinion both of men and women; and did not think that there was either sincerity or chastity in the world out of principle, but that some had either the one or the other out of humour or vanity. He thought that no body did serve him out of love: And so he was quits with all the world, and loved others as little as he thought they loved him. He hated business, and could not be easily brought to mind any: But when it was necessary, and he was set to it, he would stay as long as his Ministers had work for him. The ruine of his reign, and of all his affairs, was occasioned chiefly by his delivering himself up at his first coming over to a mad range of pleasure. One of the race of the *Villers*, then married to *Palmer*, a Papist, soon after made Earl of *Castlemain*, who afterwards being separated from him was advanced to be Duchess of *Cleveland*, was his first and longest mistress, by whom he had five children. She was a

1. Charles II.

woman of great beauty, but most enormously vitious and ravenous; foolish but imperious, very uneasy to the King, and always carrying on intrigues with other men, while yet she pretended she was jealous of him. His passion for her and her strange behaviour towards him, did so disorder him, that often he was not master of himself, nor capable of minding business: But he did then so entirely trust the Earl of *Clarendon*, that he left all to his care, and submitted to his advices as to so many oracles.

The Earl of *Clarendon* was bred to the Law, and was like to grow eminent in his profession when the wars began. He distinguished himself so in the House of Commons, that he became considerable, and was much trusted all the while the King was at Oxford. He stayed beyond sea following the King's fortune till the Restoration; and was now an absolute favourite, and the chief or the only Minister, but with too magisterial a way. He was always pressing the King to mind his affairs, but in vain. He was a good Chancellour, only a little too rough, but very impartial in the administration of justice. He never seemed to understand foreign affairs well: And yet he meddled too much in them. He had too much levity in his wit, and did not always observe the decorum of his post. He was high, and was apt to reject those who addressed themselves to him with too much contempt. He had such a regard to the King, that when places were disposed of, even otherwise than as he advised, yet he would justify what the King did, and disparage the pretensions of others, not without much scorn; which created him many enemies. He was indefatigable in business, tho' the gout did often disable him from waiting on the King: Yet, during his credit, the King came constantly to him when he was laid up by it.

Gilbert Burnet

History of his Own Time (1724). Written 1683–1704

GEORGE SAVILLE, MARQUESS OF HALIFAX

(1633–95)

HE was a man of a great and ready wit; full of life, and very pleasant; much turned to satyr. He let his wit run much on matters of religion: So that he passed for a bold and determined Atheist; tho' he often protested to me, he was not one; and said, he believed there was not one in the world : He confessed, he could not swallow down every thing that divines imposed on the world: He was a Christian in submission: He believed as much as he could, and he hoped that God would not lay it to his charge, if he could not digest iron, as an ostrich did, nor take into his belief things that must burst him: If he had any scruples, they were not sought for, nor cherished by him; for he never read an atheistical book. In a fit of sickness, I knew him very much touched with a sense of religion. I was then often with him. He seemed full of good purposes: But they went off with his sickness. He was always talking of morality and friendship. He was punctual in all payments, and just in all his private dealings. But, with relation to the publick, he went backwards and forwards, and changed sides so often, that in conclusion no side trusted him. He seemed full of Common-wealth notions: Yet he went into the worst part of King *Charles*'s reign. The liveliness of his imagination was always too hard for his judgment. A severe jest was preferred by him to all arguments whatsoever. And he was endless in consultations: For when after much discourse a point was settled, if he could find a new jest, to make even that which was suggested by himself seem ridiculous, he could not hold, but would study to raise the credit of his wit, tho' it made others call his judgment in question. When he talked to me as a philosopher of his contempt of the world, I asked him, what he meant by getting so many new titles, which I call'd the hanging himself about with bells and tinsel. He had no other excuse for it, but this, that, since the world were such fools as to value those matters, a man must be a fool for company: He considered them but as rattles: Yet rattles please children: So these might be of use to his family. His heart was much set on raising his family. But, tho' he made a vast estate for them, he buried two of his sons himself, and almost all his grandchildren. The son that survived was an honest man, but far inferior to him.

Gilbert Burnet
History of his Own Time (1724). Written 1683–1704

THE NEW QUEEN

(1688)

6 FEB... There was much contest about the King's abdication, and whether he had vacated the government. The *Earle of Nottingham* and about 20 Lords, and many Bps. enter'd their protests, but the concurrence was greate against them... 21 Feb. Dr. *Burnett* preach'd at *St. James's*, on the obligation to walke worthy of God's particular and signal deliverance of the Nation and Church.

I saw the *new Queene* and *King* proclaim'd the very next day after her coming to *Whitehall*, Wednesday 13 Feb., with greate acclamation and generall good reception. Bonfires, bells, guns, &c. It was believ'd that both, especialy the Princesse, would have shew'd some (seeming) reluctance at least, of assuming her father's Crown, and made some apology, testifying by her regret, that he should by his mismanagement necessitate the Nation to so extraordinary a proceeding, wch would have shew'd very handsomely to the world, and according to the character given of her piety; consonant also to her husband's first declaration, that there was no intention of deposing the King, but of succouring the Nation; but nothing of all this appear'd; she came into *Whitehall* laughing and jolly, as to a wedding, so as to seem quite transported. She rose early the next morning, and in her undresse, as it was reported, before her women were up, went about from roome to roome to see the convenience of *Whitehall*; lay in the same bed and apartm^t where the late Queene lay, and within a night or two sate down to play at basset, as the Queene her predecessor us'd to do. She smil'd upon and talk'd to every body, so that no change seem'd to have taken place at Court since her last going away, save that infinite crouds of people throng'd to see her, and that she went to our prayers. This carriage was censur'd by many. She seems to be of a good nature, and that she takes nothing to heart; whilst the Prince her husband has a thoughtful countenance, is wonderfull serious and silent, and seems to treat all persons alike gravely, and to be very intent on affaires: *Holland*, *Ireland*, and *France* calling for his care.

John Evelyn

Memoirs Illustrative of the Life and Writings of John Evelyn, Esq., F.R.S. (1818)

A SAD EXAMPLE AND A NEW SADDLE

(1694)

July 21st 1694

... WEE have had many strange disasters within this weeke as to untimely deaths: some making away themselves and others suddainly struck by the immediate hand of God. I will only mention two because remarkable. one was neer us. A Bricklayers apprentice Sunday night last his mistris giving him victualls for his supper told him what hee could not eat if hee gave it to the Cat hee had better bee hanged, it seemes hee used so to doe, but the next morning the boy not coming out of the chamber to goe to work when they came into it they found him hanging by the neck and the Cat hanging in another cord by him both dead. And also the same day, viz: the Lords day after the Afternoons sermon a mayd formerly our servant but now lives neer the Tower coming to see us sayd that as shee came by the Thames side neer the Custom house a fellow was at work on shipboard and having a Barrell on his shoulders by some accedent the Barrell broak his neck and dyed. she sayd she saw the man. a sad example for Sabboth breakers. I intend God willing within a moneth to come into Devonshire, haveing some few houses at Plymouth, I have been on Horseback but once these 7 yeares and how I shall endure the journey I know not, but if I have oppertunity and strenght I think to make bold to wayt on you. I never was yet in that part of the Cuntry and its not probable I may ever see Devonshire againe.

July 28th 1694

Wee heare that since our fyring of deepe and Haver de Grace French privateers have burnt a village or two in Scotland. Wee heare of some disturbances in Cheshire and adjacent Counties against the Government by some gents of ye cheepest note and that neere 20 are seized and severall of them charged with High Treason.

Yisterday one Captaine Riffington killed one Mr. Dod by runing him through with his sword neer Chayring Cross.

August 4th 1694

I have this day sent by the Exeter Carier a Box directed to your selfe at Portledge neer Torrington because I suppose the Torrington Carrier brings it from Exeter. in the box are the sadle stirrups Girts fore paterne and crupper and black cover

deepe] Dieppe

and Bridle. also in the same box is Mr. Coffins perriwig, Ashmole's 'Order of the Garter' and Mr. Bamfeilds and Dr Wallis their controversies bound in one vollum. As for the sadle I have as neer as I could literally observed your last directions according as you have set down the perticulars and have bin with most of the eminentest sadlers both in the Citty and suburbs. I could have bought severall sadles that looked more gaudy for a lesser price but then I must have ventured on my own head. I met with severall with gould silver and silk trimings but none that were for your purpose with gould triming alone unless embroidred and those were very gay and highprised and was forced to fix on this which I had formerly in my eyes, but thought it too deare. I bought it of the Queens sadler neer the Pall mell. hee is reputed a very honest man but a stranger to mee. hee gave mee his lowest price when I first saw him but when I went againe to consummate the bargaine, thinking to have had it cheaper, hee was gon to Winchester and his servants sayd that the perticulars proposed were without the Sadle-cloath . . . Its a new sadle very good velvet and frenge but without gould or silver. as for the other furniture its fashionable but plaine as it is now worne by most gentlemen. They tell mee by reason of the warr velvet and frenge is much rissen which makes it the dearer. I hope the Box wilbe at your house by Tuesday.

Richard Lapthorne
The Portledge Papers (1928). Written 1683–95

LEEDS

(1698)

LEEDS is a large town, severall large streetes cleane and well pitch'd and good houses all built of stone, some have good gardens and steps up to their houses and walls before them; this is esteemed the wealthyest town of its bigness in the Country, its manufacture is the woollen cloth the Yorkshire Cloth in which they are all employ'd and are esteemed very rich and very proud; they have provision soe plentifull that they may live with very little expense and get much variety; here if one calls for a tankard of ale which is allwayes a groate –its the only dear thing all over Yorkshire, their ale is very strong – but for paying this groat for your ale you may have a slice of meate either hott or cold according to the tyme of day you call, or else butter and cheese gratis into the bargaine, this was a generall custom in most parts of Yorkshire but now they have almost changed it, and tho' they still retaine the great price for the ale yet make Strangers pay for their meate, and at some places at great rates, notwithstanding how cheape they have all their provision; there is still this custome on a Market day at Leeds the sign of the Bush just by the bridge, any body that will goe and call for one tanckard of ale and a pinte of wine and pay for these only, shall be set to a table to eate with 2 or 3 dishes of good meate and a dish of sweet-meates after; had I known this and the day which was their Market, I would have come then but I happened to come a day after the Market, however I did only pay for 3 tankards of ale and what I eate and my servants was gratis; this town is full of Discenters there are 2 large Meeting places, here is also a good schoole for young Gentlewomen; the streetes are very broad the Market large.

Celia Fiennes

'My Great Journey to Newcastle and Cornwall' [in 1698] in *Journeys* (1888). Text from Morris's edition (London, 1947). Written 1685–1703

THE MOVEMENT OF IDEAS: REFLECTION, ARGUMENT, EXHORTATION, SATIRE

PRINCIPLE AND FEELING IN THE CIVIL CONFLICT

ONE Day after Dinner, *Nathaniel Fiennes*, who that Day likewise dined there, asked Mr. *Hyde*, whether He would ride into the Fields, and take a little Air, it being a fine Evening; which the other consenting to, They sent for their Horses, and riding together in the Fields, between *Westminster* and *Chelsea*, Mr. *Fiennes* asked him, what it was that inclined him to adhere so passionately to the Church, which could not possibly be supported. He answered, that He could have no other Obligation than that of his own Conscience, and his Reason, that could move with him; for He had no Relation, or Dependance upon any Churchmen, that could dispose him to it; that He could not conceive, how Religion could be preserved without Bishops; nor how the Government of the State could well subsist, if the Government of the Church were altered; and asked him what Government They meant to introduce in its Place: To which He answered, that there would be Time enough to think of that; but assured him, and wished him to remember what He said, that if the King resolved to defend the Bishops, it would cost the Kingdom much Blood; and would be the Occasion of as sharp a War, as had ever been in *England*: for that there was a great Number of good Men, who resolved to lose their Lives, before They would ever submit to that Government. Which was the first positive Declaration He had ever heard from any particular Man of that Party; very few of them having at that Time that Resolution, much less avowing it; and if They had, the Kingdom was in no Degree at that Time infected with that Poison, how much soever it was spread afterwards.

Within two Days after this Discourse from Mr. *Fiennes*, Mr. *Hyde*, walking between the Parliament House, and *Westminster*, in the Church-Yard met with *Harry Martin*, with whom He lived very familiarly; and speaking together about the Proceedings of the Houses, *Martin* told him, that He would undo himself by his adhering to the Court; to which He replied that He had no Relation to the Court, and was only concerned to maintain the Government, and preserve the Law: and then told him He could not conceive what He proposed to himself, for He did not think him to be of the Opinion, or Nature with those Men, who governed the House; and asked him, what He thought of such, and such Men; and He very frankly answered, that He thought them Knaves; and that when They had done as much as They intended to do, They should be used as They had used others. The other pressed him then to say what He desired; to which, after a little Pause, He very roundly answered, *I do not think one Man wise enough to govern us all*: which was the first Word He had ever heard any Man speak to that Purpose; and would without Doubt, if it had been then communicated, or attempted, been the most abhorred by the whole Nation, of any Design that could be mentioned; and yet it appears it had even so early entered into the Hearts of some desperate Persons; that Gentleman being at that Time possessed of a very great Fortune, and having great Credit in his Country. . . .

Mr. *Hyde* was wont often to relate a Passage in that melancholick Time, when the Standard was set up at *Nottingham*, with which He was much affected. Sir *Edmund Varney*, Knight-

Marshal, who was mentioned before as Standard Bearer, with whom He had great Familiarity, who was a Man of great Courage, and generally beloved, came one Day to him and told him, "He was very glad to see him, in so universal a Damp, under which the Spirits of most Men were oppressed, retain still his natural Vivacity and Chearfulness; that He knew that the Condition of the King, and the Power of the Parliament, was not better known to any Man than to him; and therefore He hoped that He was able to administer some Comfort to his Friends, that might raise their Spirits, as well as it supported his own." He answered, "that He was in Truth beholden to his Constitution, which did not incline him to Despair; otherwise, that He had no pleasant Prospect before him, but thought as ill of Affairs as most Men did; that the other was as far from being melancholick as He, and was known to be a Man of great Courage (as indeed He was of a very cheerful, and a generous Nature, and confessedly Valiant) and that They could not do the King better Service, than by making it their Business to raise the dejected Minds of Men; and root out those Apprehensions which disturbed them, of Fear and Despair, which could do no Good, and did really much Mischief."

He replied smiling, "I will willingly join with you the best I can, but I shall act it very scurvily. My Condition, *said He*, is much worse than yours, and different I believe from any other Man's, and will very well justify the Melancholick that, I confess to you, possesses me. You have Satisfaction in your Conscience that you are in the Right; that the King ought not to grant what is required of him; and so you do your Duty, and your Business together: But for my Part, I do not like the Quarrel, and do heartily wish that the King would yield and consent to what They desire; so that my Conscience is only concerned in Honour, and in Gratitude to follow my Master. I have eaten his Bread, and served him near thirty years, and will not do so base a Thing, as to forsake him; and chuse rather to lose my Life (which I am sure I shall do) to preserve and defend those Things, which are against my Conscience to preserve and defend: For I will deal freely with you, I have no Reverence for the Bishops, for whom this Quarrel subsists." It was not a Time to Dispute; and his Affection to the Church had never been suspected. He was as Good as his Word; and was killed in the Battle of *Edgehill*, within two Months after this Discourse. And if those who had the same and greater Obligations, had observed the same Rules of Gratitude, and Generosity, whatever their other Affections had been, that Battle had never been fought, nor any of that Mischief been brought to pass, that succeeded it.

Edward Hyde, Earl of Clarendon
*The Life of Edward Earl of Clarendon . . . written
by himself* (1759). Written 1668–70

THE KING HAS HIS POWER IN TRUST

THE name of a King is great I confesse, and worthy of great honour, but is not the name of people greater? let not meere tearms deceave us, let us weigh names and things together, admit that God sheds here some rayes of Majesty upon his vicegerents on earth, yet except we thinke he doth this out of particular love to Princes themselves, and not to communities of men, wee must not hence invert the course of nature, and make nations subordinate in end to Princes. My Lord of *Strafford*, sayes that the Law of Prerogative is like that of the first table, but the Law of Common safety and utility like that of the second, and hence concludes, that precedence is to be given to that which is more sacred, (that is) Regall Prerogative. Upon this ground all Parasites build when they seeke to hood-winke Princes for their owne advantages, and when they assay to draw that esteeme to themselves, which they withdraw from the people: and this doctrin is common, because 'tis so acceptable: for as nothing is more pleasant to Princes then to be so deified, so nothing is more gainefull to Courtiers then so to please. But to look into termes a little more narrower, and dispell umbrages; *Princes are called Gods, Fathers, Husbands, Lords, Heads, &c. and this implyes them to be of more worth and more unsubordinate in end, then their Subjects are, who by the same relation must stand as Creatures, Children, Wives, Servants, Members, &c.* I answer, these termes do illustrate some excellency in Princes by way of similitude, but must not in all things be applyed, and they are most truly applyed to Subjects taken *divisim*, but not *conjunctim*: Kings are Gods to particular men, *secumdum quid*, and are sanctified with some of Gods royaltie; but it is not for themselves, it is for an extrinsecall end, and that is the prosperitie of Gods people, and that end is more sacred than the meanes, as to themselves they are most unlike God; for God cannot be obliged by any thing extrinsecall, no created thing whatsoever can be of sufficient value or excellencie to impose any dutie or tye upon God, as Subjects upon Princes: therefore granting Prerogative to be but mediate, and the Weale Publike to be finall, wee must rank the Lawes of libertie in the first Table, and Prerogative in the second, as Nature doth require; and not after a kind of blasphemy ascribe that unsubordination to Princes, which is only due to God; so the King is a Father to his People, taken singly, but not universally; for the father is more worthy than the son in nature, and the son is wholly a debtor to the father, and can by no merit transcend his dutie, nor chalenge any thing as due from his father; for the father doth all his offices meritoriously, freely, and unexactedly. Yet this holds not in the relation betwixt King and Subject, for its more due in policie, and more strictly to be chalenged, that the King should make happy the People, than the People make glorious the King. This same reason is also in relation of Husband, Lord, &c. for the wife is inferiour in nature, and was created for the assistance of man, and servants are hired for their Lords meere attendance; but it is otherwise in the State betwixt man and man, for that civill difference which is for civill ends, and those ends are, that wrong and violence may be repressed by one for the good of all, not that servilitie and drudgerie may be imposed upon all, for the pomp of one.

Henry Parker
Observations upon Some of His Majesties
Late Answers and Expresses (1642)

AGAINST THE BISHOPS, AND THEIR STYLE

WE need not the autority of *Pliny* brought to tell us, the people cannot judge of a minister. Yet that hurts not. For as none can judge of a Painter, or Statuary but he who is an Artist, that is, either in the *Practick* or the *Theory*, which is often separated from the practick, and judges learnedly without it, so none can judge of a Christian teacher, but he who hath, either the practize, or the knowledge of Christian religion, though not so artfully digested in him. And who almost of the meanest Christians hath not heard the Scriptures often read from his childhood, besides so many Sermons and Lectures more in number then any student hath heard in Philosophy, whereby he may easily attaine to know when he is wisely taught and when weakly. Whereof three wayes I remember are set down in Scripture. The one is to read often that best of books written to this purpose, that not the wise only but the simple and ignorant may learne by them; the

other way to know of a minister, is by the life he leads, whereof the meanest understanding may be apprehensive. The last
way to judge aright in this point is when he who judges, lives
a Christian life himselfe. Which of these three will the Con-
futer affirme to exceed the capacity of a plaine artizan? And
what reason then is there left wherefore he should be deny'd
his voice in the election of his minister, as not thought a
competent discerner? It is but arrogance therefore, and the
pride of a *metaphysicall* fume, to thinke that *the mutinous
rabble* (for so he calls the Christian congregation) *would be so
mistaken in a Clerk of the University* that were to be their
minister. I doubt me those Clerks that think so, are more mistaken in themselves, and what with truanting and debaushery,
what with false grounds and the weaknesse of naturall faculties in many of them (it being a maxim in some men to send
the simplest of their sonnes thither) perhaps there would be
found among them as many unsolid and corrupted judgements
both in doctrine and life, as in any other two Corporations
of like bignesse. This is undoubted that if any Carpenter,
Smith, or Weaver, were such a bungler in his trade, as the
greater number of them are in their profession, he would
starve for any custome. And should he exercise his manifac-
ture, as little as they do their talents, he would forget his art:
and should he mistake his tools as they do theirs, he would
marre all the worke he took in hand. How few among them
know to write, or speak in a pure stile, much lesse to distinguish the *idea's*, and various kinds of stile: in Latine barbarous,
and oft not without *solecisms*, declaming in rugged and miscellaneous geare blown together by the foure winds, and in
their choice preferring the gay ranknesse of *Apuleius, Arno-
bius*, or any moderne fustianist, before the native *Latinisms* of
Cicero. In the Greek tongue most of them unletter'd, or un-
enter'd to any sound proficiency in those *Attick* maisters of
morall wisdome and eloquence. In the Hebrew text, which is

so necessary to be understood except it be some few of them, their lips are utterly uncircumcis'd. No lesse are they out of the way in philosophy; pestring their heads with the saplesse dotages of old *Paris and Salamanca*. And that which is the main point, in their Sermons affecting the comments and postils of Friers and Jesuits, but scorning and slighting the reformed writers. In so much that the better sort among them will confesse it a rare matter to heare a true edifying Sermon in either of their great Churches; and that such as are most humm'd and applauded there, would scarce be suffer'd the second hearing in a grave congregation of pious Christians. Is there cause why these men should overween, and be so queasie of the rude multitude, lest their deepe worth should be undervalu'd for want of fit umpires? No my *matriculated confutant* there will not want in any congregation of this Island, that hath not beene altogether famisht, or wholly perverted with Prelatish leven, there will not want divers plaine and solid men, that have learnt by the experience of a good conscience, what it is to be well taught, who will soone look through and through both the lofty nakednesse of your *Latinizing* Barbarian, and the finicall goosery of your neat Sermon-actor.

John Milton

*An Apology against a Pamphlet call'd a Modest
Confutation of the Animadversions upon the
Remonstrant against Smectymnuus* (1642)

A Plea for the Separatists, against the Bishop's Intolerance

I MOST affectionately entreat men not to contemne all things in those they now brand with their usuall staine of *Separatisme*; which phrase many use in such scorne, as if with one stab (of

postils] commentaries or marginal notes

that Italian dagger) they could run through Body and Soule at once.

These whom they so brand, may maintaine some errors, may not carry on the truth in the glory of it; who is so perfect? but oft-times in the midst of thickest ore we finde the purest gold: discover their errors and reject them; but doe not refuse what is good, because they hold it forth but darkly: no truth can shine in its perfect lustre at the first: light is darknesse when it first appeareth.

Yet *Light* was on the first Creatures, and yet not perfected till the Fourth Day, (and perhaps not fully then;) so was spirituall *Light* the beginning of *Reformation*, That *New Creation*; yet it was not perfect at first dawning, but encreaseth still by degrees, till it have quite chased away darknesse, and there be no more Night. All men yeeld there must be an encrease of light in the world; Now whether that be more probable to be in *Doctrine* or *Discipline*, judge yee.

At the first Rising out of Popery, the Church-lesse Church of the *Albigenses*, and *Waldenses* (Holy Good men) began an admirable Reformation. This was much advanced by *Jerome* of *Prague*, and *John Hus*. *Luther* had many grosse errours, yet must not lose his place among these glorious Lights. After these appeareth *Calvin*, shining yet brighter both in Doctrine and Discipline. Since him our God hath raised up a more glorious Light among these Northern Iles. And yet some went from us lately with a candle burning brighter perhaps than ours; though it were lighted here. Thus Light dilating, and enlarging it selfe, seemeth to become more pure, more Light, more Glorious; and yet it seemes not to be Noone. The Light, still, will, must, cannot but encrease; why then doe wee shut our eyes? Let it not bee said of us, that Light came in & grew up among us, yet we would not use it (for we cannot but receive it) because we loved darknesse . . .

We are too apt to slight the sweet breathings of Gods

Spirit, which He is pleased to communicate to others when wee are destitute of the same Workings. Some Christians are as it were wholly legall; they Fast, they Pray, receive Sacraments, heare Sermons, pay every one his own, live inoffensively: This is well done, but This is not All; yet this they take for enjoying God in Christ Jesus. But alas! *Quantum distat ab illo*, How far from that is it? *Non est vivere, sed valere vita*, Life consists in being healthfull, and not barely in living. These men may well be saved hereafter, but in the mean time, they lose the sweetest part of their life here.

On the other side, if God please to communicate himself in any manner of sweetnesse, so that a man begins to taste and see how good Communion and acquaintance with God is; how easily it is interrupted by loose walking; how sweet it is when enjoyed; so that it ravisheth the soul, and filleth the whole Heart, that it cannot but flow out at the Lips, in sweet breathings of, for, and after God in Christ Jesus, God in Christ Jesus. This man is presently stained with a taint of *Madnesse*, and I know not what *Enthusiasme*. If one that hath tasted and experimentally found the sweetnesse of Peace of Conscience, and knows how unpossible it is to keep it, but by close walking with God; how easily it is broken; and how hardly it is made up again when broken: so that he is content to leave Friends, Living, Liberty, All, rather than to break his Peace, wound his Conscience, sin against God, in sinning against light, or acting against Doubts, O that man is beyond all Rule of Reason; He hath a Tang of Phrensie; one puft up with a spirit of self conceit; a Rank *Separatist*.

But sure it should not be so among Christians. Can we not dissent in judgment (specially in these lower points of *Discipline*, while we agree *Doctrine*) but we must also disagree in *Affection*? A hard case!

I confesse there are many now that turn the Light of Truth, into a Life of loosenesse, vanity, and profanenesse; and we are all too too prone to This. There are some *Enthusiasticks*, who profane the Spirit. This I would resist with all my might. But let not all suffer with the wicked. Some without warrant run away from their Callings, and take up a bare, empty, fruitlesse Profession of Christianity, without the least dramme of life or power; These men my soul hateth.

But when God shall so enlarge his Hand, and unveil his face, that the poore creature is brought into communion and acquaintance with his Creator: steered in all his wayes, by his spirit; and by it carried up above shame, feare, pleasure, comfort, losses, grave, and death it selfe; Let us not censure such Tempers, but blesse God for them. So far as Christ is in us, we shall love, prise, honour Christ, and the least particle of his Image in others: For we never prove ourselves true members of Christ more, than when we embrace his members with most enlarged, yet straitest Affections.

To this end, God assisting me, my desire, prayer, endeavour shall still be, as much as in me lies, to follow peace and holinesse; and though there may haply be some little dissent betweene my darke judgement, weake conscience, and other Good men, that are much more cleare and strong; yet my prayer still shall be, to *keepe the Unity of the Spirit in the Bond of Peace*. And as many as walke after this Rule, Peace I hope shall still be on them, and the whole Israel of God.

Robert Greville, Lord Brooke
*A Discourse opening the Nature of that Episcopacie
which is Exercised in England* (1641). Text from
the second edition (1642)

LIBERTY OF SPEAKING AND WRITING

BEHOLD now this vast City; a City of refuge, the mansion house of liberty, encompast and surrounded with his protection;

the shop of warre hath not there more anvils and hammers waking, to fashion out the plates and instruments of armed Justice in defence of beleaguer'd Truth, then there be pens and heads there, sitting by their studious lamps, musing, searching, revolving new notions and idea's wherewith to present, as with their homage and their fealty the approaching Reformation: others as fast reading, trying all things, assenting to the force of reason and convincement. What could a man require more from a Nation so pliant and so prone to seek after knowledge. What wants there to such a towardly and pregnant soile, but wise and faithfull labourers, to make a knowing people, a Nation of Prophets, of Sages, and of Worthies. We reck'n more then five months yet to harvest; there need not be five weeks, had we but eyes to lift up, the fields are white already. Where there is much desire to learn, there of necessity will be much arguing, much writing, many opinions; for opinion in good men is but knowledge in the making. Under these fantastic terrors of sect and schism, we wrong the earnest and zealous thirst after knowledge and understanding which God hath stirr'd up in this City. What some lament of, we should rather rejoyce at, should rather praise this pious forwardnes among men, to reassume the ill deputed care of their Religion into their own hands again. A little generous prudence, a little forbearance of one another, and som grain of charity might win all these dilegences to joyn, and unite into one generall and brotherly search after Truth; could we but forgoe this Prelaticall tradition of crowding free consciences and Christian liberties into canons and precepts of men. I doubt not, if some great and worthy stranger should come among us, wise to discern the mould and temper of a people, and how to govern it, observing the high hopes and aims, the diligent alacrity of our extended thoughts and reasonings in the pursuance of truth and freedom, but that he would cry out as *Pirrhus* did, admiring the Roman docility and courage, if such were my *Epirots*, I would not despair the greatest design that could be attempted to make a Church or Kingdom happy. Yet these are the men cry'd out against for schismaticks and sectaries; as if, while the Temple of the Lord was building, some cutting, some squaring the marble, others hewing the cedars, there should be a sort of irrationall men who could not consider there must be many schisms and many dissections made in the quarry and in the timber, ere the house of God can be built. And when every stone is laid artfully together, it cannot be united into a continuity, it can but be contiguous in this world; neither can every peece of the building be of one form; nay rather the perfection consists in this, that out of many moderat varieties and brotherly dissimilitudes that are not vastly disproportionall arises the goodly and gracefull symmetry that commends the whole pile and structure. Let us therefore be more considerat builders, more wise in spirituall architecture, when great reformation is expected. For now the time seems come, wherein *Moses* the great Prophet may sit in heav'n rejoycing to see that memorable and glorious wish of his fulfill'd, when not only our sev'nty Elders, but all the Lords people are become Prophets. No marvell then though some men, and some good men too perhaps, but young in goodnesse, as *Joshua* then was, envy them. They fret, and out of their own weaknes are in agony, lest these divisions and subdivisions will undoe us. The adversarie again applauds, and waits the hour, when they have brancht themselves out, saith he, small anough into parties and partitions, then will be our time. Fool! he sees not the firm root, out of which we all grow, though into branches: nor will beware untill he see our small divided maniples cutting through at every angle of his ill united and unweildy brigade. And that we are to hope better of all these supposed sects and schisms. and that we shall not need that solicitude honest perhaps though over timorous of them that vex in this behalf, but shall laugh in the end, at those malicious applauders of our differences, I have these reasons to perswade me.

First, when a City shall be as it were besieg'd and blockt about, her navigable river infested, inrodes and incursions round, defiance and battell oft rumor'd to be marching up ev'n to her walls, and suburb trenches, that then the people, or the greater part, more then at other times, wholly tak'n up with the study of the highest and most important matters to be reform'd, should be disputing, reasoning, reading, inventing, discoursing, ev'n to a rarity, and admiration, things not before discourst or writt'n of, argues first a singular good will, contentednesse and confidence in your prudent foresight, and safe government, Lords and Commons; and from thence derives itself to a gallant bravery and well grounded contempt of their enemies, as if there were no small number of as great spirits among us, as his was, who when Rome was nigh besieg'd by *Hanibal*, being in the City, bought that peece of ground at no cheap rate, whereon *Hanibal* himself encampt his own regiment. Next it is a lively and cherfull presage of our happy successe and victory. For as in a body, when the blood is fresh, the spirits pure and vigorous, not only to vital, but to rationall faculties, and those in the acutest, and the pertest operations of wit and suttlety, it argues in what good plight and constitution the body is, so when the cherfulnesse of the people is so sprightly up, as that it has, not only wherewith to guard well its own freedom and safety, but to spare, and to bestow upon the solidest and sublimest points of controversie, and new invention, it betok'ns us not degenerated, nor drooping to a fatall decay, but casting off the old and wrincl'd skin of corruption to outlive these pangs and wax young again, entring the glorious waies of Truth and prosperous vertue destin'd to become great and honourable in these latter ages. Methinks I see in my mind a noble and puissant

Nation rousing herself like a strong man after sleep, and shaking her invincible locks: Methinks I see her as an Eagle muing her mighty youth, and kindling her undazl'd eyes at the full midday beam; purging and unscaling her long abused sight at the fountain it self of heav'nly radiance; while the whole noise of timorous and flocking birds, with those also that love the twilight, flutter about, amaz'd at what she means, and in their envious gabble would prognosticat a year of sects and schisms.

John Milton

Areopagitica; A Speech . . . for the Liberty of Vnlicenc'd Printing . . . (1644)

INDEPENDENTS VERSUS PRESBYTERIANS: AN INDEPENDENT'S PLEA FOR PEACEFUL CO-EXISTENCE

IF matters were duly and fairly examined between the two Combatants in this case, the *way* we plead for, would be found *via lactea*, the candid, harmlesse, and peaceable *way*; and her corrivall and competitresse, *via sanguinea*, the trouble and strife-making way. *Onely by pride* (saith *Solomon*) *cometh contention*. Surely that way which commandeth homage and subjection unto her from all her fellowes, and threatens to breake them all in pieces like a potters vessell with a rod of iron, if they will not bow, and deny themselves for her sake, is the way of *pride*, and so of *contention*, (according to *Solomons* Logique) not that which is gentle, and easie to be entreated by all others, claiming no superioritie or jurisdiction over any. If there be any clashing or unkindnesse between the two wayes, *Independency* (so called) and *Presbyterie*, when they

muing] renewing by the process of moulting (?)

meet together, either in a relation, familie &c. the very complexion of the latter bewrayes that to be still the foundresse of the quarrell. To me it is a wonder of the first magnitude, how men come to have so much ground of hope as to set their foot upon, of composing differences and distractions, of setling peace and love throughout the Nation, by exalting one way of Discipline, of Church-Government, for the treading downe and trampling under foot all others. If *Ephraim be against Manasseh*, is it any wayes like but that *Manasseh* will be *against Ephraim*? And God himselfe prophecying of *Ishmael*, told his mother, that he would *be a wild man:* and *that his hand should be against every man; and every mans hand against him.* Undoubtedly that way, whose hand shall be against every way, will find that the hand of every way will be against it: and then what manner of peace can reasonably be expected under the predominancy of such a way? That *way* which shall be able to *out-reason*, not that which shall *out-clubbe* all other wayes, will at last exalt unitie, and be it selfe exalted by gathering in all other wayes unto it. *Solomon* tells us, that all that is *taken in hunting*, is not alwayse *roasted*; and that *an inheritance may be hastily gotten, and yet the end thereof not be blessed:* and the Prophet *Habbakuk* denounceth a *woe* against him that *shall build a towne with bloud*. But,

I would gladly know what the plaintiffe in the objection means, by distractions, rents, divisions, in relations, families, Congregations, &c. If he means onely this, that the father goes to heare one Minister in one place, and the son another Minister, in another, and that some within the same parochiall line goe to this Minister, or are members of this Church, others to another Minister, and are members of another Church, and the like &c. I answer, That in this case, I know no more occasion, (at least no more necessitie) of any distraction, rent, or division then when the father being free of one Company, as suppose of Merchant-taylors, shall still upon occasion of the meeting of this Company, repaire to the hall belonging to it; and the son being free of another, as perhaps of the company of Grocers, shall upon the like occasion repaire to the hall appertaining to them. Who knows not that the members of all the severall Companies in *London*, dwell scatteringly and promiscuously up and downe the Citie, with the greatest irregularitie of intermixture that lightly can be, and without any observation of their relations to their respective Companies, sundry members of twenty severall Companies (it may be) inhabiting within one and the same parish; and yet without any complaint or inconvenience of *rents, distractions, or divisions*? Or if by *rents, distractions, and divisions*, he means distances or alienations in affections; nor can these with any face of reason be charged upon that *way*, whose cause we plead; because it is a maine principle and maxime in this *way*, to hold terms of love and Christian correspondence, with all persons of what judgement soever in point of Government, if they be godly, as well as with her owne children.

John Goodwin
ΘEOMAXIA; or the Grand Imprudence ...
of Fighting against God ... (1644)

THE SECTS VERSUS THE PRESBYTERIANS: A DEFENCE OF THE BROWNISTS AND ANABAPTISTS

I WILL make no Apologie for my selfe, but desire, that every man would give his reason scope, boldly to examine, what [Learning] is, what good the World receives from it, whether the most learned, or unlearned men have been the troublers of the World. How presumptsious and confident the learned Scribes, Priests, and Doctors of the Law were, that they best understood the Scriptures: How the poore and unlearned

Fishermen and Tentmakers were made choyce of for Christs Disciples and Apostles, before any of them: How in processe of time they that tooke upon them to be Ministers, when they had acquired to themselves the mysterie of Arts and Learning, & confounded thereby the cleare streames of the Scripture, and perverted the true Gospell of Jesus Christ, and by politicke Glosses, and Comments introduced an other Gospell sutable to the covetous, ambitious, and persecuting spirit of the Clergie (which their esteeme with the people made authentick) they then began to scorne the simplicity and meanesse of the Apostles, to call that the Infancy of the Church, and to engrosse great Livings, Lordships, Territories and Dominions; to embroyle States in warres, to supplant one an other and divert the people from the prosecution of their owne interest, (which is their safety and libertie) to maintaine their quarrells, and erect that Government the then rising part of them could agree upon. So that the Preists and Ministers of Christendome (though others have the name) yet they are indeed the Lords and leaders thereof, as at present by Englands sad experience may evidently appeare: For I would have all wise men consider, whether the party who are now in armes to make us slaves, consists not cheifly of such as have had esteeme for the most learned Arts men in the Kingdome; or of others, (who if not learned themselves) are admirers of such as are. Yea, to examine whence most of the warres of Christendome have sprung, and whether these artificiall Clergie men have not been the cheife causers and still are the grand Incendiaries of our present miseries which threaten our utter ruine, and although the Episcopall Clergie pretend to strive for the Regall Prerogative on the one side, and the Presbiterian Prelacy for Reformation, and the Liberty of the Subiect on the other side; yet both of these mainely intend their owne respective profits, and advancements; so that which side soever prevaile, if such may have their wills (both aiming at their own greatnesse and Dominion over the consciences of their Brethren) extremeast miserie, and basest kind of slavery will unavoydably follow; whilst each of them by all slye insinuations and cunning contrivances seeke to obtaine authority to compell the whole Nation to be subject to their doubtfull, yea groundlesse determinations, which of all other is the greatest and worst sort of oppression and tyranny. The people may, if they please, dote upon that which ever hath been, and will be their destruction: It would be more safe for them (I am sure) to distinguish of Knowledge, and to reject what is uselesse (as most of that which hath hitherto borne the name of learning, will upon impartiall examination prove to be) and esteeme that only which is evidently usefull to the people; to account better of them that having no by-ends or respects, have studied the Scriptures for their owne and others information, and doe impart the same to the people out of a desire of their good, for nothing, (as the Anabaptists doe to their Congregations) than of such men as use all meanes to augment their tythes and profits, who being rich and abundantly provided for, yet exact them from poore people, even such whose very bellies can hardly spare it; whose necessities ought to be releeved by them, and not the fruite of their labours so unreasonably wrested from them, as oft it is, and the same so superfluously spent, or so covetously hoarded up, as for the most part is knowne to be. When they commend Learning, it is not for learnings sake, but their owne; her esteeme gets them their Livings and preferments; and therefore she is to be kept up, or their Trade will goe downe. *Have a care therefore, O yee Clergie, as you esteem your honour and preferment, your profit and observance, that you keep this Diana of yours high in the peoples esteem: Rouze up your selves, and imagine some new wayes to quicken the admiration of this your Goddesse; for I can assure you, mens eyes begin to open, they find that she is not so beautifull as she once seemed to be; that her lustre is not naturall, but painted and artificiall: Bestirre your selves, or your Diana will downe...*

I will adde one thing more to the Brownists and Anabaptists glory; that in the times of the Bishops domineering, when many of the Presbyterians complyed, some to the very top of *Wrens* Conformity, and preached for those things they now pretend cheifly to reforme, and the Independants fled to places where they might live at ease, and enjoy their hundred pounds a yeare, without danger; the Brownist and Anabaptist endured the heate and brunt of persecution, and notwithstanding the severall wayes of vexing them, continued doing their duties, counting it to the glory of a Christian to endure tribulation for the name of Christ: And the times altering the Presbyterian soon comes about, and the Independant comes over, to be leaders in the Reformation, when forgetting the constancie and integrity of those who bore the heat and burden of the day, they hold the same heavy hand over them, that their fathers the Bishops did. And so the Brownists & Anabaptists affection to the common good of all, was then firme, & able to endure the triall of persecution, so hath it in these present searching times continued constant & unshaken, notwithstanding the many almost unsufferable Injuries & provocations of the Divines on the one side, & the faire promises & frequent invitations of the King on the other...

William Walwyn
The Compassionate Samaritane ... (1644)

THE SAFETY OF THE PEOPLE IS THE SUPREME LAW OF ALL COMMONWEALTHS

IT is in vaine for our Members of Parliament to think that we will justifie or tollerate the same among them, which we would not indure in the King, to pluck off the *Garments of Royalty* from oppression and tyranny, to dresse up the same in *Parlament Robes*: No, no, that was ever and is farre from our hearts, and wee shall justifie or allow the same no more in the one then in the other, for it is equally unequall in both, and in itself resistable wheresoever it is found. . . .

All degrees and titles Magisteriall, whether emperiall, regall, Parliamentarie, or otherwise are all subservient to *popular safety*, all founded and grounded thereon, all instituted and ordained only for it, for without it can be no humane society, cohabitation or being, which above all earthly things must be maintained, as the earthly sovereign good of mankind, let what or who will perish, or be confounded, for mankind must be preserved upon the earth, and to this preservation, all the Children of men have an equall title by Birth, none to be deprived thereof, but such as are enemies thereto, and this is the *ground-worke* that God *in nature* hath laid for all commonwealths, for all Governours and Governments amongst men, for all their Lawes, executions and Administrations: therefore all contrary Governments and Governours are ungodly, unnatural, diabolicall, and trayterous, to be abhorred, condemned and resisted by all possible wayes and meanes whatsoever: And from hence ariseth the true *definition of Treason*, for indeed Treason is no other then a *destruction to humane society or actions overwhelming or apparently tending to the utter overthrow of publick safety co-habitation and peace, or to the vassalage, bondage and thraledome of a people or Country*; such actions and Actors are only treasonable and trayterous and no other, although it be the custome of tyrants and opressors unhappily intrusted with Imperial Regal or Parliament Authority to proclaim, condemne and execute such cheifly for traytors as are enemies to their opressions and tyrannies, their boundlesse prerogatives, arbitrary *Domination*, or the like, even as our degenerate Members dissembled at Westminster have done in the late Petitioners case of the Armie, making it a matter of Treason to petition for justice and right.

Now in regard, the *Body naturall* for its owne safety may prune, amputate and cut of the corrupt putrified Members from the *Body Representative*, yea utterly renounce, oppose, resist, and dissolve all the Members therein upon *totall forfeiture* of, and *reall Apostacy* from the true *representative capacity* of Parliament, and that this is most evident and cleare; it then inevitable followeth, that this *naturall Body*, by vertue of its instincted, inherent naturall Soveraignity, may *create*, or *depute* any *person* or *persons* for their *Deputy* or *Deputies* for the removall of those dead, corrupt, putrified Members from the *seat* and *name* of their *Formall Authority*, and for the supression of injustice and tyranny, recovery of liberty and freedome; but it may be, it will be objected, that by reason of distraction, confusion and disorder at such an exigency in the *Body naturall*, such a new deputation is not likely, or cannot possibly be formally effected, and therefore those forementioned Members though never so corrupt and destructive, must be continued and subjected unto. I answer that the *Body naturall* must never be without a mean to save it selfe, and therefore by the foresaid permanent unalterable *rule of Necessity and safety*, any *person* or *persons* (in discharge of their duty to God, themselves and their Countrey) may warrantably rise up in the cause and behalfe of the people, to preserve them from imminent ruine and destruction, such person or persons, doing in that act no more then everie man by nature is bound to performe.

Richard Overton

An Appeale from the degenerate Representative Body the
Commons of England assembled at Westminster: to the
Body Represented the free people in generall (1647)

A Leveller Tradesman's Protest

Oh that the cravings of our Stomacks could be heard by the Parliament and City! Oh that the Tears of our poor famishing Babes were botled! Oh that their tender Mothers Cryes for bread to feed them were ingraven in Brasse! Oh that our pined Carkasses were open to every pitifull Eye! Oh that it were known that we sell our Beds and Cloaths for Bread! Oh our Hearts faint, and we are ready to swoon in the top of every Street!

O you Members of Parliament, and rich men in the City, that are at ease, and drink Wine in Bowls, and stretch your selves upon Beds of Down, you that grind our faces, and flay off our skins, Will no man amongst you regard, will no man behold our faces black with Sorrow and Famine? Is there none to pity? The Sea Monster drawes out the brest, and gives suck to their young ones, and are our Rulers become cruell *like* the Ostrich in the Wildernesse? *Lament.* 4.3.

Oh ye great men of *England*, will not (think you) the righteous God behold our Affliction, doth not he take notice that you devour us as if our Flesh were Bread? are not most of you either Parliament-men, Customers, Excise-men, Treasurers, Governors of Towns and Castles, or Commanders in the Army, Officers in those Dens of Robbery, the Courts of Law? and are not your Kinsmen and Allies, Colectors of the Kings Revenue, or the Bishops Rents, or Sequestratours? What then are your russling Silks and Velvets, and your glittering Gold and Silver Laces? are they not the sweat of our brows, & the wants of our backs & bellies?

Its your Taxes, Customs, and Excize, that compells the Countrey to raise the price of food, and to buy nothing from us but meer absolute necessaries; and then you of the City that buy our Work, must have your Tables furnished, and your Cups overflow; and therefore will give us little or nothing for our Work, even what you please, because you know we must sell for moneys to set our Families on work, or else we famish: Thus our Flesh is that whereupon you Rich men live, and wherewith you deck and adorn yourselves. Ye great men, is it not your plenty and abundance which begets you Pride and Riot? And doth not your Pride beget Ambition, and your Ambition Faction, and your Faction these Civil broyles? What else but your Ambition and Faction continue our Distractions and Oppressions? Is not all the Controversie whose *Slaves* the poor shall be? Whether they shall be the Kings Vassals, or the Presbyterians, or the Independent Factions? And is not the Contention nourished, that you whose Houses are full of the spoils of your Countrey, might be secure from Accounts, while there is nothing but Distraction? and that by the tumultuousnesse of the people under prodigious oppression, you might have fair pretences to keep up an Army, and garrisons? and that under pretence of necessity, you may uphold your arbitrary Government by Committees, &c.

Have you not upon such pretences brought an Army into the bowels of the City? and now Exchange doth rise already beyond the Sea, and no Merchants beyond Sea will trust their Goods hither, and our own Merchants conveigh their Estates from hence, so there is likely to be no importing of Goods, and then there will be no Exporting, and then our Trade will be utterly lost, and our Families perish as it were in a moment. . . .

O Parliament men, and Souldiers! *Necessity dissolves all Laws and Government*, and *Hunger will break through stone Walls*; Tender Mothers will sooner devour You, then the Fruit of their own womb, and Hunger regards no Swords nor Canons. It may be so great oppressours intend tumults, that they may escape in a croud, but your food may then be wanting as well as ours, and your Arms will be hard dyet. O heark, heark at our doors, how our children cry Bread, Bread, Bread; and we now with bleeding hearts, cry, once more to you, pity, pity an oppressed, inslaved People: carry our cries in the large Petition to the Parliament, and tell them, if they be still deaf, the Teares of the oppressed will wash away the foundations of their houses. Amen, Amen, so be it.

Anonymous [?John Lilburne]
The mournfull Cryes of many thousand poor Tradesmen,
who are ready to famish through decay of Trade (1648)

LILBURNE'S SPEECH TO THE JURY, TREASON TRIAL OF 1649

Lilburne. O Lord, Sir! What strange Judges are you, that you will neither allow me Counsel to help me to plead; nor suffer me my self to speak for my own life? Is this your law and Justice Sir? I have no more to say but this, seeing you straiten me; although you said you would hear me till midnight: I hope I have made it evident to all rationall men, that all or any part of the testimony given in against me, does not in the exact eye of the law, in the least, touch me; although I have been most unjustly imprisoned, and most barbarously used and tyrannized over; yea, and my estate by will and power taken from me, that should have kept me and mine alive; and the legal and customary allowance of the Tower denied me to this day; and although I have used all Christian and fair means, to compose my differences with my Adversaries; but nothing would serve their turns, but I must have oppression upon oppression laid upon me, enough to break the back of a horse; and then if I cry out of my oppressions in any kind, I must have new Treason-snares made to catch me, many moneths after their oppressions were first laid upon me, that if I so much as whimper or speak, in the least, of their unjust dealing with me, I must dye therefore as a traytor. O miserable servitude! and miserable bondage, in the first year of

Englands Freedom! I have now no more to say unto you, but onely this; your own law tels me, Sir *Edw. Cook* speaks it three or four times over in his 3rd part [of] *Institutes, That it is the Law of England that any by-stander may speak in the prisoners behalf, if he see any thing urg'd against him contrary to Law, or do apprehend he fals short of urging any material thing that may serve for his defence and preservation.* Here's your own law for it, Sir; *Cook* is full and pregnant to this purpose in his 3rd part [of] *Institutes*, fol. 29, 34, 37. But this hath several times been denyed me in the case of Mr. *Sprat* my Soliciter; and now I demand it again, as my right by law, that he may speak a few words for me, according to his often desire, both to me, and the Court. I have almost done Sir, onely once again, I claim that as my right which you have promised, that I should have Councel to matter of law; and if you give me but your own promise, which is my undoubted right by your own law, and I fear not my life; But if you again shall deny both these legal priviledges, I shall desire my Jury to take notice, that I aver, you rob me of the benefit of the law, and go about to murther me, without and against law: and therefore as a free-born English man, and as a true Christian that now stands in the sight and presence of God, with an upright heart and conscience, & with a chearfull countenance, cast my life, and the lives of all the honest free-men of *England*, into the hands of God, and his gracious protection, and into the care and conscience of my honest Jury and Fellow-Citizens; who I again declare by the law of *England*, are the Conservators and sole Judges of my life, having inherent in them alone, the judicial power of the law, as well as fact: you Judges that sit there, being no more, if they please, but Ciphers to pronounce the Sentence or their Clarks to say *Amen*, to them, being at the best, in your Original, but the Norman Conqueror's Intruders; and therefore, you Gentlemen of the Jury [are] my sole Judges, the Keepers of my life; at whose hands, the Lord

will require my bloud, in case you leave any part of my
indictment to the cruell and bloudy men: And therefore, I
desire you to know your power, and consider your duty
both to God, to Me, and to your own Selves, and to your
Country; And the gracious assisting Spirit, and presence of
the Lord God omnipotent, the Governour of Heaven and
Earth, and all things therein contained, go along with you,
give counsell, and direct you, to do that which is just, and for
his glory.

[*The People with a loud voyce cryed,* Amen, Amen, *And gave
an extraordinary great hum, which made the Judges look something untowardly about them, and caused Major General* Skippon
to send for three more fresh Companies of Foot Souldiers.]

The Triall of Lieut. Collonell John Lilburne By an
extraordinary or speciall Commission . . . as exactly
pen'd and taken in short hand (1649)

THE EARTH IS THE COMMON TREASURY OF
ALL MANKIND

THEN they came privately by day to *Gerrard Winstanleys*
house, and drove away four Cowes; I not knowing of it and
some of the Lords Tenants rode to the next Town shouting
the diggers were conquered, the diggers were conquered.
Truly it is an easie thing to beat a man, and cry conquest over
him after his hands are tied, as they tyed ours. But if their
cause be so good, why will they not suffer us to speak, and
let reason and equity, the foundation of righteous Lawes,
judge them and us. But strangers made rescue of those Cowes,
and drove them astray out of the Bailiffes hands, so that the
Bailiffes lost them; but before the Bailiffes had lost the Cowes,
I hearing of it went to them and said here is my body, take
me that I may come to speak to those *Normans* that have

stolne our land from us; and let the Cowes go, for they are none of mine; and after some time, they telling me that they had nothing against my body, it was my goods they were to have; then said I take my goods, for the Cowes are not mine; and so I went away and left them, being quiet in my heart, and filled with comfort within my self, that the King of righteousnesse would cause this to work for the advancing of his own Cause, which I prefer above estate or livelyhood,

Saying within my heart as I went along, that if I could not get meat to eat, I would feed upon bread, milk and cheese; and if they take the Cowes, that I cannot feed on this, or hereby make a breach between me and him that ownes the Cowes, then Ile feed upon bread and beere, till the King of righteousnesse clear up my innocency, and the justice of his own cause: and if this be taken from me for maintaining his Cause, Ile stand still and see what he will doe with me, for as yet I know not.

Saying likewise within my heart as I was walking along, O thou King of righteousnesse shew thy power, and do thy work thy self, and free thy people now from under this heavy bondage of miserie, *Pharaoh* the covetous power. And the answer in my heart was satisfactory, and full of sweet joy and peace: and so I said Father, do what thou wilt, this cause is thine, and thou knowest that the love to righteousnesse makes me do what I do.

I was made to appeal to the Father of life in the speakings of my heart likewise thus: Father thou knowest that what I have writ or spoken, concerning this light, that the earth should be restored and become a common Treasurie for all mankind, without respect of persons, was thy free revelation to me, I never read it in any book, I heard it from no mouth of flesh till I understood it from thy teaching first within me. I did not study nor imagine the conceit of it; self-love to my own particular body does not carry me along in the mannaging of this businesse; but the power of love flowing forth to the liberty and peace of thy whole Creation, to enemies as well as friends: nay towards those that oppresse me, endeavouring to make me a beggar to them. And since I did obey thy voice, to speak and act this truth, I am hated, reproached and oppressed on everie side. Such as make profession of thee, yet revile me. And though they see I cannot fight with fleshly weapons, yet they will strive with me by that power. And so I see Father, that *England* yet does choose rather to fight with the Sword of Iron, and covetousnesse, then by the Sword of the Spirit which is love: and what thy purpose is with this land, or with my body, I know not; but establish thy power in me, and then do what pleases thee.

These and such like sweet thoughts dwelt upon my heart as I went along, and I feel my self now like a man in a storm, standing under shelter upon a hill in peace, waiting till the storm be over to see the end of it, and of many other things that my eye is fixed upon: But I will let this passe.

And return again to the Dragons Den, or Hornets nest, the selfish murdering fleshly Lawes of this Nation, which hangs some for stealing, and protects others in stealing; Lords of Mannours stole the land from their fellow creatures formerly in the conquests of Kings, and now they have made Lawes to imprison and hang all those that seek to recover the land again out of their thieving murdering hands.

Gerrard Winstanley
A Watch-Word to the City of London and the Armie (1649)

LAST CONSTITUTIONAL PROPOSALS

FOR the ground and basis of every just and free government (since men have smarted so oft for committing all to one person) is a general councel of ablest men, chosen by the people to consult of publick affairs from time to time for the common good. This Grand Councel must have the forces by sea and land in thir power, must raise and mannage the Publick revenue, make lawes, as need requires, treat of commerce, peace, or war with forein nations; and for the carrying on som particular affairs of State with more secrecie and expedition, must elect, as they have already out of thir own number and others, a Councel of State. And although it may seem strange at first hearing, by reason that mens mindes are prepossessed with the conceit of successive Parlaments, I affirme that the Grand or General Councel being well chosen, should sit perpetual: for so their business is, and they will become thereby skilfullest, best acquainted with the people, and the people with them. The ship of the Commonwealth is alwaies undersail; they sit at the stern; and if they stear well, what need is ther to change them; it being rather dangerous? Adde to this, that the Grand Councel is both foundation and main pillar of the whole State; and to move pillars and foundations, unless they be faultie, cannot be safe for the building. I see not therefor, how we can be advantag'd by successive Parlaments; but that they are much likelier continually to unsettle rather then to settle a free government, to breed commotions, changes, novelties and uncertainties; and serve only to satisfie the ambition of such men, as think themselves injur'd, and cannot stay till they be orderly chosen to have thir part on government. If the ambition of such be at all to be regarded, the best expedient will be, and with least danger, that everie two or three years a hundred or some such number may go out by lot or suffrage of the rest, and the like number be chosen in thir places; (which hath bin already thought on heer, and done in other Commonwealths:) but in my opinion better nothing mov'd, unless by death or just accusation.

John Milton

The Readie & Easie Way to Establish a Free
Commonwealth . . . (February–March, 1660)

REFLECTIONS ON THE PAST

HE[1] had originally in his Nature so great a Tenderness and Love towards Mankind, that He did not only detest all calumniating and Detraction towards the lessening the Credit or Parts or Reputation of any Man, but did really believe that all Men were such as They seemed or appeared to be; that They had the same Justice and Candour and Goodness in their Nature, that They professed to have; and thought no Men to be wicked and dishonest and corrupt, but those who in their Manners and Lives gave unquestionable Evidence of it; and even amongst those He did think most to err and do amiss, rather out of Weakness and Ignorance, for Want of Friends and good Counsel, than out of the Malice and Wickedness of their Natures.

But now, upon the Observation and Experience He had in the Parliament (and He believed He could have made the Discovery no where else, without Doubt not so soon), He reformed all those Mistakes, and mended that Easiness of his Understanding. He had seen those there, upon whose Ingenuity and Probity He would willingly have deposited all his Concernments of this World, behave themselves with that signal Uningenuity and Improbity that must pull up all Confidence by the Roots; Men of the most unsuspected Integrity, and of the greatest Eminence for their Piety and Devotion, most industrious to impose upon and to cozen Men of weaker Parts and Understanding, upon the Credit of their Sincerity, to concur with them in mischievous Opinions, which They did not comprehend, and which conduced to dishonest Actions They did not intend. He saw the most bloody and inhuman Rebellion contrived by them who were generally believed to be the most solicitous and zealous for the Peace and Prosperity of the Kingdom, with such Art and Subtilty,

1. i.e. Clarendon himself.

and so great Pretences to Religion, that it looked like Ill-nature to believe that such sanctified persons could entertain any but holy Purposes. In a Word, Religion was made a Cloak to cover the most impious Designs; and Reputation of Honesty, a Stratagem to deceive and cheat others who had no Mind to be wicked. The Court was as full of Murmuring, Ingratitude and Treachery, and as willing and ready to rebel against the best and most bountiful Master in the World, as the Country and the City. A barbarous and bloody Fierceness and Savageness had extinguished all Relations, hardened the Hearts and Bowels of all Men; and an universal Malice and Animosity had even covered the most innocent and best-natured People and Nation upon the Earth.

These unavoidable Reflections first made him discern, how weak and foolish all his former Imaginations had been, and how blind a Surveyor He had been of the Inclinations and Affections of the Heart of Man; and it made him likewise conclude from thence, how uncomfortable and vain the Dependance must be upon any Thing in this World, where whatsoever is good and desirable *suddenly perisheth*, and Nothing is lasting but *the Folly and Wickedness of the Inhabitants thereof*.

Edward Hyde, Earl of Clarendon
*The Continuation of the Life of Edward Earl
of Clarendon* (1759). Written 1672

MAN IN THE STATE OF NATURE

NATURE hath made men so equall, in the faculties of body, and mind; as that though there bee found one man sometimes manifestly stronger in body, or of quicker mind then another; yet when all is reckoned together, the difference between man, and man, is not so considerable, as that one man can thereupon claim to himselfe any benefit, to which another may not pretend, as well as he. . . .

From this equality of ability, ariseth equality of hope in the attaining of our Ends. And therefore if any two men desire the same thing, which neverthelesse they cannot both enjoy, they become enemies; and in the way to their End, (which is principally their owne conservation, and sometimes their delectation only,) endeavour to destroy, or subdue one another. And from hence it comes to passe, that where an Invader hath no more to feare than another mans single power; if one plant, sow, build, or possesse a convenient Seat, others may probably be expected to come prepared with forces united, to dispossesse, and deprive him, not only of the fruit of his labour, but also of his life, or liberty. And the Invader again is in like danger of another.

And from this diffidence of one another, there is no way for any man to secure himselfe, so reasonable, as Anticipation; that is, by force, or wiles, to master the persons of all men he can, so long, till he see no other power great enough to endanger him: And this is no more than his own conservation requireth, and is generally allowed. . . .

Againe, men have no pleasure, (but on the contrary a great deal of griefe) in keeping company, where there is no power able to over-awe them all. For every man looketh that his companion should value him, at the same rate he sets upon himselfe: And upon all signs of contempt, or undervaluing, naturally endeavours, as far as he dares (which amongst them that have no common power to keep them quiet, is far enough to make them destroy each other,) to extort a greater value from his contemners, by dammage; and from others, by the example.

So that in the nature of man, we find three principall causes of quarrell. First, Competition; Secondly, Diffidence; Thirdly, Glory.

The first, maketh men invade for Gain; the second, for Safety; and the third, for Reputation. The first use Violence, to make themselves Masters of other mens persons, wives, children, and cattell; the second, to defend them; the third, for trifles, as a word, a smile, a different opinion, and any other signe of undervalue, either direct in their Persons, or by reflexion in their Kindred, their Friends, their Nation, their Profession, or their Name.

Hereby it is manifest, that during the time men live without a common Power to keep them all in awe, they are in that condition which is called Warre; and such a warre, as is of every man, against every man. For WARRE consisteth not in Battell onely, or the act of fighting; but in a tract of time, wherein the Will to contend by Battell is sufficiently known: and therefore the notion of *Time*, is to be considered in the nature of Warre; as it is in the nature of Weather. For as the nature of Foule weather, lyeth not in a showre or two of rain; but in an inclination thereto of many dayes together: So the nature of War, consisteth not in actuall fighting; but in the known disposition thereto, during all the time there is no assurance to the contrary. All other time is PEACE.

Whatsoever therefore is consequent to a time of Warre, where every man is Enemy to every man; the same is consequent to the time, wherein men live without other security, than what their own strength, and their own invention shall furnish them withall. In such condition, there is no place for Industry; because the fruit thereof is uncertain: and consequently no Culture of the Earth; no Navigation, nor use of the commodities that may be imported by Sea; no commodious Building; no Instruments of moving, and removing such things as require much force; no Knowledge of the face of the Earth; no account of Time; no Arts; no Letters; no Society; and which is worst of all, continuall feare, and danger of violent death; And the life of man, solitary, poore, nasty, brutish, and short.

Thomas Hobbes
*Leviathan, or the Matter, Forme, and Power of a
Commonwealth Ecclesiastical and Civil* (1651)

THE GENERATION OF A COMMONWEALTH

... the Lawes of Nature, (as *Justice, Equity, Modesty, Mercy,* and, (in summe) *doing to others, as wee would be done to,*) of themselves, without the terrour of some Power, to cause them to be observed, are contrary to our naturall Passions, that carry us to Partiality, Pride, Revenge, and the like. And Covenants, without the Sword, are but Words, and of no strength to secure a man at all. Therefore notwithstanding the Lawes of Nature, (which every one hath then kept, when he has the will to keep them, when he can do it safely,) if there be no Power erected, or not great enough for our security; every man will, and may lawfully rely on his own strength and art, for caution against all other men. And in all places, where men have lived by small Families, to robbe and spoyle one another, has been a Trade, and so farre from being reputed against the Law of Nature, that the greater spoyles they gained, the greater was their honour; and men observed no other Lawes therein, but the Lawes of Honour; that is, to abstain from cruelty, leaving to men their lives, and instruments of husbandry. And as small Familyes did then; so now do Cities and Kingdomes which are but greater Families (for their own security) enlarge their Dominions, upon all pretences of danger, and fear of Invasion, or assistance that may be given to Invaders, [and] endeavour as much as they can, to subdue or weaken their neighbours, by open force, and

113

secret arts, for want of other Caution, justly; and are remembred for it in after ages with honour. . .

Nor is it enough for the security, which men desire should
last all the time of their life, that they be governed, and
directed by one judgement, for a limited time; as in one
Battell, or one Warre. For though they obtain a Victory by
their unanimous endeavour against a forraign enemy; yet
afterwards, when either they have no common enemy, or he
that by one part is held for an enemy, is by another part held
for a friend, they must needs by the difference of their interests
dissolve, and fall again into a Warre amongst themselves.

It is true, that certain living creatures, as Bees, and Ants,
live sociably one with another, (which are therefore by *Aristotle* numbred amongst Politicall creatures;) and yet have no
other direction, than their particular judgements and ap-
petites; nor speech, whereby one of them can signifie to
another, what he thinks expedient for the common benefit:
and therefore some man may perhaps desire to know, why
Man-kind cannot do the same. To which I answer,

First, that men are continually in competition for Honour
and Dignity, which these creatures are not; and consequently
amongst men there ariseth on that ground, Envy and Hatred,
and finally Warre; but amongst these not so.

Secondly, that amongst these creatures, the Common good
differeth not from the Private; and being by nature enclined
to their private, they procure thereby the common benefit.
But man, whose Joy consisteth in comparing himselfe with
other men, can relish nothing but what is eminent.

Thirdly, that these creatures, having not (as man) the use
of reason, do not see, nor think they see any fault, in the administration of their common businesse; whereas amongst
men, there are very many, that think themselves wiser, and
abler to govern the Publique, better than the rest; and these
strive to reforme and innovate, one this way, another that

way; and thereby bring it into Distraction and Civill warre.

Fourthly, that these creatures, though they have some use of voice, in making knowne to one another their desires, and other affections; yet they want that art of words, by which some men can represent to others, that which is Good, in the likenesse of Evill; and Evill in the likenesse of Good; and augment, or diminish the apparent greatnesse of Good and Evill; discontenting men, and troubling their Peace at their pleasure.

Fiftly, irrationall creatures cannot distinguish between *Injury*, and *Dammage*; and therefore as long as they be at ease, they are not offended with their fellowes: whereas Man is then most troublesome, when he is most at ease: for then it is that he loves to shew his Wisdome, and controule the Actions of them that governe the Common-wealth.

Lastly, the agreement of these creatures is Naturall; that of men, is by Covenant only, which is Artificiall: and therefore it is no wonder if there be somewhat else required (besides Covenant) to make their Agreement constant and lasting; which is a Common Power, to keep them in awe, and to direct their actions to the Common Benefit.

The only way to erect such a Common Power, as may be able to defend them from the invasion of Forraigners, and the injuries of one another, and thereby to secure them in such sort, as that by their owne industrie, and by the fruites of the Earth, they may nourish themselves and live contentedly; is, to conferre all their power and strength upon one Man, or upon one Assembly of men, that may reduce all their Wills, by plurality of voices, unto one Will: which is as much as to say, to appoint one Man, or Assembly of men, to beare their Person; and every one to owne, and acknowledge himself to be Author of whatsoever he that so beareth their Person, shall Act, or cause to be Acted, in those things which concerne the Common Peace and Safetie; and therein to submit their Wills, every one to his Will, and their Judgements to his Judgment. This is more than Consent, or Concord; it is a reall Unitie of them all, in one and the same Person, made by Covenant of every man with every man, in such manner, as if every man should say to every man, *I Authorize and give up my Right of Governing my selfe, to this Man, or to this Assembly of men, on this condition, that thou give up thy Right to him, and Authorise all his Actions in like manner.* This done, the multitude so united in one person, is called a COMMON-WEALTH, in latine CIVITAS. This is the generation of that great LEVIATHAN, or rather (to speak more reverently) of that *Mortall God*, to which wee owe under the *Immortall God*, our peace and defence. For by this Authoritie, given him by every particular man in the Common-Wealth, he hath the use of so much Power and Strength conferred on him, that by terror thereof, he is inabled to conforme the wills of them all, to Peace at home, and mutuall ayd against their enemies abroad. And in him consisteth the Essence of the Common-wealth; which (to define it,) is *One Person, of whose Acts a great Multitude, by mutuall Covenants one with another, have made themselves every one the Author, to the end he may use the strength and means of them all, as he shall think expedient, for their Peace and Common Defence.*

And he that carryeth this Person, is called SOVER-AIGNE, and said to have *Soveraigne Power;* and every one besides, his SUBIECT.

Thomas Hobbes

Leviathan, or the Matter, Forme, and Power of a Commonwealth Ecclesiastical and Civil (1651)

THE IMMORTAL GOVERNMENT

Rome was said (*Mole sua ruere*) to bee broken by her own weight, but poetically. For that weight by which she was pretended to bee ruined, was supported in her Emperors, by a farre slighter foundation. And in the Common experience of good Architecture, there is nothing more known, than that buildings, stand the firmer and the longer for their own weight; nor ever swerve through any other internal cause, than that their materials are corruptible; but the people never dyes, nor, as a Political Body, are subject unto any other corruptions than that which deriveth from their Government. Unlesse a man will deny the chain of causes in which hee denies God, hee must also acknowledge the chain of effects; wherefore there can bee no effect in Nature, that is not from the first Cause, and those successive lincks of the chain, without which it could not have been. Now except a man can shew the contrary in a Commonwealth, if there bee no cause of corruption in the first make of it, there can never bee any such effect. Let no mans superstition, impose prophanenesse upon this assertion; for as Man is sinful, but yet the world is perfect, so may the Citizen bee sinfull, and yet the Commonwealth bee perfect. And as man seeing the World is perfect, can never commit any such sin as can render it imperfect, or bring it unto a natural dissolution; so the Citizen, where the common Wealth is perfect can never commit any such crime, as can render it imperfect, or bring it unto a natural dissolution. To come unto experience, *Venice*, notwithstanding that wee have found some flaws in it, is the only Commonwealth, in the make wherof, no man can find a cause of dissolution; for which reason wee behold her (albeit she consist of men that are not without sin) at this day with one thousand years upon her back, for any internal cause, as young, as fresh, and free from decay, or any appearance of it, as shee was born, but what ever in nature, is not sensible of decay by the course of a thousand years, is capable of the whole age of nature: by which calculation for any check that I am able to give my self; a Commonwealth rightly ordered, may for any internal causes be as immortal, or longlived as the World. But if this be true, those Commonwealths that are naturally fallen, must have derived their ruine from the rise of them. *Israel* and *Athens*, died not naturall, but violent deaths, in this manner the World is to dye; wee are speaking of those causes of dissolution which are naturall unto government; and they are but two, either *Contradiction* or *Inequality*, if a Commonwealth be a contradiction she must needs destroy her self; and if she be unequal, it tends to strife, and strife to ruine. By the former of these fell *Lacedemon*, by the latter *Rome*. *Lacedemon* being made altogether for war, and yet not for increase, her natural progresse, became her natural dissolution, and the building of her own victorious hand, too heavy for her foundation; so shee indeed fell by her own weight.

But *Rome* through her native Inequality, which how it inveterate the bosomes of the Senate and the people each against each other, and even unto death hath been shewn at large.

Look well unto it my Lords, for if there be a contradiction of equality in your Commonwealth it must fall; but if it have neither of these, it hath no principle of mortality, do not think me impudent; if this be truth, I should commit a grosse indiscretion, in concealing it. Sure I am that *Machiavil*, is for the immortality of a Commonwealth upon far weaker principles.

James Harrington
The Common-Wealth of Oceana (1656)

POWER AND LIBERTY

OUR *Trimmer* admires our blessed Constitution, in which Dominion and Liberty are reconciled; it gives to the Prince the glorious Power of commanding Free-men, and to the Subject, the satisfaction of seeing the Power so lodged, as that their Liberties are secure; it do's not allow the Crown such a Ruining Power, as that no grass can grow where e'er it treads, but a Cherishing and Protecting Power; such a one as hath a grim Aspect only to the offending Subjects, but is the joy and the Pride of all the good ones; their own interest being so bound up in it, as to engage them to defend and support it; and tho in some instances the King is restrained, yet nothing in the Government can move without him: our Laws make a distinction between Vassalage and Obedience; between devouring Prerogatives, and a licentious ungovernable Freedom: and as of all the Orders of Building, the Composite is the best, so ours by a happy mixture and a wise choice of what is best in others, is brought into a Form that is our Felicity who live under it, and the envy of our Neighbour that cannot imitate it.

The Crown has power sufficient to protect our Liberties. The People have so much Liberty as is necessary to make them useful to the Crown.

Our Government is in a just proportion, no Tympany, no unnatural swelling either of Power or Liberty; and whereas in all overgrown Monarchies, Reason, Learning, and Enquiry are hang'd in Effigy for Mutineers; here they are encouraged and cherished as the surest Friends to a Government establish'd upon the Foundation of Law and Justice. When all is done, those who look for Perfection in this World, may look as the *Jews* have for their *Messias*, and therefore our *Trimmer* is not so unreasonably Partial as to free our Government from all objections; no doubt there have been fatal Instances of its Sickness, and more than that, of its Mortality, for sometime, tho' by a Miracle, it hath been reviv'd again: but till we have another race of Mankind, in all Constitutions that are bounded there will ever be some matter of Strife, and Contention, and rather than want pretensions, Mens Passions and Interests will raise them from the most inconsiderable Causes.

Our Government is like our Climate, there are Winds which are sometimes loud and unquiet, and yet with all the Trouble they give us, we owe great part of our Health unto them, they clear the Air, which else would be like a standing Pool, and in stead of Refreshment would be a Disease unto us.

There may be fresh Gales of asserting Liberty, without turning into such storms of Hurricane, as that the State should run any hazard of being Cast away by them; these struglings which are natural to all mixed Governments, while they are kept from growing into Convulsions, do by a mutual agitation from the several parts, rather support and strengthen, than weaken or maim the Constitution; and the whole frame, instead of being torn or disjointed, comes to be the better and closer knit by being thus exercised; but what ever faults our Government may have, or a discerning Critick may find in it, when he looks upon it alone; let any other be set against it, and then it shews its Comparative Beauty; let us look upon the most glittering outside of unbounded Authority, and upon a nearer enquiry, we shall find nothing but poor and miserable deformity within; let us imagine a Prince living in his Kingdom, as if in a great Gally, his Subjects tugging at the Oar, laden with Chains, and reduced to real Rags, that they may gain him imaginary Lawrels; let us Represent him gazing among his Flatterers, and receiving their false Worship, like a Child never Contradicted, and therefore always Cozen'd: or like a Lady complemented only to be abused, condemned never to hear Truth, and Consequently never to do Justice, wallowing in the soft Bed of wanton and unbridled Greatness, not less odious to the Instruments themselves, than to the Objects of his Tyranny; blown up into an Ambitious Dropsy, never to be satisfied by the Conquest of other People, or by the Oppression of his own; by aiming to be more than a Man, he falleth lower than the meanest of 'em, a mistaken Creature, swelled with

Panegyricks, and flattered out of his Senses, and not only an Incumbrance, but a Nuisance to Mankind, a hardened and unrelenting Soul, and like some Creatures that grow fat with Poisons, he groweth great by other Mens Miseries; an Ambitious Ape of the Divine Greatness, an unruly Gyant that would storm even Heaven it self, but that his scaling Ladders are not long enough; in short, a Wild and devouring Creature in rich Trappings, and with all his Pride, no more than a Whip in God Almighty's hand, to be thrown into the Fire when the World has been sufficiently scourged with it: This Picture laid in right Colours would not incite Men to wish for such a Government, but rather to acknowledge the happiness of our own, under which we enjoy all the Privilege Reasonable Men can desire, and avoid all the Miseries many others are subject to; so that our *Trimmer* would keep it with all its faults, and doth as little forgive those who give the occasion of breaking it, as he doth those that take it.

George Savile, Marquess of Halifax
The Character of a Trimmer (1688)
Text from *Miscellanies* (1700)

OF THE STATE OF NATURE

To understand Political Power aright, and to derive it from its Original, we must consider what Estate all men are naturally in, and that is, a State of perfect Freedom to order their Actions, and dispose of their Possessions, and Persons as they think fit, within the bounds of the Law of Nature, without asking leave, or depending upon the Will of any other Man.

A State also of Equality, wherein all the Power and Jurisdiction is reciprocal, no one having more then another, there being nothing more evident then that Creatures of the same species and rank promiscuously born to all the same advantages of Nature, and the use of the same faculties, should also be equal one amongst another without Subordination or Subjection, unless the Lord and Master of them all, should by any manifest Declaration of his Will set one one above another, and confer on him by an evident and clear appointment an undoubted Right to Dominion and Sovereignty.

This equality of Men by Nature, the Judicious *Hooker* looks upon as so evident in it self, and beyond all question, that he makes it the Foundation of that Obligation to mutual Love amongst Men, on which he Builds the Duties they owe one another, and from whence he derives the great Maxims of *Justice* and *Charity* . . .

But though this be a State of Liberty, yet it is not a State of Licence, though Man in that State have an uncontroleable Liberty, to dispose of his Person or Possessions, yet he has not Liberty to destroy himself, or so much as any Creature in his Possession, but where some nobler use, then its bare Preservation calls for it. The State of Nature has a Law of Nature to govern it, which obliges every one, and reason, which is that Law, teaches all Mankind, who will but consult it; That being all equal and independent, no one ought to harm another in his Life, Health, Liberty or Possessions; for Men being all the Workmanship of one Omnipotent, and infinitely wise maker: All the Servants of one Sovereign Master, sent into the World by his order and about his business; they are his Property, whose Workmanship they are made to last during his, not one anothers Pleasure. And being Furnished with like Faculties, sharing all in one Community of Nature, there cannot be supposed any such Subordination among us, that may Authorize us to destroy one another, as if we were made for one anothers uses, as the inferior ranks of Creatures are for ours, every one as he is bound to preserve himself, and not to quit his Station wilfully, so by the like reason, when his own Preservation comes not in competition, ought he as much as he can to preserve the rest of Mankind, and not unless it be to do Justice on an offender, take away, or impair the Life, or what tends to the Preservation of the Life, the Liberty, Health, Limb or Goods of another.

And that all Men may be restrained from invading others Rights, and from doing hurt to one another, and the Law of Nature be observed, which willeth the Peace and Preservation of all Mankind, the Execution of the Law of Nature is in that State put into every Mans hands, whereby every one has a Right to punish the transgressors of that Law to such a Degree, as may hinder its Violation. For the Law of Nature would, as all other Laws that concern Men in this World, be in vain, if there were no body that in the State of Nature had a power to Execute that Law, and thereby preserve the innocent and restrain offenders and if any one in the State of Nature may punish another for any evil he has done, every one may do so. For in that State of perfect Equality, where naturally there is no superiority of jurisdiction of one over another, what any one may do in Prosecution of that Law, every one must needs have a Right to do.

John Locke
'An Essay concerning . . . Civil Government'
from *Two Treatises of Government* (1690)

THE BEGINNING OF POLITICAL SOCIETIES

MEN being, as has been said, by Nature, all free, equal and independent no one can be put out of this Estate, and subjected to the Political Power of another, without his own Consent, which is done by agreeing with other Men to joyn and unite into a Community, for their comfortable, safe, and peaceable living one amongst another in a secure Enjoyment of their Properties, and a greater Security against any that are not of it. This any number of Men may do, because it injures not the Freedom of the rest; they are left as they were in the Liberty of the State of Nature. When any number of Men have so consented to make one Community or Government, they are thereby presently incorporated, and make one Body politick, wherein the Majority have a Right to act and conclude the rest.

For, when any number of Men have by the consent of every individual made a Community, they have thereby made that Community one Body, with a power to act as one Body, which is only by the will and determination of the majority. For that which acts any Community, being only the consent of the individuals of it, and it being one Body must move one way; it is necessary the Body should move that way whither the greater force carries it, which is the consent of the majority: or else it is impossible it should act or continue one Body, one Community, which the consent of every individual united into it, agreed that it should; and so every one is bound by that consent to be concluded by the majority. And therefore we see, that in Assemblies impowred to act by positive Laws where no number is set by that positive Law which impowers them, the act of the majority passes for the act of the whole and of course determines, as having by the Law of Nature and Reason, the power of the whole.

And thus every Man by consenting with others to make one Body Politick, under one Government, puts himself under an Obligation to every one of that Society, to submit to the determination of the majority, and to be concluded by it; or else this original Compact, whereby he with others incorporates into one Society, would signifie nothing, and be no Compact if he be left free and under no other ties than he was before in the state of Nature. For what appearance would there be of any Compact? What new engagement if he were no farther tied by any Decrees of the Society than he himself thought fit, and did actually consent to? This would be still as great a liberty as he himself had before his Compact, or any one else in the state of Nature, who may submit himself and consent to any acts of it if he thinks fit.

For if the consent of the majority shall not in reason be received as the act of the whole, and conclude every individual; nothing but the consent of every individual can make anything to be the act of the whole, which, considering the infirmities of health, and the avocations of business, which in a number, though much less than that of a Commonwealth, will necessarily keep many away from the publick Assembly; and the variety of Opinions and contrariety of interests which unavoidably happen in all Collections of Men, 'tis next impossible ever to be had. And therefore if coming into Society be upon such terms, it will be only like *Cato's* coming into the Theatre, *tantum ut exiret*. Such a Constitution as this would make the mighty *Leviathan* of a shorter duration than the feeblest Creatures; and not let it outlast the day it was born in, which cannot be suppos'd till we think that rational Creatures should desire and constitute Societies only to be dissolved. For where the majority cannot conclude the rest, there they cannot act as one Body, and consequently will be immediately dissolved again.

Whosoever therefore, out of a state of Nature, unite into a Community, must be understood to give up all the power necessary to the ends for which they unite into Society, to the majority of the Community, unless they expressly agreed in any number greater than the majority. And this is done by barely agreeing to unite into one political Society, which is all the Compact that is, or needs be, between the individuals that enter into or make up a Commonwealth. And thus that which begins and actually constitutes any Political Society, is nothing but the consent of any number of Freemen capable of majority, to unite and incorporate into such a Society. And this is that, and that only, which did or could give beginning to any lawful Government in the World.

John Locke
'An Essay concerning . . . Civil Government'
from *Two Treatises of Government* (1690)

Of Puritans

I FIND many that are called *Puritans*; yet few, or none that will own the *name*. Whereof the reason sure is this, that 'tis for the most part held a *name of infamy*; and is so new, that it hath scarcely yet obtain'd a *definition*: nor is it an *appellation* derived from one *mans* name, whose *Tenents* we may find digested into a *Volume*: whereby we do much err in the *application*. It imports a kind of *excellency* above another; which *man* (being conscious of his own fraile bendings) is ashamed to assume to himself. So that I beleeve there are men which *would be Puritans*: but indeed not any that *are*. One will have him one that lives religiously, and will not revell it in a shore-lesse excesse. Another, him that separates from our *Divine Assemblies*. Another, him that in some *tenents* only is *peculiar*. Another, him that will not *sweare*. Absolutely to define him, is a work, I thinke of *Difficulty*; some I know that rejoyce in the *name*; but sure they be such, as least *understand* it. As he is more generally in these times taken, I suppose we may call him a *Church-Rebell*, or one that would exclude *order*, that his *brain* might rule. To *decline offences*; to be careful and conscionable in our several *actions*, is a *Purity*, that every man ought to labour for, which we may well doe, without a sullen *segregation* from all *society*. If there be any *Priviledges*, they are surely granted to the Children of the *King*; which are those that are the Children of *Heaven*. If *mirth* and *recreations* be lawful, sure such a one may lawfully use it. If *Wine* were given to chear the *heart*, why should I fear to use it for that end? Surely, the *merry soul* is freer from intended *mischief* than the *thoughtfull man*. A bounded *mirth*, is a *Pattent* adding time and happinesse to the crazed life of *Man*. Yet if *Laertius* reports him rightly, *Plato* deserves a *Censure*, for allowing *drunkennesse* at *Festivals*; because, says he, as then, the *Gods* themselves reach *Wines* to present *Men*. *God* delights in nothing more, than in a *cheerfull heart*, carefull to perform him service. What *Parent* is it, that rejoyceth not to see his *Childe* pleasant, in the limits of a *filiall duety*? I know, we read of Christs *weeping*, not of his *laughter*: yet we see, he graceth a *Feast* with his *first Miracle*; and that a *Feast of joy*: And can we think that such a *meeting* could pass without the noise of *laughter*? What a lump of *quickned care* is the *melancholike man*? Change *anger* into *mirth*, and the Precept will hold good still: *Be merry, sinne not*. As there be many, that in their life assume too great a *Libertie*; so I beleeve there are some that abridge themselves of what they might lawfully use. *Ignorance* is an ill *Steward*, to provide for either *Soul*, or *Body*. A man that submits to reverent *Order*, that sometimes unbends himself in a moderate *relaxation*; and in all, labours to approve himselfe, in the serenenesse of a healthfull *Conscience*: such a *Puritane* I will love immutably. But when a man, in things but *ceremoniall*, shall spurn at the grave Authority of the *Church*, and out of a needless *nicety*, be a Thiefe to himselfe, of those benefits which GOD hath allowed him: or out of a blinde and uncharitable *Pride*, censure, and scorne others, as *reprobates*: or out of obstinacy, fill the World with *brawls*, about *undeterminable tenents*: I shall think him one of those, whose *opinion* hath fevered his *zeal* to *madness* and *distraction*. I have more faith in one *Solomon*, then in a thousand *Dutch Parlours* of such *Opinionists*. Behold then; what I have seen good! That it is comely to eat, and to drink, and to take pleasure in all his labour wherein he travaileth under the *Sun*, the whole number of the days of his life, which GOD giveth him. For, this is his *Portion*. Nay, *there is no profit to Man, but that he eat, and drink, and delight his soul with the profit of his labour*. For, he that saw other things but *vanity*, saw this also, that it was the *hand of God*. Methinks that the reading of *Ecclesiastes* should make a *Puritan* undress his brain, and lay off all those *Phanatique toyes* that gingle about his *understanding*. For my own part, I think the World has not better men, then some, that suffer under that name: nor withall, more *Scelestique Villains*. For when they are once *elated* with that *pride*, they so *contemn* others, that they infringe the Laws of all *humane society*.

Owen Felltham

Resolves: Divine, Moral, Political (?1623). Text
from the revised eighth edition (1661)

A General Character of the Presbyterian Clergy of Scotland

THEIR spirits were eager, and their tempers sour: But they had an appearance that created respect. They were related to the chief families in the countrey, either by blood or marriage; and had lived in so decent a manner, that the Gentry paid great respect to them. They used to visit their parishes much, and were so full of the scriptures, and so ready at extempore prayer, that from them they grew to practice extempore sermons: For the custom in *Scotland* was after dinner or supper to read a chapter in the scripture: And where they happened to come, if it was acceptable, they on the sudden expounded the chapter. They had brought the people to such a degree of knowledge, that cottagers and servants would have prayed extempore. I have often over heard them at it: And, tho' there was a large mixture of odd stuff, yet I have been astonished to hear how copious and ready they were in it. Their Ministers generally brought them about them on the sunday nights, where the sermons were talked over; and every one, women as well as men, were desired to speak their sense and experience: And by these means they had a comprehension of matters of religion, greater than I have seen among people of that sort any where. The preachers went all in one track, of raising observations on points of doctrine out of their text, and proving these by reasons, and then of applying those, and shewing the use that was to be made of such a point of doctrine, both for instruction and terrour, for exhortation and comfort, for trial of themselves upon it, and for furnishing them with proper directions and helps: And this was so methodical, that the people grew to follow a sermon quite through every branch of it. To this some added, the resolving of doubts concerning the state they were in, or their progress or decay in it; which they called cases of conscience: And these were taken from what their people said to them at any time, very oft being under fits of melancholy, or vapours, or obstructions, which, tho' they flowed from natural causes, were looked on as the work of the spirit of God, and a particular exercise to them and they fed this disease of weak minds too much. Thus they had laboured very diligently, tho' with a wrong method and wrong notions. But as they lived in great familiarity with their people, and used to pray and talk oft with them in private, so it can hardly be imagined to what a degree they were loved and reverenced by them. They kept scandalous persons under a severe discipline: For breach of sabbath, for an oath, or the least disorder in drunkenness, persons were cited before the Church session, that consisted of ten or twelve of the chief of the parish, who with the Minister had this care upon them, and were solemnly reproved for it: For fornication they were not only reproved before these; but there was a high place in the church called the stool or pillar of repentance, where they sate at the times of worship for three Lords-day's, receiving admonitions, and making profession of repentance on all those days; which some did with many tears, and serious exhortations to all the rest, to take warning by their fall: For adultery they were to sit six months in that place, covered with sackcloth. These things had a grave appearance. Their faults and defects were not so conspicuous. They had a very scanty measure of learning, and a narrow compass in it. They were little men, of a very indifferent size of capacity, and apt to fly out into great excess of passion and indiscretion. They were servile, and too apt to fawn upon, and flatter their admirers. They were affected in their deportment, and very apt to censure all who differed from them, and to believe and report whatsoever they heard to their prejudice. And they were superstitious and haughty. In their sermons they were apt to enlarge on the state of the present time, and to preach against the sins of Princes and Courts: A topick that naturally makes men popular. It has an appearance of courage: And the people are glad to hear their sins insisted on, in which they perceive they have no share, and to believe that all the judgments of God come down by the means and procurement of other mens sins. But their opinions about the independence of the Church and Clergy on the Civil power, and their readiness to stir up the people to tumults and wars, was that which begot so ill an opinion of them at this time in all men, that very few, who were not deeply engaged with them in these conceits, pitied them much under all the ill usage they now[1] met with. I hope this is no impertinent nor ungrateful digression. It is a just and true account of these men and those times, from which a judicious

1. In 1662.

reader will make good inferences. I will conclude this with a judicious answer that one of the wisest and best of them, *Colvil*, who succeeded *Leightoun* in the Headship of the College of *Edenburgh*, made to the Earl of *Midletoun*, when he press'd him in the point of defensive arms to tell plainly his opinion, whether they were lawful or not. He said, the question had been often put to him, and he had always declined to answer it: But to him he plainly said, he wished that Kings and their Ministers would believe them lawful, and so govern as men that expect to be resisted; but he wished, that all their subjects would believe them to be unlawful, and so the world would be at quiet.

Gilbert Burnet
History of his Own Time (1724). Written 1683–1704

An Account of the Anglican Community at Little Gidding

A FAMILY of the *Farrars*, the Mother, with Sons and Daughters of both Sexes in the plural Number, other Branches of the Kindred, with Servants fit to be about them, were collected into a House of their own at *Giding* aforesaid, purposing, and covenanting between themselves to live in as strict a way, according to the Gospel of Christ, as good Rules could chalk out, and humane Infirmity undergo. This pious Design was proposed, and perswaded to them by the eldest Son, in Holy Orders, bred in *Clare-Hall* in *Cambridge*, an humble, diligent, devout Servant of God, learned in the Theory, more in the Practice of Divinity. Their House, fit for their Contemplation, stood alone. All were single Persons in it, to the best I could learn. The Church was so near, that it was next to the Pale of their Yard: the easier for them that frequented it so often. The whole Village of *Giding* had been depopulated: or I am misinform'd: the House which contained them remaining for an whole Parish. The Tythes had been impropriated: but were restored back again by the Mother, to the use of the Rector then, her own Son; and to the succeeding Rectors, by a firm Deed, as Law could make, which in its time shall be declared. They kept much at home: their turns of Prayer, and Watching, which they observ'd, requir'd it. Yet Visits, perhaps once a Month, they made abroad: but shunning such Diversions, as much as they could, which rob us of a great part of the Employment of our Life. *Non horam tecum esse potes: non otia recte – Ponere*: as an Heathen complained, *Horat. Serm.* 7. Strangers that came to them were fairly receiv'd: all the Tribe was meek and courteous, and did let none depart, before they gave them an account of their Conversation, if they ask'd it. And withall offer'd to read to them, what was written in a Table hanging up in their Parlour, as followeth:

He that by report of our Endeavours, will remonstrate that which is more perfect, and seek to make us better, is welcome as an Angel of God. He that by chearful participating, and approbation of that which is good, confirms us in the same, is welcome as a Christian friend. He that any way goes about to divert, or disturb us in that which is, as it ought to be among Christians (though it be not usual in the World) is a Burthen while he stays, and shall bear his Judgment whosoever he be. He that faults us in absence, for that which in presence he made shew to approve, shall by a double guilt of Flattery and Slander, violate the Bands both of Friendship, and Christianity.

Subscribed,

> Mary Farrar, *Widow, Mother of this Family, aged about Fourscore Years: who bids adieu to all Hopes and Fears of this World, and only desires to serve God.*

impropriated] placed in lay hands

Their Apparel had nothing in it of Fashion, but that which was common: yet plain: and much of it for Linnen and Woollen spun at home; such as modest Christians thought to be the best Habit. *Fateor vobis de pretiosâ veste erubesco*, says St. *Austin. Inter. serm. de diver.* They gave no Entertainment but to the Poor, whom they instructed first, and then relieved, not with Fragments, but with the best they had: and having sufficiency did abound to every good work, 2 *Cor.* 11.8. Their business was, either they were at Prayer, or at work; nothing came between: the Devil had the less Power to tempt them, that he never found them idle. They had the more leisure for work, because they fasted so much: and their diet at their meals was soon drest; beside, their daily temperance was such, as they sat not long at them. It was not by fits, but by constancy, that they subdued their Bodies by Sobriety. Their Bread was course, their Drink small, and of ill relish to the Taste: that it was sure they strived for nothing, that a dainty Appetite might long for: As Alms and Fasting were frequent with them, so Prayers and Watching, with Reading and Singing Psalms, were continually in their Practice. *Note*, The Word continually: For there was no Intermission, day, nor night. Four times every day they offer'd up their Supplications to God, twice in the Words of the Common-Prayer in the Church: twice in their Family, with several Petitions for their own needs, and for such as desired, upon some special occasions, to be remembred by them to God. At all times one, or more, by their Constitutions were drawn aside to some private Holy Exercise. By night they kept watch in the House of the Lord, and two by turns did supply the Office for the rest, from whence they departed not till the Morning. Their Scope was to be ready like wise Virgins with Oil in their Lamps, when the Bridegroom came. This was the hardest part of their Discipline, that they kept Centinel at all Hours, and Seasons, to expect the second coming of the Lord Jesus ... In which, and in all the rest, What was their offensive? Nay, What not to be admir'd? To leave it off, or to lessen it for the Girds of lavish Tongues, were like the Man in the *Dutch* Epigram, *That would eat nothing but Spoon-meat, for fear of wearing out his Teeth.* God be glorified for such, whose Prayers were powerful and uncessant to pierce the Heavens. The whole Land was the better for their Sanctity. They fasted, that Famine might not be inflicted upon our common Gluttony. They abridg'd themselves of all Pleasures, that Vengeance might not come down upon the Voluptuousness of this riotous Age. They kept their Vigils all Night, that the Day of the Lord might not come upon us like a Thief unawares, that sleep in security. The whole World was the better for their Contempt of the World.

John Hacket
Scrinia Reserata: The Life of Archbishop Williams (1693)

LATITUDINARIANS AND THEIR FOLLOWERS

THESE were generally of *Cambridge*, formed under some divines, the chief of whom were Drs. *Whitchcot*, *Cudworth*, *Wilkins*, *More* and *Worthington*. Whitchcot was a man of a rare temper, very mild and obliging. He had great credit with some that had been eminent in the late times; but made all the use he could of it to protect good men of all persuasions. He was much for liberty of conscience: And being disgusted with the dry systematical way of those times, he studied to raise those who conversed with him to a nobler set of thoughts, and to consider religion as a seed of a deiform nature (to use one of his own phrases.) In order to this, he set young students much on reading the ancient Philosophers, chiefly *Plato*, *Tully*, and *Plotin*, and on considering the Christian religion as a doctrine sent from God, both to elevate and sweeten humane nature, in which he was a great example, as well as a wise and kind instructer. *Cudworth* carried this on with a great strength of genius, and a vast compass of learning. He was a man of great conduct and prudence: Upon which his enemies did very falsely accuse him of craft and dissimulation. *Wilkins* was of *Oxford*, but removed to *Cambridge*. His first rise was in the Elector Palatine's family, when he was in *England*. Afterwards he married *Cromwell's* sister; but made no other use of that alliance, but to do good offices, and to cover the University from the sourness of *Owen* and *Goodwin*. At *Cambridge* he joined with those who studied to propagate better thoughts, to take men off from being in parties, or from narrow notions, from superstitious conceits, and a fierceness about opinions. He was also a great observer and a promoter of experimental philosophy, which was then a new thing, and much looked after. He was naturally ambitious, but was the wisest Clergy-man I ever knew. He was a lover of mankind, and had a delight in doing good. *More* was an open hearted, and sincere christian philosopher, who studied to establish men in the great principles of religion against atheism, that was then beginning to gain ground, chiefly by reason of the hypocrisy of some, and the fantastical conceits of the more sincere enthusiasts.

Hobbs, who had long followed the Court, and passed there for a mathematical man, tho' he really knew little that way, being disgusted by the Court, came into *England* in *Cromwell's* time, and published a very wicked book, with a very strange title, *The Leviathan*. His main principles were, that all men acted under an absolute necessity, in which he seemed protected by the then received doctrine of absolute decrees. He seemed to think that the universe was God, and that souls were material, Thought being only subtil and unperceptible motion. He thought interest and fear were the chief principles of society: And he put all morality in the following that which was our own private will or advantage. He thought religion had no other foundation than the laws of the land. And he put all the law in the will of the Prince, or of the people: For he writ his book at first in favour of absolute monarchy, but turned it afterwards to gratify the republican party. These were his true principles, tho' he had disguised them, for deceiving unwary readers. And this set of notions came to spread much. The novelty and boldness of them set many on reading them. The impiety of them was acceptable to men of corrupt minds, which were but too much prepared to receive them by the extravagancies of the late times. So this set of men at *Cambridge* studied to assert, and examine the principles of religion and morality on clear grounds, and in a philosophical method. In this *More* led the way to many that came after him. *Worthington* was a man of eminent piety and great humility, and practised a most sublime way of self-denial and devotion. All these, and those who were formed under them, studied to examine farther into the nature of things than had been done formerly. They declared against superstition on the one hand, and enthusiasm on the other. They loved the constitution of the Church, and the Liturgy, and could well live under them: But they did not think it unlawful to live under another form. They wished that things might have been carried with more moderation. And they continued to keep a good correspondence with those who had differed from them in opinion, and allowed a great freedom both in philosophy and divinity: From whence they were called men of Latitude. And upon this men of narrower thoughts and fiercer tempers fastened upon them the name of Latitudinarians. They read *Episcopius* much. And the making out of the reasons of things being a main part of their studies, their enemies called them Socinians. They were all

Socinians] deniers of the divinity of Christ

very zealous against popery. And so, they becoming soon very considerable, the Papists set themselves against them to decry them as Atheists, Deists, or at best Socinians. And now that the main principle of religion was struck at by *Hobbs* and his followers, the Papists acted upon this a very strange part. They went in so far even into the argument for Atheism, as to publish many books, in which they affirmed, that there was no certain proofs of the Christian religion, unless we took it from the authority of the Church as infallible. This was such a delivering up of the cause to them, that it raised in all good men a very high indignation at Popery; that party shewing, that they chose to make men, who would not turn Papists, become Atheists, rather than believe Christianity upon any other ground than infallibility.

The most eminent of those, who were formed under those great men I have mention'd, were *Tillotson*, *Stillingfleet*, and *Patrick*. The first of these was a man of a clear head, and a sweet temper. He had the brightest thoughts, and the most correct style of all our divines; and was esteemed the best preacher of the age. He was a very prudent man; and had such a management with it, that I never knew any Clergyman so universally esteemed and beloved, as he was for above twenty years. He was eminent for his opposition to Popery, He was no friend to persecution, and stood up much against Atheism. Nor did any man contribute more to bring the City to love our worship, than he did. But there was so little superstition, and so much reason and gentleness in his way of explaining things, that malice was long levelled at him, and in conclusion broke out fiercely on him....

This set of men contributed more than can be well imagined to reform the way of preaching; which among the divines of *England* before them was over-run with pedantry, a great mixture of quotations from fathers and ancient writers, a long opening of a text with the concordance of every word in it, and a giving all the different expositions with the grounds of them, and the entring into some parts of controversy, and all concluding in some, but very short, practical applications, according to the subject or the occasion. This was both long and heavy, when all was pyeballed, full of many sayings of different languages. The common style of sermons was either very flat and low, or swelled up with rhetorick to a false pitch of a wrong sublime. The King had little or no literature, but true and good sense; and had got a right notion of style; for he was in *France* at a time when they were much set on reforming their language. It soon appear'd that he had a true taste. So this help'd to raise the value of these men, when the King approved of the style their discourses generally ran in; which was clear, plain, and short. They gave a short paraphrase of their text, unless where great difficulties required a more copious enlargement: But even then they cut off unnecessary shews of learning, and applied themselves to the matter, in which they opened the nature and reasons of things so fully, and with that simplicity, that their hearers felt an instruction of another sort than had commonly been observed before. So they became very much followed: And a set of these men brought off the City in a great measure from the prejudices they had formerly to the Church.

Gilbert Burnet

History of his Own Time (1724). Written 1683–1704

SLEEP AND DEATH

I sleepe not day nor night.

Naturall men have conceived a twofold use of *sleepe*; That it is a *refreshing* of the body in this life; That it is a *preparing* of the *soule* for the next; That it is a *feast*, and it is the *Grace* at that *feast*; That it is our *recreation*, and cheeres us, and it is our

Catechisme, and instructs us; wee lie downe in a hope, that wee shall rise the stronger; and wee lie downe in a knowledge, that wee may rise no more. *Sleepe* is an *Opiate* which gives us *rest*, but such an *Opiate*, as perchance, being under it, we shall wake no more. But though naturall men, who have induced secondary and figurative considerations, have found out this second, this *emblematicall* use of *sleepe*, that it should be a *representation of death*, God, who wrought and perfected his worke, before *Nature* began, (for *Nature* was but his *apprentice*, to learne in the first *seven daies*, and now is his *foreman*, and works next under him) *God*, I say, intended *sleepe* onely for the *refreshing* of man by bodily rest, and not for a *figure of death*, for he intended not *death* it selfe then. But *Man* having induced *death* upon himselfe, *God* hath taken *Mans Creature*, *death*, into his hand, and mended it; and whereas it hath in it selfe a fearefull forme and aspect, so that Man is afraid of his own *Creature*, *God* presents it to him, in a *familiar*, in an *assiduous*, in an *agreeable*, and *acceptable* forme, in *sleepe*, that so when hee awakes from *sleepe*, and saies to himselfe, shall I bee no otherwise when I am dead, than I was even now, when I was asleep, hee may bee ashamed of his waking *dreames*, and of his *Melancholique* fancying out a horrid and an affrightfull figure of that *death* which is so like sleepe. As then we need *sleepe* to live out our *threescore and ten yeeres*, so we need *death*, to live that *life* which we cannot *out-live*. And as *death* being our *enemie*, *God* allowes us to defend ourselves against it (for wee *victuall* ourselves against *death*, *twice* every day, as often as we *eat*) so *God* having so sweetned *death* unto us, as hee hath in *sleepe*, wee put ourselves into our *Enemies* hands *once* every day; so farre, as *sleepe* is *death*; and *sleepe* is as much *death*, as *meat* is *life*. This then is the *misery* of my *sicknesse*, That death as it is produced from mee, and is mine owne *Creature*, is now before mine *Eies*, but in that forme, in which *God* hath mollified it to us, and made it acceptable, in *sleepe*, I cannot see it:

how many *prisoners*, who have even hollowed themselves their *graves* upon that *Earth*, on which they have lien long under heavie fetters, yet at this *houre* are *asleepe*, though they bee yet working upon their own *graves* by their owne *waight*? hee that hath seene his *friend* die to *day*, or knowes hee shall see it to *morrow*, yet will sinke into a sleepe betweene. I cannot; and oh, if I be entring now into *Eternitie*, where there shall be no more distinction of *houres*, why is it al my businesse now *to tell Clocks*? why is none of the heavinesse of my *heart*, dispensed into mine *Eie-lids*, that they might fall as my heart doth? And why, since I have lost my delight in all obiects, cannot I discontinue the facultie of seeing them, by closing mine *Eies* in *sleepe*? But why rather being entring into that presence, where I shall wake continually and never sleepe more, doe I not interpret my continuall waking here, to bee a *parasceve*, and a *preparation* to that?

John Donne
Devotions upon Emergent Occasions . . . (1624)

THE LAST MESSAGE OF JAMES NAYLER (OCTOBER 1660)

THERE is a Spirit which I feel, that delights to do no Evil, nor to revenge any Wrong, but delights to endure all things, in hope to enjoy its own in the End: Its hope is to outlive all Wrath and Contention, and to weary out all Exaltation and Cruelty, or whatever is of a Nature contrary to it self. It sees to the End of all Temptations: As it bears no Evil in it self, so it conceives none in Thoughts to any other: If it be betrayed it bears it; for its Ground and Spring is the Mercies and Forgiveness of God. Its Crown is Meekness, its Life is Everlasting Love unfeigned, and takes its Kingdom with Intreaty, and not with Contention, and keeps it by Lowliness of Mind. In God alone it can rejoyce, though none else regard it, or can

own its Life. It's conceived in Sorrow, and brought forth
without any to pity it: nor doth it murmur at Grief and
Oppression, It never rejoyceth, but through Sufferings; for
with the World's Joy it is murthered. I found it alone, being
forsaken; I have Fellowship therein, with them who lived in
Dens, and desolate Places in the Earth, who through Death
obtained this Resurrection and Eternal Holy Life.   J.N.

James Nayler

'His Last Testimony ... two Hours before his
Departure out of this Life' from *A Collection of
Sundry Books, Epistles and Papers* (1716)

ALTERATIONS OF SOUL

AMONG Truths certain in themselves, all are not equally certain unto me; and even of the Mysteries of the Gospel, I must
needs say with Mr. *Richard Hooker Eccl. Polit.* that whatever
men may pretend, the subjective Certainty cannot go beyond
the objective Evidence: for it is caused thereby as the print on
the Wax is caused by that on the Seal: Therefore I do more of
late than ever discern a necessity of a methodical procedure in
maintaining the Doctrine of Christianity, and of beginning
at Natural Verities, as presupposed fundamentally to supernatural (though God may when he please reveal all at once,
and even Natural Truths by Supernatural Revelation): And
it is a marvellous great help to my Faith, to find it built on
so sure Foundations, and so consonant to the Law of Nature.
I am not so foolish as to pretend my certainty to be greater
than it is, meerly because it is a dishonour to be less certain;
nor will I by shame be kept from confessing those Infirmities,
which those have as much as I, who hypocritically reproach
me with them. My certainty that I am a Man, is before my
certainty that there is a God; for *Quod facit notum est magis*

notum: My certainty that there is a God, is greater than my certainty that he requireth love and holiness of his Creature: My certainty of *this* is greater than my certainty of the Life of Reward and Punishment hereafter: My certainty of that, is greater than my certainty of the endless duration of it, and of the immortality of individuate Souls: My certainty of the Deity is greater than my certainty of the Christian Faith: My certainty of the Christian Faith in its Essentials, is greater than my certainty of the Perfection and Infallibility of all the Holy Scriptures: My certainty of that is greater than my certainty of the meaning of many particular Texts, and so of the truth of many particular Doctrines, or of the Canonicalness of some certain Books. So that as you see by what Gradations my Understanding doth proceed, so that also my Certainty differeth as the Evidences differ. And they that have attained to greater Perfection, and a higher degree of Certainty than I, should pity me and produce their Evidence to help me. And they that will begin all their Certainty with that of the Truth of the Scripture, as the *Principium Cognoscendi*, may meet me at the same end; but they must give me leave to undertake to prove to a Heathen or Infidel, the Being of a God; and the necessity of Holiness, and the certainty of a Reward or Punishment, even while he yet denieth the Truth of Scripture, and in order to his believing it to be true.

In my younger years my trouble for Sin, was most about my *Actual failings* in *Thought*, *Word*, or *Action*, (except *Hardness of Heart*, of which more anon). But now I am much more troubled for *Inward Defects*, and omission or want of the Vital Duties or Graces in the Soul. My daily trouble is so much for my *Ignorance of God*, and weakness of *Belief*, and want of greater *love to God*, and *strangeness* to him, and to the Life to come, and for want of a greater willingness to die, and longing to be with God in Heaven, as that I take not some Immoralities, though very great, to be in themselves so great and odious

Sins, if they could be found as separate from these. Had I all the Riches of the World, how gladly should I give them, for a fuller Knowledge, Belief, and Love of God and Everlasting Glory! These wants are the greatest burden of my Life, which oft maketh my Life it self a burden. And I cannot find any hope of reaching so high in these, while I am in the Flesh, as I once hoped before this time to have attained: which maketh me the wearier of this sinful world, which is honoured with so little of the Knowledge of God.

Heretofore I placed much of my Religion in tenderness of heart, and grieving for sin, and penitential tears; and less of it, in the love of God, and studying his love and goodness, and in his joyful praises, than now I do. Then I was little sensible of the greatness and excellency of Love and Praise; though I coldly spake the same words in its commendations, as now I do: And now I am less troubled for want of *grief* and *tears* (though I more value *humility*, and refuse not needful *Humiliation*): But my Conscience now looketh at *Love* and *Delight* in God, and praising him, as the top of all my Religious Duties, for which it is that I value and use the rest.

My Judgment is much more for frequent and serious Meditation on the heavenly Blessedness, than it was heretofore in my younger days. I then thought that a Sermon of the Attributes of God, and the Joys of Heaven were not the most excellent; and was wont to say, *Every body knoweth this, that God is great and good, and that Heaven is a blessed place; I had rather hear how I may attain it.* And nothing pleased me so well as the Doctrine of Regeneration, and the Marks of Sincerity; which was because it was suitable to me in that state: but now I had rather read, hear or meditate, on God and Heaven, than on any other Subject: for I perceive that it is the Object that altereth and elevateth the Mind; which will be such as that is, which it most frequently feedeth on: And that it is not only useful to our *comfort*, to be much in Heaven in our believing thoughts; but that it must animate all our *other Duties*, and fortifies us against every *Temptation* and *Sin*; and that the *Love of* the *end* is it that is the *poise* or spring, which setteth every Wheel a going, and must put us on to all the *means*: And that a Man is no more a Christian indeed than he is *Heavenly*.

Richard Baxter

Reliquiæ Baxterianæ (1696). From Part I, written 1664

HIS TEMPTATION

AND now I found, as I thought, that I loved Christ dearly: Oh! me-thought my Soul cleaved unto him, my affections cleaved unto him: I felt love to him as hot as fire, and now, as *Job* said, I thought I should die in my nest; but I did quickly find, that my great love was but little; and that I, who had, as I thought, such burning love to Jesus Christ, could let him go again for a very trifle. God can tell how to abase us, and can hide pride from Man. Quickly after this, my love was tried to purpose.

For after the Lord had, in this manner, thus graciously delivered me from this great and sore temptation, and had set me down so sweetly in the Faith of his holy Gospel, and had given me such strong consolation and blessed evidence from Heaven, touching my interest in his love through Christ; the tempter came upon me again, and that with a more grievous and dreadful temptation than before.

And that was, *to sell and part with this most blessed Christ, to exchange him for the things of this life, for any thing*. The temptation lay upon me for the space of a year, and did follow me so continually, that I was not rid of it one day in a month; no, not sometimes one hour in many days together, unless when I was asleep.

And though in my judgment I was perswaded, that those who were once effectually in Christ (as I hoped, through his Grace, I had seen my self) could never lose him for ever; (*For the land shall not be sold for ever, for the land is mine*, saith God, *Lev.* 25.23.) yet it was a continual vexation to me, to think that I should have so much as one such thought within me against a Christ, a Jesus, that had done for me as he had done; and yet then I had almost none others, but such blasphemous ones.

But it was neither my dis-like of the thought, nor yet any desire and endeavour to resist it, that in the least did shake or abate the continuation, or force and strength thereof; for it did always, in almost whatever I thought, inter-mix it self therewith, in such sort, that I could neither eat my food, stoop for a pin, chop a stick, or cast mine eye to look on this or that, but still the temptation would come, *Sell Christ for this, or sell Christ for that; sell him, sell him.*

Sometimes it would run in my thoughts, not so little as an hundred times together; *Sell him, sell him, sell him*: against which, I may say, for whole hours together, I have been forced to stand as continually leaning and forcing my spirit against it, lest haply, before I were aware, some wicked thought might arise in my heart, that might consent thereto; and sometimes also the Tempter would make me believe I had consented to it, but then should I be as tortured upon a Rack for whole days together.

This temptation did put me to such scares, lest I should at some times, I say, consent thereto, and be overcome therewith, that by the very force of my mind, in labouring to gain-say and resist this wickedness, my very body would be put into action, or motion, by way of pushing or thrusting with my hands or elbows; still answering, as fast as the destroyer said, *sell him; I will not, I will not, I will not, I will not; no, not for thousands, thousands, thousands of Worlds:* Thus reckoning,

lest I should, in the midst of these assaults, set too low a value
of him, even until I scarce well knew where I was, or how to
be composed again.

At these seasons he would not let me eat my food at quiet;
but, forsooth, when I was set at the table, at my meat, I must
go hence to pray; I must leave my food now, just now; so
counterfeit holy also would this Devil be. When I was thus
tempted, I should say in my self, *Now I am at meat, let me make
an end. No*, said he, *you must do it now, or you will displease God,
and despise Christ*. Wherefore I was much afflicted with these
things; and because of the sinfulness of my nature (imagining
that these things were impulses from God) I should deny to
do it, as if I denied God; and then should I be as guilty because
I did not obey a temptation of the Devil, as if I had broken the
Law of God indeed.

But to be brief, one morning as I did lie in my bed, I was,
as at other times, most fiercely assaulted with this temptation,
to sell, and part with Christ; the wicked suggestion still running
in my mind, *Sell him, sell him, sell him, sell him, sell him*, as fast as
a man could speak: Against which also, in my mind, as at
other times, I answered, *No, no, not for thousands, thousands,
thousands*, at least twenty times together: But at last, after
much striving, even until I was almost out of breath, I felt
this thought pass through my heart, *Let him go, if he will*;
and I thought also that I felt my heart freely consent thereto.
Oh, the diligence of Satan! Oh, the desperateness of Man's
heart!

Now was the battle won, and down fell I, as a Bird that is
shot from the top of a tree, into great guilt, and fearful despair.
Thus getting out of my bed, I went mopeing into the field;
but, God knows, with as heavy an heart as mortal man, I
think, could bear; where for the space of two hours, I was like
a man bereft of life, and as now past all recovery, and bound
over to eternal punishment.

And withal, that Scripture did sieze upon my Soul, *Or pro-phane person, as* Esau, *who for one morsel of meat, sold his birthright: for ye know, how that afterwards, when he would have inherited the blessing, he was rejected; for he found no place of repentance, though he sought it carefully, with tears,* Heb.12.16.17.

Now was I as one bound, I felt my self shut up unto the Judgment to come; nothing now, for two years together, would abide with me, but damnation, and an expectation of damnation: I say, nothing now would abide with me but this, save some few moments for relief, as in the sequel you will see.

John Bunyan
Grace Abounding to the Chief of Sinners (1666)
Text from the revised sixth edition (1688)

THE WORKING OF THE INNER LIGHT

. . . yea if it fall out, that several met together, be straying in their minds, though outwardly silent, and so wandering from the measur of Grace *in* themselves, (which through the work-ing of the enemy, and negligence of some, may fall out) if either one come in, or may be in, who is watchfull, and *in* whom the *Life* is raised in a great measur, as that one keeps his place, he will feel a secret travel for the rest, in a sympathy with the *Seed*, which is oppressed *in* the other, and kept from arising by their thoughts and wanderings; and as such a faith-full one waits in the *Light*, and keeps in this *Divine* work, God often-times answers the secret travel and breathings of his own Seed through such a one, so that the rest will find them-selves secretly smitten without words, and that one will be as a midwife, through the secret travel of his Soul, to bring forth the life *in* them, just as a little water, thrown into a pump brings up the rest, whereby *Life* will come to be raised *in* all, and the vain imaginations brought down, and such a one is felt by the rest to minister life unto them without words; yea sometimes, when there is not a word in the meeting, but all are silently waiting, if one come in, that is rude and wicked, and in whom the power of darkness prevaileth much, perhaps with an intention to mock, or do mischief, if the whole meeting be gathered into the *Life*, and it be raised in a good measur, it will strike terror into such an one, and he will feel himself unable to resist, but by the secret strength and vertue thereof the power of darkness in him will be chained down, and, if the day of his visitation be not expired, it will reach to the measur of Grace *in* him, and raise it up to the redeeming of his Soul, and this we often bear witness of, so as we had hereby frequent occasion, in this respect, since God hath gathered us to be a people, to renew this old saying, of many, *Is Saul also among the Prophets?* For not a few have come to be convinced of the Truth, after this manner, Of which I my self in a part am a true Witness, who not by the strength of arguments, or by a particular disquisition of each doctrine, and convincement of my understanding thereby, came to receive and bear witness of the Truth, but by being secretly Reached by this *Life*: for, when I came into the *silent assembly* of God's people, I felt a secret Power among them, which touched my heart; and as I gave way unto it, I found the evil weakening in me, and the good raised up, and so I became thus knit and united unto them, hungering more and more after the increase of this Power and Life, whereby I might feel my self perfectly redeemed.

Robert Barclay

An Apology for the True Christian Divinity, As the same is held forth, and preached by the people Called, in Scorn, QUAKERS (1678)

DEATH AND RESURRECTION

I NEED not call in new Philosophy, that denies a settlednesse, an acquiescence in the very body of the Earth, but makes the Earth to move in that place, where we thought the Sunne had moved; I need not that helpe, that the Earth it selfe is in Motion, to prove this, That nothing upon Earth is permanent; The Assertion will stand of it selfe, till some man assigne me some instance, something that a man may relie upon, and find permanent. Consider the greatest Bodies upon Earth, The Monarchies; Objects, which one would thinke, Destiny might stand and stare at, but not shake; Consider the smallest bodies upon Earth, The haires of our head, Objects, which one would thinke, Destiny would not observe, or could not discerne; And yet, Destiny, (to speak to a naturall man) And God, (to speake to a Christian) is no more troubled to make a Monarchy ruinous, then to make a haire gray. Nay, nothing needs to be done to either, by God, or Destiny; A Monarchy will ruine, as a haire will grow gray, of it selfe. In the Elements themselves, of which all sub-elementary things are composed, there is no acquiescence, but a vicissitudinary transmutation into one another; Ayre condensed becomes water, a more solid body, And Ayre rarified becomes fire, a body more disputable, and in-apparant. It is so in the Conditions of men too; A Merchant condensed, kneaded and packed up in a great estate, becomes a Lord; and a Merchant rarified, blown up by a perfidious Factor, or by a riotous Sonne, evaporates into ayre, into nothing, and is not seen. And if there were any thing permanent and durable in this world, yet we got nothing by it, because howsoever that might last in it selfe, yet we could not last to enjoy it; If our goods were not amongst Moveables, yet we our selves are; if they could stay with us, yet we cannot stay with them; which is another Consideration in this part.

The world is a great Volume, and man the Index of that Booke; Even in the body of man, you may turne to the whole world; This body is an Illustration of all Nature; Gods recapitulation of all that he said before in his *Fiat lux*, and *Fiat firmamentum*, and in all the rest, said or done, in all the six dayes. Propose this body to thy consideration in all the highest exaltation thereof; as it is the *Temple of the Holy Ghost*: Nay, not in a Metaphor, or comparison of a Temple, or any other similitudinary thing, but as it was really and truly the very body of God, in the person of Christ, and yet this body must wither, must decay, must languish, must perish. When *Goliah* had armed and fortified this body, And *Iezabel* had painted and perfumed this body, And *Dives* had pampered and larded this body, As God said to *Ezekiel*, when he brought him to the *dry bones, Fili hominis, Sonne of Man, doest thou thinke these bones can live?* They said in their hearts to all the world, Can these bodies die? And they are dead. *Iezabels* dust is not Ambar, nor Goliahs dust *Terra sigillata*, Medicinall; nor does the Serpent, whose meat they are both, finde any better relish in *Dives* dust, then in *Lazarus*. But as in our former part, where our foundation was, That in nothing, no spirituall thing, there was any perfectnesse, which we illustrated in the weaknesses of Knowledge, and Faith, and Hope, and Charity, yet we concluded, that for all those defects, God accepted those their religious services; So in this part, where our foundation is, That nothing in temporall things is permanent, as we have illustrated that, by the decay of that which is Gods noblest piece in Nature, The body of man; so we shall also conclude that, with this goodnesse of God, that for all this dissolution, and putrefaction, he affords this Body a Resurrection.

The Gentils, and their Poets, describe the sad state of Death so, *Nox una obeunda*, That it is one everlasting Night; To them, a Night; But to a Christian, it is *Dies Mortis*, and *Dies Resurrectionis*, The day of Death, and The day of Resurrection; We die in the light, in the sight of Gods presence, and we rise in the light, in the sight of his very Essence. Nay, Gods corrections, and judgements upon us in this life, are still expressed so, *Dies visitationis*, still it is a Day, though a *Day of visitation*; and still we may discerne God to be in the action. The *Lord of Life* was the first that named *Death; Morte morieris*, sayes God, Thou shalt die the Death. I doe the lesse feare, or abhorre Death, because I finde it in his mouth; Even a malediction hath a sweetnesse in his mouth; for there is a blessing wrapped up in it; a mercy in every correction, a Resurrection upon every Death. When *Iezabels* beauty, exalted to that height which it had by art, or higher then that, to that height which it had in her own opinion, shall be infinitely multiplied upon every Body; And as God shall know no man from his own Sonne, so as not to see the very righteousnesse of his own Sonne upon that man; So the Angels shall know no man from Christ, so as not to desire to looke upon that mans face, because the most deformed wretch that is there, shall have the very beauty of Christ himselfe; So shall *Goliahs* armour, and *Dives* fulnesse, be doubled, and redoubled upon us, And every thing that we can call good, shall first be infinitely exalted in the goodnesse, and then infinitely multiplied in the proportion, and againe infinitely extended in the duration. And since we are in an action of preparing this dead Brother of ours to that state, (for the Funerall is the Easter-eve, The Buriall is the depositing of that man for the Resurrection) As we have held you, with Doctrine of Mortification, by extending the Text, from *Martha* to this occasion; so shall we dismisse you with Consolation, by a like occasionall inverting the Text, from passion in *Martha's* mouth, *Lord, if thou hadst been here, my Brother had not dyed*, to joy in ours, *Lord, because thou wast here, our Brother is not dead*.

John Donne
Funeral sermon for Alderman Sir Wm. Cokayne
(1626) from *LXXX Sermons* (1640)

The Wind Bloweth Where it Listeth

. . . the *Spirit* of the *Day*, is so a spirit as in *no* sort a body. Τὸ Πνεῦμα, with an *Article* and an *Emphasis*, a Spirit above all Spirits, the prime Spirit. A Spirit by *Essence*, an essential Spirit, or essentially a Spirit. A Spirit by *Procession*, the Spirit proceeding: *personally* that Spirit which *proceedeth from the Father*, St. *John* xv.26 and *from the Son* St. *John* xvi.7 which was this *Day* breath'd first of all solemnly into the World to quicken it to a heavenly life. *Spiritus Dei*, and *Spiritus Deus*, the Spirit of God, and the Spirit which is God, and the only Spirit that can bring us all to God.

But this great Nature is too great to comprehend, too infinite to pursue. Nor can the Simile reach it. It falls short, and so must I and you when we have done our utmost. 'Tis an easier Project for us both to fall upon the *Power* and *Operations* of it, though I foresee we shall often there be at a stand too. Yet, to help our selves as well as we can, we will consider the Operations; first by *themselves*, then by their *Effects*, and then thirdly by their *Course* and *Compass*.

By *themselves* first.

1. The *wind*, you hear, *blows*, and so the *Spirit blows*. Yet the Spirit *is* not, *blows* not neither like every wind. There are whirlwinds that make a horrid noise, that whirl every way about, and turn the World up topsie turvy, upside down; the wind that is but *Spiritus*, a direct and orderly breathing does not so. *Spiritus vertiginis* is but *Vertigo Spiritus*, the spirit of giddiness that the *Prophet* speaks of, *Isa.* xix. 14 is but the *Vertigo*, or turning of the brain, an abuse of the name, not a spirit, but a meer humour that makes us giddy, – has made this nation so too long.

2. Blustring and stormy winds there are, ἄνεμοι rather than πνεύματα, *graves violento flamine venti*; but *this* is no such. *Spiritus* rather than *Ventus*, ours is here; a calm and peaceable

one, a breath rather than a wind, a Spirit proceeding from the *God* of peace, bequeathed and sent us by the *Prince* of peace; so still and even, that it did not so much as disorder a wreath of that holy flame, which this day encircled the heads of the Disciples, but let that heavenly fire sit quietly upon them *Acts* ii.3.

3. Nor is it of this wind to which this Spirit is compared, said *flat* here, but *spirat*, not said to blow by a word that signifies commonly the ordinary and natural blowing. All is supernatural here. 'Tis neither *whirling*, we told you first; nor *blustring*, we said secondly, nor *puffing* wind we tell you now; 'tis a meek, an humble Spirit; from the beginning it mov'd upon the waters, *Gen.* i but did not swell them into waves or billows, as natural winds commonly do, nor does it now; but only guides all our waters, passions, and motions, into their proper place with sweetness and order, which is meerly a supernatural work.

4. And yet, as soft and smooth as it blows, it is the *Spirit* of *Power*, a *mighty wind Acts* ii.2 and rush in it does oft times at first with a little sudden, and eager violence; yet two syllables, one single *fiat*, and all is done; strange things we know are done by a very little wind, and that *one* word of this one Spirit made the World out of nothing, and can as easily make a nothing of the World. He can remove the greatest rocks and mountains not only with the breath of his displeasure, but of his pleasure too, his easiest breath. He blew the Gods of the Heathens out of their Thrones, and spake all their Oracles dumb, blew all their spirits in a moment thence, and yet the voice of his breathing was scarce heard. He does so still, throws down all the Holds and Fortresses of the devil in us *sine strepitu* without noise. Some rushing mighty wind sometimes may go before it to rouze our dulness and awake us, but the spirit is not *there*. Some Earthquake of servile fear may shake us first, and affright us from some ill action, but the

Spirit is not *there*. Some fire or fiery trial may first burn or scorch us, and thereby make us look about us, or some kinder fire warm us into a better temper than formerly we were in, but the Spirit is not *there* neither. But when these outward dispensations have sufficiently disposed us to attention, then comes the *still small voice* 1 Kings xix.12, and there's the *Spirit* that silently glides into our souls as the small dew into a fleece of wool.

Mark Frank

The First Sermon on Whitsunday, from LI Sermons (1672)

PRAYER AND ANGER

THE first thing that hinders the prayers of a good man from obtaining its effect is a violent anger, a violent storm in the spirit of him that prayes. For anger sets the house on fire, and all the spirits are busie upon trouble, and intend propulsion, defence, displeasure or revenge; it is a short madnesse, and an eternall enemy to discourse, and sober counsels, and fair conversation; it intends its own object with all the earnestnesse of perception, or activity of designe, and a quicker motion of a too warm and distempered bloud; it is a feaver in the heart, and a calenture in the head, and a fire in the face, and a sword in the hand, and a fury all over; and therefore can never suffer a man to be in a disposition to pray. For prayer is an action and a state of entercourse, and desire, exactly contrary to this character of anger. Prayer is an action of likenesse to the holy Ghost, the Spirit of gentlenesse and dove-like simplicity; an imitation of the holy Jesus, whose Spirit is meek up to the greatnesse of the biggest example, and a conformity to God whose anger is alwaies just, and marches slowly, and is with-

calenture] fever

out transportation, and often hindred, and never hasty, and is full of mercy; prayer is the peace of our spirit, the stilnesse of our thoughts, the evennesse of recollection, the seat of meditation, the rest of our cares, and the calme of our tempest; prayer is the issue of a quiet minde, of untroubled thoughts, it is the daughter of charity, and the sister of meeknesse; and he that prayes to God with an angry, that is, with a troubled and discomposed spirit, is like him that retires into a battle to meditate, and sets up his closet in the out quarters of an army, and chooses a frontier garrison to be wise in. Anger is a perfect alienation of the minde from prayer, and therefore is contrary to that attention which presents our prayers in a right line to God. For so have I seen a lark rising from his bed of grasse and soaring upwards singing as he rises, and hopes to get to heaven, and climbe above the clouds; but the poor bird was beaten back with the loud sighings of an eastern winde, and his motion made irregular and unconstant, descending more at every breath of the tempest, then it could recover by the libration and frequent weighing of his wings; till the little creature was forc'd to sit down and pant, and stay till the storm was over, and then it made a prosperous flight, and did rise and sing as if it had learned musick and motion from an Angell as he passed sometimes through the aire about his ministeries here below: so is the prayers of a good man; when his affairs have required businesse, and his businesse was matter of discipline, and his discipline was to passe upon a sinning person, or had a design of charity, his duty met with the infirmities of a man, and anger was its instrument, and the instrument became stronger then the prime agent, and raised a tempest, and overrul'd the man; and then his prayer was broken, and his thoughts were troubled, and his words went up towards a cloud, and his thoughts pull'd them back again, and made them without

libration] balancing

intention; and the good man sighs for his infirmity, but must
be content to lose that prayer, and he must recover it when his
anger is removed and his spirit is becalmed, made even as the
brow of *Jesus*, and smooth like the heart of God; and then it
ascends to heaven upon the wings of the holy dove, and dwels
with God till it returnes like the usefull Bee, loaden with a
blessing and the dew of heaven.

Jeremy Taylor

'The Return of Prayers' in XXV Sermons Preached at Golden-
Grove (1653) as included in ΕΝΙΑΥΤΟΣ: A Course of
Sermons for all the Sundays of the Year (1655)

Man's Nature and Creation

THESE[1] are certainly the Magisteriall & master pieces of the
Creator, the Flower or (as we may say) the best part of nothing, actually existing, what we are but in hopes, and proba-
bilitie; we are only that amphibious piece betweene a corporall and spirituall essence, that middle forme that linkes those
two together, and makes good the method of God and
nature, that jumps not from extreames, but unites the incom-
patible distances by some middle and participating natures;
that wee are the breath and similitude of God, it is indisput-
able, and upon record of holy Scripture, but to call our selves
a Microcosme, or little world, I thought it onely a pleasant
trope of Rhetorick, till my nearer judgement and second
thoughts told me there was a reall truth therein: for first wee
are a rude masse, and in the ranke of creatures, which only are,
and have a dull kinde of being not yet priviledged with life, or
preferred to sense or reason; next we live the life of plants, the
life of animals, the life of men, and at last the life of spirits,

1. i.e. Spirits.

running on in one mysterious nature those five kinds of existences, which comprehend the creatures not onely of the world, but of the Universe; thus is man that great and true *Amphibium*, whose nature is disposed to live not onely like other creatures in divers elements, but in divided and distinguished worlds; for though there bee but one world to sense, there are two to reason; the one visible, the other invisible, whereof *Moses* seemes to have left description, and of the other so obscurely, that some parts thereof are yet in controversie; and truely for the first chapters of *Genesis*, I must confesse a great deale of obscurity, though Divines have to the power of humane reason endeavoured to make all goe in a literall meaning, yet those allegoricall interpretations are also probable, and perhaps the mysticall method of *Moses* bred up in the Hieroglyphicall Schooles of the *Egyptians*.

Now for that immateriall world, me thinkes wee need not wander so farre as the first moveable, for even in this materiall fabricke the spirits walke as freely exempt from the affections of time, place, and motion, as beyond the extreamest circumference: doe but extract from the corpulency of bodies, or resolve things beyond their first matter, and you discover the habitation of Angels, which if I call the ubiquitary, and omnipresent essence of God, I hope I shall not offend Divinity; for before the Creation of the world God was really all things. For the Angels hee created no new world, or determinate mansion, and therefore they are every where where is his essence, and doe live at a distance even in himselfe: that God made all things for man, is in some sense true, yet not so farre as to subordinate the creation of those purer creatures unto ours, though as ministring spirits they doe, and are willing to fulfil the will of God in these lower and sublunary affaires of man; God made all things for himself, and it is impossible hee should make them for any other end than his owne glory; it is all he can receive, and all that is without himselfe;

for honour being an externall adjunct, and in the honourer rather than in the person honoured, it was necessary to make a creature, from whom hee might receive this homage; and that is, in the other world Angels, in this, man; which when we neglect, we forget the very end of our creation, and may justly provoke God, not onely to repent that hee hath made the world, but that hee hath sworne he would not destroy it. That there is but one world, is a conclusion of faith. *Aristotle* with all his Philosophy hath not beene able to prove it, and as weakely that the world was eternall; that dispute much troubled the penne of the antient Philosophers, but *Moses* decided that question, and all is salved with the new terme of a creation, that is, a production of something out of nothing; and what is that? Whatsoever is opposite to something or more exactly, that which is truely contrary unto God: for he onely is, all others have an existence with dependency, and are something but by a distinction; and herein is Divinity conformant unto Philosophy, and generation not onely founded on contrarieties, but also creation; God being all things is contrary unto nothing out of which were made all things, and so nothing becomes something, and *Omneity* informed *Nullity* into an essence.

The whole Creation is a mystery, and particularly that of man; at the blast of his mouth were the rest of the creatures made, and at his bare word they started out of nothing: but in the frame of man (as the text describes it) he played the sensible operator, and seemed not so much to create, as make him; when hee had separated the materials of other creatures, there consequently resulted a forme and soule, but having raised the wals of man, he was driven to a second and harder creation of a substance like himselfe, an incorruptible and immortall soule.

Sir Thomas Browne

Religio Medici (1642). Text from the
first authorized edition (1643)

AGAINST THE ATHEIST

POOR intricated soule! Riddling, perplexed, labyrinthicall soule! Thou couldest not say, that thou beleevest not in God, if there were no God; Thou couldest not not[1] beleeve in God, if there were no God; If there were no God, thou couldest not speake, thou couldest not thinke, not a word, not a thought, no not against God; Thou couldest not blaspheme the Name of God, thou couldest not sweare, if there were no God: For, all thy faculties, how ever depraved, and perverted by thee, are from him; and except thou canst seriously beleeve, that thou art nothing, thou canst not beleeve that there is no God. If I should aske thee at a Tragedy, where thou should-est see him that had drawne blood, lie weltring, and sur-rounded in his owne blood, Is there a God now? If thou couldst answer me, No, These are but Inventions, and Re-presentations of men, and I beleeve a God never the more for this; If I should aske thee at a Sermon, where thou shouldest heare the Judgements of God formerly denounced, and executed, re-denounced, and applied to present occasions, Is there a God now? If thou couldest answer me, No, These are but Inventions of State, to souple and regulate Congrega-tions, and keep people in order, and I beleeve a God never the more for this; Bee as confident as thou canst, in company; for company is the Atheists Sanctuary; I respit thee not till the day of Judgement, when I may see thee upon thy knees, upon thy face, begging of the hills, that they would fall downe and cover thee from the fierce wrath of God, to aske thee then, Is there a God now? I respit thee not till the day of thine own death, when thou shalt have evidence enough, that there is a God, though no other evidence, but to finde a Devill, and evidence enough, that there is a Heaven, though no other evidence, but to feele Hell; To aske thee then, Is there a God

1. The original omits the second *not*.

now? I respit thee but a few houres, but six houres, but till midnight. Wake then; and then darke, and alone, Heare God aske thee then, remember that I asked thee now, Is there a God? and if thou darest, say No.

John Donne
Sermon for the Feast of the Conversion of
St Paul (1628) in *LXXX Sermons* (1640)

MAN BY HIMSELF

CONSIDER Man by himself, and from under the conduct and protection of a superior and more powerful Being, and he is in a most disconsolate and forlorn condition: Secure of nothing that he enjoys, and liable to be disappointed of every thing that he hopes for: He is apt to grieve for what he cannot help, and perhaps the justest cause of his grief is that he cannot help it; for if he could, instead of grieving for it, he would help it: He cannot refrain from desiring a great many things which he would fain have, but is never likely to obtain, because they are out of his power; and it troubles him both that they are so, and that he cannot help his being troubled at it. . . .

And when we are grown up, we are liable to a great many mischiefs and dangers, every moment of our lives; and, without the Providence of God, continually insecure not only of the good things of this life, but even of life it self: So that when we come to be men, we cannot but wonder how ever we arrived at that state, and how we have continued in it so long, considering the infinite difficulties and dangers which have continually attended us: That in running the *gantlope* of a long life, when so many hands have been lifted up against

gantlope] gauntlet

us, and so many strokes levell'd at us, we have escaped so free, and with so few marks and scars upon us: That when we are besieged with so many dangers, and so many arrows of death are perpetually flying about us, to which we do so many ways lie open, we should yet hold out *twenty*, *forty*, *sixty* years, and some of us perhaps longer, and do still stand at the mark untouch'd, at least not dangerously wounded by any of them: And considering likewise this fearful and wonderful frame of a human Body, this infinitely complicated Engine; in which, to the due performance of the several functions and offices of life, so many strings and springs, so many receptacles and channels are necessary, and all in their right frame and order; and in which, besides the infinite imperceptible and secret ways of mortality, there are so many sluices and flood-gates to let Death in and Life out, that it is next to a miracle, tho' we take but little notice of it, that every one of us did not die every day since we were born: I say, considering the nice and curious frame of our Bodies, and the innumerable contingencies and hazards of human Life, which is set in so slippery a place, that we still continue in the land of the living, we cannot ascribe to any thing but the watchful Providence of Almighty God, *who holds our soul in life, and suffers not our foot to be moved.*

To the same merciful Providence of God we owe, that whilst we continue in life we have any comfortable possession and enjoyment of our selves and of that which makes us Men, I mean our Reason and Understanding: That our Imagination is not let loose upon us, to haunt and torment us with melancholick freaks and fears: That we are not deliver'd up to the horrors of a gloomy and guilty mind: That every day we do not fall into frenzy and distraction, which next to wickedness and vice is the sorest calamity, and saddest disguise of human Nature: I say, next to wickedness and vice, which is a wilful frenzy, a madness not from misfortune but from choice; whereas the *other* proceeds from natural and necessary causes, such as are in a great measure out of our power; so that we are perpetually liable to it, from any secret and sudden disorder of the Brain, from the violence of a Disease, or the vehement transport of any Passion.

Now if things were under no government, what could hinder so many probable evils from breaking in upon us, and from treading upon the heels of one another? like the calamities of *Job*, when *the hedge which God had set about him and all that he had, was broken down and removed*.

So that if there were no God to take care of us, we could be secure of no sort, no degree of happiness in this World; no not for one moment; And there would be no other World for us to be happy in, and to make amends to us for all the fears and dangers, all the troubles and calamities of this present life: For God and another World stand and fall together: Without *Him* there can be no Life after this, and if our hopes of happiness were only in this Life, Man of all other Beings in this lower World would certainly be the most miserable.

John Tillotson

Sermon XL (1692) in *Works* (1696)
Text from the eighth edition (1720)

DIVINE THINGS ARE TO BE UNDERSTOOD
BY A SPIRITUAL SENSATION

To seek our Divinity meerly in Books and Writings, *is to seek the living among the dead*: we doe but in vain seek God many times in these, where his Truth too often is not so much *enshrin'd*, as *entomb'd*: no; *intra te quaere Deum*, seek for God within thine own soul; he is best discern'd νοερᾷ ἐπαφῇ, as *Plotinus* phraseth it, by an *Intellectual touch* of him: we must *see with our eyes, and hear with our ears, and our hands must handle the word of life*, that I may express it in S. John's words. ᾿Εστι καὶ ψυχῆς ἄισθησίς τις, The Soul it self hath its sense, as well as the Body: and therefore *David*, when he would teach us how to know what the Divine Goodness is, calls not for *Speculation* but *Sensation*, *Tast and see how good the Lord is*. That is not the best & truest knowledge of God which is wrought out by the labour and sweat of the Brain, but that which is kindled within us by an heavenly warmth in our Hearts. As in the natural Body it is the Heart that sends up good Blood and warm Spirits into the Head, whereby it is best enabled to its several functions; so that which enables us to know and understand aright in the things of God, must be a living principle of Holiness within us. When the *Tree of Knowledge* is not planted by the *Tree of Life*, and sucks not up sap from thence, it may as well be fruitful with *evil* as with *good*, and bring forth *bitter* fruit as well as *sweet*. If we would indeed have our Knowledge thrive and flourish, we must water the tender plants of it with Holiness. When *Zoroaster's* Scholars asked him what they should doe to get *winged Souls*, such as might soar aloft in the bright beams of Divine Truth, he bids them bathe themselves in *the waters of Life*: they asking what they were; he tells them, the *four Cardinal Vertues*, which are *the four Rivers of Paradise*. It is but a thin, aiery knowledge that is got by meer Speculation, which is usher'd in by Syllogisms and Demonstrations; but that which springs forth from true Goodness, is θειότερόν τι πάσης ἀποδείξεως, as *Origen* speaks, it brings such a Divine Light into the Soul, as is more clear and convincing then any Demonstration. The reason why, notwithstanding all our acute reasons and subtile disputes, Truth prevails no more in the world, is, we so often disjoyn *Truth* and true *Goodness*, which in themselves can never be disunited; they grow both from the same Root, and live in one another. We may, like those in *Plato's* deep pit with their faces bended downwards, converse with *Sounds* and *Shadows*; but not with the *Life* and *Substance* of Truth, while our Souls remain defiled with any vice or lusts. These are the black *Lethe*-lake, which drench the Soules of men: he that wants true Vertue, in heaven's Logick *is blind, and cannot see afar off*. Those filthy mists that arise from impure and terrene minds, like an *Atmospheare*, perpetually encompass them, that they cannot see that Sun of Divine Truth that shines *about* them, but never shines *into* any *unpurged* Souls; the darkness comprehends it not, the foolish man understands it not. All the Light and Knowledge that may seem sometimes to rise up in unhallowed mindes, is but like those fuliginous flames that arise up from our culinary fire, that are soon quench'd in their own smoak; or like those foolish fires that fetch their birth from terrene exudations, that doe but hop up & down, and flit to and fro upon the surface of this earth where they were first brought forth; and serve not so much to enlighten, as to delude us; nor to direct the wandring traveller into his way, but to lead him farther out of it. While we lodge any filthy vice in us, this will be perpetually twisting up it self into the thread of our finest-spun Speculations; it will be continually climbing up into the *Tò Ἡγεμονικόν* the *Hegemonicall* powers of the Soul, into the bed of Reason, and defile it: like the wanton Ivie twisting it self about the Oak, it will twine about our Judgments and Understandings till it hath suck'd out the Life and Spirit of them . . . This is that venemous *Solanum*, that deadly *Nightshade*, that derives its cold poyson into the Understandings of men.

John Smith

'Of the true Way . . . of attaining to Divine
Knowledge' in *Select Discourses* (1660)

OUR KNOWLEDGE OF THE EXISTENCE OF A GOD

I THINK it is beyond Question, that *Man has a clear Perception of his own Being*; he knows certainly, that he exists, and that he is something. He that can doubt, whether he be any thing, or no, I speak not to, no more than I would argue with pure nothing, or endeavour to convince Non-entity that it were something. If any one pretend to be so sceptical, as to deny his own Existence, (for really to doubt of it, is manifestly impossible,) let him for me enjoy his beloved Happiness of being nothing, until Hunger, or some other Pain convince him of the contrary. This then, I think, I may take for a Truth, which every ones certain Knowledge assures him of, beyond the liberty of doubting, *viz.* that he is something that actually exists.

In the next place, Man knows by an intuitive Certainty, that bare *nothing can no more produce any real Being, than it can be equal to two right Angles.* If a Man knows not that Non-entity, or the Absence of all Being, cannot be equal to two right Angles, it is impossible he should know any demonstration in *Euclid.* If therefore we know there is some real Being, and that Non-entity cannot produce any real Being, it is an evident demonstration, that from Eternity there has been something. Since what was not from Eternity, had a Beginning; and what had a Beginning, must be produced by something else.

Next, it is evident, that what had its Being and Beginning from another, must also have all that which is in, and belongs to its Being from another too. All the Powers it has, must be owing to, and received from the same Source. This eternal Source then of all being must also be the Source and Original of all Power; and so *this eternal Being must be also the most powerful.*

Again, a Man finds in himself Perception, and Knowledge.

We have then got one step further; and we are certain now, that there is not only some Being, but some knowing intelligent Being in the World.

There was a time then, when there was no knowing Being, and when Knowledge began to be; or else, there has been also a *knowing Being from Eternity*. If it be said, there was a time when no Being had any Knowledge, when that eternal Being was void of all Understanding—I reply, that then it was impossible there should ever have been any Knowledge: It being as impossible, that Things wholly void of Knowledge, and operating blindly, and without any Perception, should produce a knowing Being, as it is impossible, that a Triangle should make it self three Angles bigger than two right ones. For it is as repugnant to the *Idea* of sensless Matter, that it should put into it self Sense, Perception, and Knowledge, as it is repugnant to the *Idea* of a Triangle, that it should put into it self greater Angles than two right ones.

Thus from the Consideration of our selves, and what we infallibly find in our own Constitutions, our Reason leads us to the Knowledge of this certain and evident Truth, That *there is an eternal, most powerful, and most knowing Being*; which whether any one will please to call God, it matters not. The thing is evident, and from this *Idea* duly considered, will easily be deduced all those other Attributes, which we ought to ascribe to this eternal Being.

John Locke

An Essay concerning Humane Understanding (1690)

REASON

LETS hear awhile what are the offences of *Reason*; are they so hainous, and capital? what has it done? what lawes has it violated? whose commands has it broken? what did it ever do against the crown and dignity of heaven, or against the peace and tranquillity of men? Why are a weak and perverse generation, so angry and displeased with it? Is it because this daughter of the morning is fallen from her primitive glory? from her original vigour, and perfection? Far be it from me to extenuate that great and fatal overthrow, which the sons of men had in their first and original apostasie from their God; that under which the whole Creation sighs and groans: but this we are sure, it did not annihilate the soul, it did not destroy the essence, the powers and faculties, nor the operations of the soul; though it did defile them, and disorder them, and every way indispose them.

Well then, because the eye of *Reason* is weakened, and vitiated, will they therefore pluck it out immediately? and must *Leah* be hated upon no other account, but because she is blear-ey'd? The whole head is wounded, and akes, and is there no other way, but to cut it off? *The Candle of the Lord* do's not shine so clearly as it was wont, must it therefore be extinguisht presently? is it not better to enjoy the faint and languishing light of this *Candle of the Lord*, rather then to be in palpable and disconsolate darknesse? There are indeed but a few seminal sparks left in the ashes, and must there be whole floods of water cast on them to quench them? 'Tis but an old imperfect Manuscript, with some broken periods, some letters worn out, must they therefore with an unmerciful indignation rend it and tear it asunder? 'Tis granted that the picture has lost its glosse and beauty, the oriency of its colours, the elegancy of its lineaments, the comelinesse of its proportion; must it therefore be totally defac'd? must it be made one great blot? and must the very frame of it be broken in pieces? Would you perswade the Lutanist to cut all his strings in sunder, because they are out of tune? And will you break the Bowe upon no other account, but because it's unbended? because men have not so much of *Reason* as they should, will they therefore resolve to have none at all? will you throw away your gold, because it's mix't with drosse? Thy very being that's imperfect too, thy graces, they are imperfect, wilt thou refuse these also? And then consider, that the very apprehending the weaknes of *Reason*, even this in some measure comes from *Reason*. *Reason*, when awaken'd, it feels her own wounds, it hears her own jarrings, she sees the dimnesse of her own sight. 'Tis a glasse that discovers its own spots, and must it therefore be broke in peices? *Reason* her self has made many sad complaints unto you; she has told you often, and that with teares in her eyes, what a great shipwrack she has suffered, what goods she has lost, how hardly she escaped with a poor decayed being; she has shewn you often some broken reliques as the sad remembrancers of her former ruines; she told you how that when she swam for her life, she had nothing, but two, or three Jewels about her, two or three common notions; and would you rob her of them also? is this all your tendernesse and compassion? Is this your kindness to your friend? will you trample upon her now she is low? Is this a sufficient cause to give her a Bill of Divorcement, because she has lost her former beauty and fruitfulnesse?

Or is *Reason* thus offensive to them, because she cannot grasp and comprehend the things of God? Vain men, will they pluck out their eyes because they cannot look upon the Sun in his brightnesse and glory? What though *Reason* cannot reach to the depths, to the bottomes of the Ocean, may it not therefore swim, and hold up the head as well as it can? What though it cannot enter into the *Sanctum Sanctorum*, and pierce within the Veile; may it not notwithstanding lie in the Porch, *at the gate of the Temple called beautiful, and be a door-keeper in the house of its God?* Its wings are clipt indeed, it cannot flie so high as it might have done, it cannot flie so swiftly, so strongly as once it could, will they not therefore allow it to move, to stirre, to flutter up and down as well as it can? the turrets and pinacles of the stately structure are fallen, will they therefore demolish the whole fabrick, and shake the very foundations of it? and down with it to the ground? though it be not a *Jacob's* ladder to climbe up to heaven by, yet may they not use it as a staffe to walk upon the earth withall? and then *Reason* it self knows this also and acknowledges, that 'tis dazled with the Majesty and Glory of God; that it cannot pierce into his mysterious and unsearchable wayes; it never was so vain as to go about to measure immensity by its own finite Compasse, or to span out absolute eternity by its more imperfect duration. True *Reason* did never go about to comprize the Bible in its own Nutshel. And if *Reason be content* with its own sphere, why should it not have the liberty of its proper motion?

Nathanael Culverwel

An Elegant . . . Discourse of the Light of Nature (1652)

THE FOURTH CAUSE OF COMMON ERRORS

THE fourth is a supinity or neglect of enquiry, even in matters whereof we doubt, rather beleeving, as we say, then going to see, or doubting with ease and gratis, than beleeving with difficulty or purchase; whereby either by a temperamentall inactivity we are unready to put in execution the suggestions or dictates of reason, or by a content and acquiescence in every species of truth we embrace the shadow thereof, or so much as may palliate its just and substantiall acquirements. Had our forefathers sat downe in these resolutions, or had their curiosities been sedentary, who pursued the knowledge of things through all the corners of nature, the face of truth had been obscure unto us, whose lustre in some part their industries have revealed.

Certainly the sweat of their labours was not salt unto them, and they took delight in the dust of their endeavours. For questionlesse in knowledge there is no slender difficulty, and truth which wise men say doth lye in a well, is not recoverable but by exantlation. It were some extenuation of the Curse, if *in sudore vultus tui* were confineable unto corporall exercitations, and there still remained a Paradise, or unthorny place of knowledge; but now our understandings being eclipsed, as well as our tempers infirmed, we must betake our selves to wayes of reparation, and depend upon the illumination of our endeavours; for thus we may in some measure repaire our primarie ruins, and build our selves men againe. And though the attempts of some have been precipitous, and their enquiries so audacious as to come within command of the flaming swords, and lost themselves in attempts above humanity, yet have the inquiries of most defected by the way, and tyred within the sober circumference of knowledge.

And this is the reason why some have transcribed any thing, and although they cannot but doubt thereof, yet neither make experiment by sence or enquiry by reason, but live in doubts of things whose satisfaction is in their owne power, which is indeed the inexcusable part of our ignorance, and may perhaps fill up the charge of the last day. For not obeying the dictates of Reason, and neglecting the cryes of truth, we faile not onely in the trust of our undertakings, but in the intention of man it selfe, which although more veniall unto ordinary constitutions, and such as are not framed beyond the capacity of beaten notions, yet will it inexcusably condemne some men, who having received excellent endowments and such as will accuse the omissions of perfection, have yet sat down by the way, and frustrated the intention of their habilities. For certainely as some men have sinned, in the principles of humanity, and must answer, for not being men,

exantlation] drawing out

so others offend if they be not more; *Magis extra vitia quam cum virtutibus*, would commend those, These are not excusable without an Excellency. For great constitutions, and such as are constellated unto knowledge, do nothing till they outdoe all; they come short of themselves if they go not beyond others, and must sit downe under the degree of worthies. God expects no lustre from the minor Stars, but if the Sun should not illuminate all, it were a sin in Nature. *Ultimus bonorum*, will not excuse every man, nor is it sufficient for all to hold the common levell; Mens names should not onely distinguish them: A man should be something that men are not, and individuall in somewhat beside his proper nature. Thus, while it exceeds not the bounds of reason, and modesty, we cannot condemn singularity. *Nos numerus sumus*, is the motto of the multitude, and for that reason are they fooles. For things as they recede from unity, the more they approach to imperfection, and deformity; for they hold their perfection in their simplicities, and as they neerest approach unto God.

Sir Thomas Browne

Pseudodoxia Epidemica: or, Enquiries into Very many received Tenents, And commonly presumed Truths (1646)

THE PHOENIX

CONCERNING its generation, that without all conjunction, it begets and reseminates it self, hereby we introduce a vegetable production in animalls, and unto sensible natures, transferre the propriety of plants, that is to multiply among themselves, according to the Law of the Creation, Gen.1. Let the earth bring forth grasse, the herbe yeelding seed, and the tree yeelding fruit, whose seed is in it selfe; which way is

constellated] predestined

indeed the naturall way of plants, who having no distinction of sex, and the power of the species contained in every *individuum*, beget and propagate themselves without commixtion, and therefore their fruits proceeding from simpler roots, are not so unlike, or distinguishable from each other, as are the off-springs of sensible creatures and prolifications descending from double originalls; But animall generation is accomplished by more, and the concurrence of two sexes is required to the constitution of one; and therefore such as have no distinction of sex, engender not at all, as Aristotle conceives of Eeles, and testaceous animalls; and though plant animalls do multiply, they doe it not by copulation, but in a way analogous unto plants; So Hermaphrodites although they include the parts of both sexes, and may be sufficiently potent in either, yet unto a conception require a separated sex, and cannot impregnate themselves; and so also though Adam included all humane nature, or was (as some opinion) an Hermaphrodite, yet had hee no power to propagate himselfe; and therefore God said, It is not good that man should be alone, let us make him an help meet for him, that is, an help unto generation; for as for any other help, it had been fitter to have made another man.

Now whereas some affirme that from one Phœnix there doth not immediatly proceed another, but the first corrupteth into a worme, which after becommeth a Phœnix, it will not make probable this production; For hereby they confound the generation of perfect animalls with imperfect, sanguineous with exanguious, vermiparous, with oviparous, and erect Anomalies, disturbing the lawes of Nature; Nor will this corruptive production be easily made out, in most imperfect generations; for although we deny not that many animals are vermiparous, begetting themselves at a distance, & as it were at the second hand, as generally insects, and more

exanguious] bloodless (exsanguineous)

172

remarkably Butterflies and Silkwormes; yet proceeds not this generation from a corruption of themselves, but rather a specificall, and seminall diffusion, retaining still the Idea of themselves, though it act that part a while in other shapes: and this will also hold in generations equivocall, and such as are not begotten from Parents like themselves; so from Frogs corrupting, proceed not Frogs againe; so if there be anatiferous trees, whose corruption breaks forth into Bernacles, yet if they corrupt, they degenerate into Maggots, which produce not them againe; for this were a confusion of corruptive and seminall production, and a frustration of that seminall power committed to animalls at the creation. The probleme might have beene spared, Why wee love not our Lice as well as our Children, Noahs Arke had been needlesse, the graves of animals would be the fruitfullest wombs; for death would not destroy, but empeople the world againe.

Since therefore we have so slender grounds to confirm the existence of the Phœnix, since there is no ocular witnesse of it, since as we have declared, by Authors from whom the Story is derived, it rather stands rejected, since they who have seriously discoursed hereof, have delivered themselves negatively, diversly, or contrarily, since many others cannot be drawne into Argument as writing Poetically, Rhetorically, Enigmatically, Hieroglyphically, since holy Scripture alleadged for it duly perpended, doth not advantage it, and lastly since so strange a generation, unity and long life hath neither experience nor reason to confirme it, how farre to rely on this tradition, wee referre unto consideration.

Sir Thomas Browne

Pseudodoxia Epidemica: or, Enquiries into Very many received Tenents, And commonly presumed Truths (1646)

anatiferous] geese-producing. A common belief was that 'barnacle geese' were generated from barnacles growing on certain trees.

The Triumph of the Telescope

THAT the *Galaxy* is a *Meteor*, was the account of *Aristotle*: But the *Telescope* hath autoptically confuted it: And he, who is not *Pyrrhonian* to the dis-belief of his Senses, may see, that it's no exhalation from the Earth, but an heap of smaller *Luminaries*. That the *Heavens* are void of *corruption*, is *Aristotles* supposal: But the Tube hath betray'd their impurity; and *Neoterick Astronomy* hath found *spots* in the *Sun*. The discoveries made in *Venus*, and the *Moon*, disprove the *Antique Quintessence*; and evidence them of as course *materials*, as the *Globe* we belong to. The *Perspicil*, as well as the *Needle*, hath enlarged the *habitable World*; and that the *Moon* is an *Earth*, is no improbable conjecture. The *inequality* of its surface, *Mountanous protuberance*, the nature of its *Maculæ*, and infinite other circumstances (for which the world's beholding to *Galilæo*) are Items not contemptible: *Hevelius* hath *graphically* described it: That *Comets* are of nature Terrestrial, is allowable: But that they are material'd of vapours, and never flamed beyond the *Moon*; were a concession unpardonable. That in Cassiopæa was in the *Firmament*, and another in our age above the *Sun*. Nor was there ever any as low as the highest point of the *circumference*, the Stagyrite allows them. So that we need not be appall'd at *Blazing Stars*, and a *Comet* is no more ground for *Astrological presages* then a *flaming* Chimney. The unparallel'd *Des-Cartes* hath unridled their dark *Physiology*, and to wonder solv'd their *Motions*. His *Philosophy* gives them transcursions beyond the *Vortex* we breath in; and leads them through others, which are only known in an *Hypothesis*. *Aristotle* would have fainted before he had flown half so far, as that *Eagle-wit*; and have lighted on a *hard name*, or *occult quality*, to rest him.

Joseph Glanvill

Scepsis Scientifica: Or, Confest Ignorance, the Way to Science (1665)

autoptically] by personal observation
Neoterick] modern   *Perspicil*] telescope

The Royal Society

If I could fetch my Materials whence I pleas'd, to fashion the *Idea* of a perfect Philosopher; he should not be all of one *Clime*, but have the different Excellencies of several Countries. First, he should have the *Industry, Activity*, and *inquisitive Humor* of the *Dutch, French, Scotch*, and *English*, in laying the Ground work, the Heap of Experiments: And then he should have added the cold, and *circumspect*, and *wary* Disposition of the *Italians* and *Spaniards*, in meditating upon them, before he fully brings them into Speculation. All this is scarce ever to be found in one single Man; seldom in the same Countrymen: It must then be supplied, as well it may, by a *publick Council*, wherein the various Dispositions of all these Nations may be blended together. To this purpose, the *Royal Society* has made no Scruple to receive all inquisitive Strangers of all Countries into its Number . . .

All Places and Corners are now busy and warm about this Work: and we find many noble Rarities to be every Day given in not only by the Hands of learned and professed Philosophers; but from the Shops of *Mechanicks*; from the Voyages of *Merchants*; from the Ploughs of *Husbandmen*; from the Sports, the Fishponds, the Parks, the Gardens of *Gentlemen* . . . What Reason then have we to bode ill alone to this *Institution*, which is now so earnestly embraced; and which, the older it grows, cannot but still appear more inoffensive? If we only required *perfect Philosophers* to manage this Employment, it were another Case. For then I grant it were improbable, that threescore, or an hundred such should meet in one Time. But here it is far otherwise; if we cannot have sufficient Choice of those that are skill'd in all *Divine* and *Human* Things (which was the ancient Definition of a Philosopher) it suffices, if many of them be plain, diligent, and laborious Observers: such, who though they bring not much Knowledge, yet bring their Hand, and their Eyes uncorrupted: such as have not their Brains infected by false Images, and can honestly assist in the *examining* and *registering* what the others represent to their View. It seems strange to me, that Men should conspire to believe all things more perplexed, and difficult, than indeed they are. This may be shewn in most other Matters; but in this particular in hand, it is most evident, Men did generally think, that no Man was fit to meddle in Matters of this Consequence, but he that had bred himself up in a long course of Discipline for that Purpose; that had the Habit, the Gesture, the Look of a Philosopher: Whereas Experience, on the contrary, tells us, that greater Things are produc'd by the *free* way, than the *formal*. This Mistake may well be compar'd to the Conceit we had of *Soldiers*, in the beginning of the civil Wars. None was thought worthy of that Name, but he that could shew his Wounds, and talk aloud of his Exploits in the *Low Countries*: Whereas the whole Business of fighting, was afterwards chiefly perform'd by *untravel'd Gentlemen, raw Citizens*, and *Generals* that had scarce ever before seen a Battle. But to say no more, it is so far from being a Blemish, that it is rather the Excellency of this Institution, that *Men of various Studies* are introduced. For so there will be always many sincere Witnesses standing by, whom Self-love will not persuade to report falsly, nor Heat of Invention carry to swallow a Deceit too soon; as having themselves no Hand in the making of the Experiment, but only in the *Inspection*. So cautious ought Men to be, in pronouncing even upon Matters of Fact. The whole Care is not to be trusted to *single* Men; not to a *Company* all of *one Mind*; not to *Philosophers*; not to *devout* and religious Men *alone*: By all these we have been already deluded; even by those whom I last named, who ought most of all to abhor Falshood; of whom yet many have multiplied upon us infinite Stories and false Miracles, without any regard to Conscience or Truth.

Thomas Sprat

*The History of the Royal Society of London, for
the Improving of Natural Knowledge* (1667)

SCIENTIFIC CORRESPONDENTS: MARTIN LISTER, JOHN RAY, HANS SLOANE

Dr. Lister *to Mr.* Ray

York, Decemb. 13. 1674.

Dear Friend,

I HAD a Letter from the *Barbadoes* from a learned and ingenious Physician of that Island the other Week: He practis'd long in *Cleveland*; and in his Passage this Summer to the *Barbadoes*, gives me an Account of two Birds he met with at Sea. I thought to ask your Opinion of them. I shall transcribe that Part of Dr. *Town's* Letter to me that mentions those Birds.

"One Night, when the Mariners were disagreeing about "our Distance from *Barbadoes*, a Bird, by the Seamen usually "called a *Booby*, lighted upon a Man sleeping on the Quarter- "Deck, which, from its stupidness, has its Name, for it sate "very quietly, looking about it, until it was taken by a Sea- "man's Hands; and by the Cry of this (which is like, and "almost as loud as the Sound a *Buck* makes upon the "*Rut*) immediately came another *Booby*, which was taken "after the same Manner: And many more might have been "so taken (the Seamen said) had there been more about the "Ship; but they were welcome Guests, because they put us "out of doubt, as usually appearing about 40 or 50 Leagues "from Land: They are of no Beauty at all, yet I'll send them "to you, because they are great Enemies to the *Flying Fish*. As "soon as we crossed the *Tropic*, we were met by a Bird called "the *Tropic-Bird*, because they commonly are first seen at 22 "or 23 Degrees of Latitude. They are about the Bigness of a "*Parrot*; the Feathers appeared white, with red intermix'd; "the *Beak* crooked, and of a Scarlet Colour; their *Tail* at a "Distance not to be seen, but, nigh at hand, about the Thick- "ness and Length of an ordinary Tobacco-Pipe. I wonder "what their Food may be so far from Land; for I cannot learn

"that they have been observed to prey upon any Fish, or Birds,
"unless they resort to some small Island yet undiscovered. I
"heard, since I came hither, that they frequent the Rocks on
"the Windward (or East-part) of this Island; which, if true,
"I'll endeavour to procure some, &c.

Mr. Ray to Dr. Lister.

Middleton, Dec. 19. 1674

Dear SIR,

I Thank you for the Information sent about the Birds. I have
read of the one in some Books of voyages, *viz.* the *Booby*, but
know nothing else of it but the Name. I wish I had a particular
Description of it, that so I might insert it in our *Ornithology*. The
Doctor, your Friend, seems to promise you the Bird dried;
which, when you receive, I shall beg a Description of it from you.

The *Tropic Bird* dried I have seen in the *Repository* of the
Royal Society, and have described as well as I can. I find it to
belong to that Sort of Birds which I call *Palmiped*, with all
the four Toes webbed together, such as are the *Cormorant* and
Soland-Goose; and therefore, without doubt, preys upon
Fishes, and lives only upon them. That which I observed most
remarkable in it was, that the Tail consisted only of two very
long Feathers: At least, I was informed that it had only two
Feathers in the Tail, and there were but two left remaining
in the Case, which accords well with what Dr. *Towne* writes:
Yet I am suspicious, that besides those two long Feathers, there
are other shorter in the Tail.

Having finished the *History of Birds*, I am now beginning
that of *Fishes*, wherein I shall crave your Assistance, especially
as to the *flat cartilagineous* Kind, and the several Sorts of
Aselli: Especially I desire Information about the Cole-fish of
Turner, which I suppose may sometimes come to *York*. When
I was in *Northumberland* I saw of them salted and dried, but
could not procure any of them new taken. . . .

Sir Hans Sloane *to Mr.* Ray.

London, June 21. 1687.

SIR,

I Send you here inclosed the Specimen of a Plant growing on *New-market Heath,* and in *Surry,* known by the Name of *Star of the Earth* in those parts. It is particularly taken Notice of on the Account of its extraordinary and admirable Virtue in curing the *Bitings of Mad Dogs,* either in Beasts or Men. One of his Majesty's Huntsmen having prov'd it a great many times, gave the King his Way of using it, which was an Infusion in Wine with Treacle, and one or two more Simples. His Majesty was pleased to communicate it to *Gresham* College to the *Royal Society;* and no body knowing the Plant by that Name, some there present confirming its Use in that Disease in some places of *England,* and procuring the Herb it self, it is as little known here as if it had come from the *Indies.* I told the Society I would let you have this best Specimen of it, which I question not but 'tis known to you. If you please to give your Sentiments about it, you'll extremely oblige, *&c.*

Mr. Ray's *Answer.*

SIR,

I Receiv'd your Letter with the Specimen enclosed, which seems to me to be the *Sesamoides Salamanticum magnum* of *Clusius,* or *Lychnis viscosa flore muscoso* of *C.B.* which I have observed to grow plentifully upon *Newmarket Heath,* that Part I mean that is in *Suffolk;* for on *Cambridgeshire* Side I have not found it. I wonder it should have such a Virtue as you mention; but it seems it is well attested. Dr. *Hulse* writes to me he finds it in *Grayes Farrier.*

If you go to *Jamaica,* I pray you a safe and prosperous Voyage. We expect great Things from you, no less than the resolving all our Doubts about the Names we meet with of

Plants in that Part of *America*, as the *Dildoe, Mammee, Man-grove, Manchinello, Avellanæ purgatrices*, the *Sower-sop*, and *Custard-apple*. Of most of which tho' I am pretty well informed and satisfied by Dr. *Robinson*, yet I shall be glad to be either confirmed, or better informed by so knowing and curious an Observer as your self. I should be glad to know what manner of Fruit the *Mandioca* bears; for (whatever some have written) that it is not without, I am confident. You may also please to observe whether there be any Species of Plants common to *America* and *Europe*, and whether *Amber-grise* be the Juice of any Sort of *Metal* or *Aloe* dropt into the Sea, as *Trapham* would have it. What Kind of *Arundo* it is, the same Author calls the *Dumb-cane*; as also what his Animal Seeds may be. The *Shining-Barks* of *Trees* which he mentions deserve Observation, because I find nothing of them in other Writers. I shall not instance in more Particulars. I wish your Voyage had so long prevented the Publication of my History, that I might have been satisfied and informed by you of these and a thousand other Particulars, and had so great an Accession of new and nondescript Species as your Inquisitions and Observations would have enriched it withal. I take Leave, and rest, &c.

> *Philosophical Letters Between . . . Mr. Ray And*
> *Several of his Ingenious Correspondents.* Edited
> by William Derham, F.R.S. (1718)

THE USES OF THE CREATURES

THOSE Philosophers indeed, who hold Man to be the only Creature in this sublunary World, endued with Sense and Perception, and that all other Animals are meer Machines or Puppets, have some Reason to think, that all things here below were made for Man. But this Opinion seems to me too mean, and unworthy the Majesty, Wisdom, and Power of

God; nor can it well consist with his Veracity, instead of a multitude of Noble Creatures, endued with Life and Sence, and spontaneous Motion, as all Mankind 'till of late Years believed, and none ever doubted of (so that it seems we are naturally made to think so) to have stocked the Earth with divers Sets of *Automata*, without all Sense and Perception, being wholly acted from Without, by the impulse of external Objects.

But be this so, there are infinite other Creatures without this Earth, which no considerate Man can think, were made only for Man, and have no other use. For my part, I cannot believe, that all the things in the World were so made for Man, that they have no other use.

For it seems to me highly absurd and unreasonable, to think that Bodies of such vast magnitude as the fix'd Stars, were only made to twinkle to us; nay, a multitude of them there are, that do not so much as twinkle, being either by reason of their distance or of their smalness, altogether invisible to the naked Eye, and only discoverable by a Telescope, and it is likely perfecter Telescopes than we yet have, may bring to light many more; and who knows, how many lie out of the ken of the best Telescope that can possibly be made? And I believe there are many Species in Nature, even in this sublunary World, which were never yet taken notice of by Man, and consequently of no use to him, which yet we are not to think were created in vain; but may be found out by, and of use to those who shall live after us in future Ages. But though in this Sence it be not true, that all things were made for Man; yet thus far it is, that all the Creatures in the World may be some way or other useful to us, at least to exercise our Wits and Understandings, in considering and contemplating of them, and so afford us Subjects of Admiring and Glorifying their and our Maker. Seeing then, we do believe, and assert, that all things were in some Sence made for us, we are therby obliged to make use of them for those Purposes for which they serve us, else we frustrate this End of their Creation. Now some of them serve only to exercise our Minds: Many others there be, which might probably serve us to good purpose, whose Uses are not discovered, nor are they ever like to be, without Pains and Industry. True it is, many of the greatest Inventions have been accidentally stumbled upon, but not by Men supine and careless, but busie and inquisitive. Some Reproach methinks it is to Learned Men, that there should be so many Animals still in the World, whose outward shape is not yet taken notice of, or describ'd, much less their way of Generation, Food, Manners, Uses, observed.

John Ray

The Wisdom of God Manifested in the Works of the Creation (1691). Text from the revised fourth edition (1704)

REFLECTIONS UPON A MICROSCOPICAL EXAMINATION OF THYME-SEEDS

THESE pretty fruits here represented,[1] are nothing else, but nine several seeds of Tyme; they are all of them in differing posture, both as to the eye and the light; nor are they all of them exactly of the same shape, there being a great variety both in the bulk and figure of each seed; but they all agreed in this, that being look'd on with a *Microscope*, they each of them exactly resembled a Lemmon or Orange dry'd; and this both in shape and colour. . . .

The Grain affords a very pretty Object for the *Microscope*, namely, a Dish of Lemmons plac'd in a very little room; should a Lemmon or Nut be proportionably magnify'd to

1. i.e. in an accompanying plate in the original.

what this seed of Tyme is, it would make it appear as bigg as a large Hay-reek, and it would be no great wonder to see *Homers Iliads*, and *Homer* and all, cramm'd into such a Nutshell. We may perceive even in these small Grains, as well as in greater, how curious and carefull Nature is in preserving the seminal principle of Vegetable bodies, in what delicate, strong and most convenient Cabinets she lays them and closes them in a pulp for their safer protection from outward dangers, and for the supply of convenient alimental juice, when the heat of the Sun begins to animate and move these little *automatons* or Engines; as if she would, from the ornaments wherewith she has deckt these Cabinets, hint to us, that in them she has laid up her Jewels and Master-pieces. And this, if we are but diligent in observing, we shall find her method throughout. There is no curiosity in the Elemental kingdom, if I may so call the bodies of Air, Water, Earth, that are comparable in form to those of Minerals; Air and Water having no form at all, unless a potentiality to be form'd into Globules; and the clods and parcels of Earth are all irregular, whereas in Minerals she does begin to *Geometrize*, and practise, as 'twere, the first principles of *Mechanicks*, shaping them of plain regular figures, as triangles, squares, &c. and *tetra-edons*, cubes, &c. But none of their forms are comparable to the more compounded ones of Vegetables; For here she goes a step further, forming them both of more complicated shapes, and adding also multitudes of curious Mechanick contrivances in their structure; for whereas in Vegetables there was no determinate number of the leaves or branches, nor no exactly certain figures of leaves, or flowers, or seeds, in Animals all those things are exactly defin'd and determin'd; and where-ever there is either an excess or defect of those determinate parts or limbs, there has been some impediment that has spoil'd the principle which was most regular: Here we shall find, not onely most curiously compounded shapes, but most stupendious Mechanisms and contrivances, here the ornaments are in the highest perfection, nothing in all the Vegetable kingdom that is comparable to the deckings of a Peacock; nay, to the curiosity of any feather, as I elsewhere shew; nor to that of the smallest and most despicable Fly. But I must not stay on these speculations, though perhaps it were very well worth while for one that had leisure, to see what Information may be learn'd of the nature, or use, or virtues of bodies, by their several forms and various excellencies and properties. Who knows but *Adam* might from some such contemplation, give names to all creatures? If at least his names had any significancy in them of the creature's nature on which he impos'd it; as many (upon what grounds I know not) have suppos'd: And who knows, but the Creator may, in those characters, have written and engraven many of his most mysterious designs and counsels, and given man a capacity, which, assisted with diligence and industry, may be able to read and understand them.

Robert Hooke

Micrographia: or Some Physiological Descriptions of Minute Bodies made by Magnifying Glasses (1665)

JOHN EVELYN'S SPIDER

OF all the sorts of Insects, there is none has afforded me more divertisements then the *Venatores*, which are a sort of *Lupi*, that have their Denns in the rugged walls, and crevices of our houses; a small brown and delicately spotted kind of Spiders, whose hinder leggs are longer then the rest.

Such I did frequently observe at *Rome*, which espying a Fly at three or four yards distance, upon the Balcony (where I stood) would not make directly to her, but craul under the Rail, till being arriv'd to the *Antipodes*, it would steal up, seldom missing its aim; but if it chanced to want any thing of being perfectly opposite, would at first peep, immediatly slide down again, till taking better notice, it would come the next time exactly upon the Fly's back: But, if this hapn'd not to be within a competent leap, then would this Insect move so softly, as the very shadow of the Gnomon seem'd not to be more imperceptible, unless the Fly mov'd; and then would the Spider move also in the same proportion, keeping that just time with her motion, as if the same Soul had animated both those little bodies; and whether it were forwards, backwards, or to either side, without at all turning her body, like a well mannag'd Horse: But, if the capricious Fly took wing, and pitch'd upon another place behind our Huntress, then would the Spider whirle its body so nimbly about, as nothing could be imagin'd more swift; by which means, she always kept the head towards her prey, though to appearance, as immovable, as if it had been a Nail driven into the Wood, till by that indiscernable progress (being arriv'd within the sphere of her reach) she made a fatal leap (swift as Lightning) upon the Fly, catching him in the pole, where she never quitted hold till her belly was full, and then carried the remainder home. I have beheld them instructing their young ones, how to hunt, which they would sometimes discipline for not well observing: but, when any of the old ones did (as sometimes) miss a leap, they would run out of the field, and hide them in their crannies, as asham'd, and haply not be seen abroad for four or five hours after; for so long have I watched the nature of this strange Insect, the contemplation of whose so wonderfull sagacity and address has amaz'd me; nor do I find in any chase whatsoever, more cunning and Stratagem observ'd.

John Evelyn

Quoted by Robert Hooke in Micrographia (1665)

SIR NICHOLAS GIMCRACK'S SPIDER

Characters: Sir Nicholas Gimcrack (the Virtuoso), Sir Formal Trifle (his friend), and Bruce and Longvil (Gentlemen of Wit and Sense).

Sir *Nic.* I think I have found out more Phænomena's or Appearances of Nature in Spiders, than any man breathing: Wou'd you think it? there are in *England* six and thirty several sorts of Spiders; there's your Hound, Grey-hound, Lurcher, Spaniel-Spider.

Longv. But above all, your Tumbler-Spider is most admirable.

Sir *Nic.* O Sir, I am no Stranger to't: it catches Flies as Tumblers do Conies.

Bruce. Good! how these Fools will meet a lie half-way.

Longv. Great Liars are always civil in that point; as there is no lie too great for their telling, so there's none too great for their believing.

Sir *Nic.* The Fabrick or Structure of this Insect, with its Texture, is most admirable.

Sir *Form.* Nor is its Sagacity, or Address, less to be wonder'd at, as I have had the honour to observe under my noble Friend; as soon as it has spi'd its Prey, as suppose upon a Table, it will crawl under-neath till it arrive to the Antipodes of the Fly, which it discovers by sometimes peeping up; and if the capricious Fly happens not to remove it self by crural motion, or the vibration of its wings, it makes a fatal leap upon the heedless prey, of which, when it has satisfied its appetite, it carries the remainder to its Cell, or Hermitage.

Sir *Nic.* It will teach its young ones to hunt, and discipline 'em severely when they commit faults; and when an Old one misses its Prey, it will retire, and keep its Chamber for grief, shame and anguish, ten hours together.

Sir *Form.* Upon my Integrity it is true, for I have several times, by Sir *Nicholas's* command watch'd the Animal, upon this or the like miscarriages.

Sir *Nic.* But, Sir, there is not in the world a more docible Creature, I have kept several of 'em tame.

Bruce. That's curious indeed. I never heard of a tame Spider before.

Sir *Nic.* One above all the rest, I had call'd him *Nick*, and he knew his name so well, he wou'd follow me all over the house; I fed him indeed with fair Flesh-flies. He was the best natur'd, best condition'd Spider, that ever I met with. You knew *Nick* very well, Sir *Formal*, he was of the Spaniel-breed, Sir —

Sir *Form.* Knew him! I knew *Nick* intimately well.

Longv. These Fools are beyond all that Art or Nature e'r produc'd.

Bruce. These are the admirable Secrets they find out —

Longv. Have you observed that delicate Spider, called *Tarantula*?

Sir *Nic.* Now you have hit me, now you come home to me; why I travell'd all over *Italy*, and had no other affair in the world, but to study the secrets of that harmonious Insect.

Bruce. Did you not observe the Wisdom, Policies, and Customs of that ingenuous People?

Sir *Nic.* Oh by no means! 'Tis below a Virtuoso to trouble himself with Men and Manners. I study Insects; and I have observ'd the *Tarantula* does infinitely delight in Musick, which is the reason of its poison being drawn out by it. There's your Phænomenon of Sympathy!

Longv. Does a *Tarantula* delight so in Musick?

Sir *Nic.* Oh extravagantly. There are three sorts, Black, Grey, and Red, that delight in three several sorts and modes of Musick.

Bruce. That was a curious Inquisition; how did you make it?

Sir *Nic.* Why I put them upon three several Chips in water; then caus'd a Musician to play, first a grave Pavin, or Almain, at which the black *Tarantula* onely mov'd; it danc'd to it with a kind of grave motion, much like the Benchers at the Revels.

Enter Servant

Serv. Sir, the Gentleman that's going for *Lapland*, *Russia*, and those parts, is come for your Letters and Queries which you are to send thither.

Sir *Nic.* I'll wait on him. I keep a constant correspondence with all the Virtuoso's in the North and North-East parts. There are rare Phænomena's in those Countreys. I am beholding to *Finland*, *Lapland*, and *Russia*, for a great part of my Philosophy. I send my Queries thither. Come, Sir *Formal*, will you help to dispatch him?

Sir *Form.* I am proud to serve you.

Sir *Nic.* Be pleas'd to take a turn in the Garden. When we have dispatch'd, we will impart more of our Microscopical investigations.

Thomas Shadwell
The Virtuoso (1676)

THE DEFINITION OF A CHEMICAL ELEMENT

HERE *Carneades* having Dispach't what he Thought Requisite to oppose against what the Chymists are wont to alledge for Proof of their three Principles, Paus'd a while, and look'd about him, to discover whether it were Time for him and his Friend to Rejoyne the Rest of the Company. But *Eleutherius* perceiving nothing yet to forbid Them to Prosecute their Discourse a little further, said to his Friend, (who had likewise taken Notice of the same thing) I halfe expected, *Carneades* that after you had so freely declar'd Your doubting, whether there be any Determinate Number of Elements, You would have proceeded to question whether there be any Elements at all. And I confess it will be a trouble to me if You defeat me of my Expectation; especially since you see the leasure we have allow'd us may probably suffice to examine that Paradox; because you have so largely Deduc'd already many Things pertinent to it, that you need but intimate how you would have them Apply'd, and what you would inferr from them.

Carneades having in Vain represented that their leasure could be but very short, that he had already prated very long, that he was unprepar'd to maintain so great and so invidious a Paradox, was at length prevail'd with to tell his Friend; Since, *Eleutherius*, you will have me Discourse *Ex Tempore* of the Paradox you mention, I am content, (though more perhaps to express my Obedience, than my Opinion) to tell you that (supposing the Truth of *Helmonts* and *Paracelsus*'s Alkahestical Experiments, if I may so call them) though it may seem extravagant, yet it is not absurd to doubt, whether, for ought has been prov'd, there be a necessity to admit any Elements, or Hypostatical Principles, at all.

And, as formerly, so now, to avoid the needless trouble of Disputing severally with the *Aristotelians* and the Chymists, I will address my self to oppose them I have last nam'd, Because their Doctrine about the Elements is more applauded by the Moderns, as pretending highly to be grounded upon Experience. And, to deal not only fairly but favourably with them, I will allow them to take in Earth and Water to their other Principles. Which I consent to the rather, that my Discourse may the better reach the Tenents of the Peripateticks; who cannot plead for any so probably as for those two Elements; that of fire above the Air being generally by Judicious

Alkahestical] all-dissolving

Men exploded as an Imaginary thing; And the Air not con-
curring to compose Mixt Bodies as one of their Elements, but
only lodging in their pores, or rather replenishing, by reason
of its Weight and Fluidity, all those Cavities of bodies here
below, whether compounded or not, that are big enough to
admit it, and are not fill'd up with any grosser substance.

And, to prevent mistakes, I must advertize You, that I now
mean by Elements, as those Chymists that speak plainest do
by their Principles, certain Primitive and Simple, or perfectly
unmingled bodies; which not being made of any other bodies,
or of one another, are the Ingredients of which all those call'd
perfectly mixt Bodies are immediately compounded, and into
which they are ultimately resolved: now whether there be
any one such body to be constantly met with in all, and each,
of those that are said to be Elemented bodies, is the thing I
now question.

By this State of the controversie you will, I suppose, Guess,
that I need not be so absurd, as to deny that there are such
bodies as Earth, and Water, and Quicksilver, and Sulphur:
But I look upon Earth and Water, as component parts of the
Universe, or rather of the Terrestrial Globe, not of all mixt
bodies. And though I will not peremptorily deny that there
may sometimes either a running Mercury, or a Combustible
Substance be obtain'd from a Mineral, or even a Metal; yet I
need not Concede either of them to be an Element in the sence
above declar'd; as I shall have occasion to shew you by and by.

To give you then a brief account of the grounds I intend to
proceed upon, I must tell you, that in matters of Philosophy,
this seems to me a sufficient reason to doubt of a known and
important proposition, that the Truth of it is not yet by any
competent proof made to appear. And congruously hereunto,
if I shew that the grounds, upon which men are perswaded
that there are Elements, are unable to satisfie a considering
man, I suppose my doubts will appear rational.

Now the Considerations that induce me to think, that there are Elements, may be conveniently enough referr'd to two heads. Namely, the one, that it is necessary that Nature make use of Elements to constitute the bodies that are reputed Mixt. And the other, That the Resolution of such bodies manifests that Nature had compounded them of Elementary ones.

Robert Boyle

The Sceptical Chymist . . . (1661). Text
from the revised second edition (1680)

SOME CONCLUSIONS

ALL these things being consider'd, it seems probable to me, that God in the Beginning form'd Matter in solid, massy, hard, impenetrable, moveable Particles, of such Sizes and Figures, and with such other Properties, and in such Proportion to Space, as most conduc'd to the End for which he form'd them; and that these primitive Particles being Solids, are incomparably harder than any porous Bodies compounded of them; even so very hard, as never to wear or break in pieces; no ordinary Power being able to divide what God himself made one in the first Creation. While the Particles continue entire, they may compose Bodies of one and the same Nature and Texture in all Ages: But should they wear away, or break in pieces, the Nature of Things depending on them, would be changed. Water and Earth, composed of old worn Particles and Fragments of Particles, would not be of the same Nature and Texture now, with Water and Earth composed of entire Particles in the Beginning. And therefore, that Nature may be lasting, the Changes of corporeal Things are to be placed only in the various Separations and new Associations and Motions of these permanent Particles;

Resolution] dissolution

compound Bodies being apt to break, not in the midst of solid Particles, but where those Particles are laid together, and only touch in a few Points.

It seems to me farther, that these Particles have not only a *Vis inertiæ*, accompanied with such passive Laws of Motion as naturally result from that Force, but also that they are moved by certain active Principles, such as is that of Gravity, and that which causes Fermentation, and the Cohesion of Bodies. These Principles I consider, not as occult Qualities, supposed to result from the specifick Forms of Things, but as general Laws of Nature, by which the Things themselves are form'd; their Truth appearing to us by Phænomena, though their Causes only are occult. And the *Aristotelians* gave the Name of occult Qualities, not to manifest Qualities, but to such Qualities only as they supposed to lie hid in Bodies, and to be the unknown Causes of manifest Effects: Such as would be the Causes of Gravity, and of magnetick and electrick Attractions, and of Fermentations, if we should suppose that these Forces or Actions arose from Qualities unknown to us, and uncapable of being discovered and made manifest. Such occult Qualities put a stop to the Improvement of Natural Philosophy, and therefore of late Years have been rejected. To tell us that every Species of Things is endow'd with an occult specifick Quality by which it acts and produces manifest Effects, is to tell us nothing: But to derive two or three general Principles of Motion from Phænomena, and afterwards to tell us how the Properties and Actions of all corporeal Things follow from those manifest Principles, would be a very great step in Philosophy, though the Causes of those Principles were not yet discover'd: And therefore I scruple not to propose the Principles of Motion abovemention'd, they being of very general Extent, and leave their Causes to be found out.

Now by the help of these Principles, all material Things

seem to have been composed of the hard and solid Particles above-mention'd, variously associated in the first Creation by the Counsel of an Intelligent Agent. For it became him who created them to set them in order. And if he did so, it's unphilosophical to seek for any other Origin of the World, or to pretend that it might arise out of a Chaos by the mere Laws of Nature; though being once form'd, it may continue by those Laws for many Ages.

Sir Isaac Newton

Opticks: or, A Treatise of the Reflections, Refractions, Inflections and Colours of Light (1704). Text from the revised fourth edition (1730).[1]

1. As a copy of this edition was unobtainable, the extract follows a modern reprint of the 1730 text.

THE WORLD OF IMAGINATION, FEELING AND COMIC INVENTION: FICTION AND OCCASIONAL WRITING

The Solitary Man

VOLUNTARY solitariness is that which is familiar with Melancholy, and gently brings on like a Siren, a shooing-horn, or some Sphinx to this irrevocable gulf, a primary cause *Piso* calls it; most pleasant it is at first, to such as are melancholy given, to lie in bed whole days, and keep their chambers, to walk alone in some solitary Grove, betwixt Wood and Water, by a Brook side, to meditate upon some delightsom and pleasant Subject, which shall affect them most; *amabilis insania*, and *mentis gratissimus error*: A most incomparable delight it is so to melancholize, and build castles in the air, to go smiling to themselves, acting an infinite variety of parts, which they suppose, and strongly imagine they represent, or that they see acted or done: *Bland[um] quidem ab initio*, saith *Lemnius*, to conceive and meditate of such pleasant things, sometimes, *Present, past or to come*, as *Rhasis* speaks. So delightsom these toyes are at first, they could spend whole days and nights without sleep, even whole yeers alone in such contemplations, and phantastical meditations, which are like unto dreams, and they will hardly be drawn from them, or willingly interrupt, so pleasant their vain conceits are, that they hinder their ordinary tasks and necessary business, they cannot address themselves to them, or almost to any study or imployment, these phantastical and bewitching thoughts so covertly, so feelingly, so urgently, so continually set upon, creep in, insinuate, possess, overcome, distract, and detain them, they cannot I say go about their more necessary business, stave off or extricate themselves, but are ever musing, melancholizing, and carried along, as he (they say) that is led round about an Heath with a *Puck* in the night, they run earnestly on in this labarinth of anxious and solicitous melancholy meditations, and cannot wel or willingly refrain, or easily leave off, winding and unwinding themselves, as so many clocks, and still pleasing their humors, until at last the Scene is turned upon a sudden, by some bad object, and they being now habituated to such vain meditations and solitary places, can endure no company, can ruminate of nothing but harsh and distastfull subjects. Fear, sorrow, suspition, *subrusticus pudor*, discontent, cares, and weariness of life surprize them in a moment, and they can think of nothing else, continually suspecting, no sooner are their eyes open, but this infernal plague of Melancholy seizeth on them, and terrifies their souls, representing some dismal object to their minds, which now by no means, no labour, no perswasions they can avoid, *hæret lateri lethalis arundo* they may not be rid of it, they cannot resist. . . *Homo solus aut Deus, aut Dæmon:* a man alone is either a Saint or a Devil, *mens ejus languescit, aut tumescit*; and *Væ soli* in this sense, woe be to him that is so alone.

Robert Burton

The Anatomy of Melancholy (1621). Text
from the revised sixth edition (1651)

Thou Art a Man

A MAN is a Bubble (said the Greek Proverb); which *Lucian* represents with advantages and its proper circumstances, to this purpose; saying, that all the world is a storm, and Men rise up in their several generations like bubbles descending *à Jove pluvio*, from God, and the dew of Heaven, from a tear and drop of Man, from Nature and Providence: and some of those instantly sink into the deluge of their first parent, and are hidden in a sheet of Water, having had no other businesse in the world, but to be born that they might be able to die: others float up and down two or three turns, and suddenly disappear and give their place to others: and they that live longest upon the face of the waters are in perpetual motion, restlesse and uneasy, and being crushed with the great drop of a cloud sink into flatnesse and a froth; the change not being great, it being hardly possible it should be more a nothing then it was before. So is every man: He is born in vanity and sin; he comes into the world like morning Mushromes, soon thrusting up their heads into the air and conversing with their kinred of the same production, and as soon they turn into dust and forgetfulnesse; some of them without any other interest in the affairs of the world, but that they made their parents a little glad, and very sorrowful: others ride longer in the storm; it may be until seven yeers of Vanity be expired, and then peradventure the Sun shines hot upon their heads and they fall into the shades below, into the cover of death, and darknesse of the grave to hide them. But if the bubble stands the shock of a bigger drop, and outlives the chances of a childe, of a carelesse Nurse, of drowning in a pail of water, of being overlaid by a sleepy servant, or such little accidents, then the young man dances like a bubble, empty and gay, and shines like a Doves neck or the image of a rainbow, which hath no substance, and whose very imagery and colours are phantastical; and so he dances out the gayety of his youth, and is all the while in a storm, and endures, onely because he is not knocked on the head by a drop of bigger rain, or crushed by the pressure of a load of indigested meat, or quenched by the disorder of an ill placed humor: and to preserve a man alive in the midst of so many chances, and hostilities, is as great a miracle as to create him; to preserve him from rushing into nothing and at first to draw him up from nothing were equally the issues of an Almighty power. And therefore the wise men of the world have contended who shall best fit mans condition with words signifying his vanity and short abode. *Homer* cals a man *a leaf*, the smallest, the weakest piece of a short liv'd, unsteady plant. *Pindar* calls him *the dream of a shadow*. Another, *the dream of the shadow of smoak*. But S. *James* spake by a more excellent Spirit, saying, *Our life is but a vapor*, viz. drawn from the earth by a cœlestial influence; made of smoak, or the lighter parts of water, tossed with every winde, moved by the motion of a superiour body, without vertue in it self, lifted up on high, or left below, according as it pleases the Sun its Foster-father. But it is lighter yet. It is but *appearing*. A phantastic vapor, an apparition, nothing real; it is not so much as a mist, not the matter of a shower, nor substantial enough to make a cloud; but it is like *Cassiopeia's* chair, or *Pelops* shoulder, or the circles of Heaven, φαινόμενα, for which you cannot have a word that can signify a veryer nothing. And yet the expression is one degree more diminutive: *A vapor*, and *phantastical*, or *a meer appearance*, and this but *for a little while* neither: the very dream, the phantasm disappears in a small time, *like the shadow that departeth*, or *like a tale that is told*, or *as a dream when one awaketh*: A man is so vain, so unfixed, so perishing a creature, that he cannot long last in the scene of fancy: a man goes off and is forgotten like the dream of a distracted person. The summe of all is this: *That thou art a man*, then whom there is not in the world any greater instance of heights and declensions, of lights and shadows, of misery and folly, of laughter and tears, of groans and death.

And because this consideration is of great usefulnesse and great necessity to many purposes of wisdom and the Spirit; all the succession of time, all the changes in nature, all the varieties of light and darknesse, the thousand thousands of accidents in the world, and every contingency to every man, and to every creature does preach our funeral sermon, and calls us to look, and see, how the old Sexton *Time* throws up the earth, and digs a Grave where we must lay our sins, or our sorrows, and sowe our bodies till they rise again in a fair, or in an intolerable eternity. Every revolution which the sun makes about the world, divides between life and death; and death possesses both those portions by the next morrow, and we are dead to all those moneths which we have already lived, and we shall never live them over again: and still God makes little periods of our age. First we change our world, when we come from the womb to feel the warmth of the sun: Then we sleep and enter into the image of death, in which state we are unconcerned in all the changes of the world; and if our Mothers, or our Nurses die, or a wilde boar destroy our vineyards, or our King be sick, we regard it not, but, during that state, are as disinterest, as if our eyes were closed with the clay that weeps in the bowels of the earth. At the end of seven years, our teeth fall and dye before us, representing a formal prologue to the Tragedie; and still every seven year it is oddes but we shall finish the last scene: and when Nature, or Chance, or Vice takes our body in pieces, weakening some parts, and loosing others, *we taste the grave* and the solemnities of our own Funerals, first in those parts that ministred to Vice, and next in those that served for Ornament; and in a short time even they that served for necessity become uselesse, and intangled like the wheels of a broken clock.

Jeremy Taylor
The Rule and Exercises of Holy Dying (1651)

By the Cross of Christ

By the Crosse of CHRIST stood the holy Virgin Mother, upon whom old *Simeons* prophesie was now verified. For now she felt a sword passing thorow her very soul; she stood without clamour and womanish noises, sad, silent, and with a modest grief, deep as the waters of the abysse, but smooth as the face of a Pool, full of love, and patience, and sorrow, and hope. Now she was put to it to make use of all those excellent discourses, her holy Son had used to build up her spirit and fortifie it against this day. Now she felt the blessings and strengths of Faith, and she passed from the griefs of the Passion to the expectation of the Resurrection, and she rested in this death as in a sad remedy; for she knew, it reconciled GOD with all the World. But her hope drew a veil before her sorrow, and though her grief was great enough to swallow her up, yet her love was greater and did swallow up her grief. But the sun also had a veil upon his face, and taught us to draw a curtain before the passion, which would be the most artificiall expression of its greatnesse, whilest by silence and wonder we confesse it great, beyond our expression, or which is all one, great as the burden and basenesse of our sins; and with this veil drawn before the face of JESUS let us suppose him at the gates of Paradise, calling with his last words in a loud voice to have them opened; *That the King of glory might come in.*

THE PRAYER

O *Holy* JESUS, *who for our sakes didst suffer incomparable anguish and paines commensurate to thy love and our miseries, which were infinite, that thou mightest purchase for us blessings upon Earth, and an inheritance in Heaven; dispose us by love, thankfulnesse, humility, and obedience to receive all the benefit of thy passion, granting unto us and thy whole Church remission of all our sinnes, integrity of minde, health of body, competent maintenance, peace in our dayes, a temperate air, fruitfulnesse of the earth, unity and integrity of faith, extirpation of Heresies, reconcilement of Schismes, destruction of all wicked counsels intended against us; and binde the hands of rapine and sacriledge, that they may not destroy the vintage and root up the Vine it self. Multiply thy blessings upon us sweetest Jesus, increase in us true religion, sincere and actual devotion in our prayers, patience in troubles, and whatsoever is necessary to our soules health, or conducing to thy glory. Amen.*

Jeremy Taylor

The Great Exemplar . . . the History of the Life and Death of . . . Jesus Christ . . . (1649)

A MEDITATION ON THE SEPULCHRAL URNS
FOUND AT OLD WALSINGHAM, 1656

NOW since these dead bones have already out-lasted the living ones of *Methuselah*, and in a yard under ground, and thin walls of clay, out-worn all the strong and specious buildings above it; and quietly rested under the drums and tramplings of three conquests; What Prince can promise such diuturnity unto his Reliques, or might not gladly say,

Sic ego componi versus in ossa velim.[1]

Time which antiquates Antiquities, and hath an art to make dust of all things, hath yet spared these *minor* monuments. In vain we hope to be known by open and visible conservatories, when to be unknown was the means of their continuation, and obscurity their protection: If they dyed by violent hands, and were thrust into their Urnes, these bones

1. *Tibullus* [This and all subsequent notes to this extract are Browne's].

become considerable, and some old Philosophers would honour them,[a] whose soules they conceived most pure, which were thus snatched from their bodies; and to retain a stronger propension unto them: whereas they weariedly left a languishing corps, and with faint desires of re-union. If they fell by long and aged decay, yet wrapt up in the bundle of time, they fall into indistinction, and make but one blot with Infants. If we begin to die when we live, and long life be but a prolongation of death; our life is a sad composition; we live with death, and die not in a moment. How many pulses made up the life of *Methuselah*, were work for *Archimedes*: Common Counters sum up the life of *Moses* his man.[b] Our dayes become considerable like petty sums by minute accumulations; where numerous fractions make up but small round numbers; and our dayes of a span long make not one little finger.[c]

If the nearnesse of our last necessity, brought a nearer conformity unto it, there were a happinesse in hoary hairs, and no calamity in half senses. But the long habit of living indisposeth us for dying; When Avarice makes us the sport of death; When even *David* grew politickly cruel; and *Solomon* could hardly be said to be the wisest of men. But many are too early old, and before the date of age. Adversity stretcheth our dayes, misery makes [d]*Alcmenas* nights, and time hath no wings unto it. But the most tedious being is that which can unwish it self, content to be nothing, or never to have been, which was beyond the *male*-content of *Job*, who cursed not the day of his life, but his Nativity: Content to have so farre

(a) *Oracula Chaldaica cum scholiis Pselli & Plethonis.* βίῃ λιπόντων σῶμα ψυχαὶ καθαρώταται. *Vi corpus relinquentium animæ purissimæ.*

(b) In the Psalme of Moses.

(c) According to the ancient Arithmetick of the hand wherein the little finger of the right hand contracted signified an hundred. *Pierius in Hieroglyph.*

(d) One night as long as three.

been, as to have a Title to future being; Although he had lived here but in an hidden state of life, and as it were an abortion.

What Song the *Syrens* sang, or what name *Achilles* assumed when he hid himself among women, though puzling Questions[e] are not beyond all conjecture. What time the persons of these Ossuaries entred the famous Nations of the dead,[f] and slept with Princes and Counsellours,[g] might admit a wide solution. But who were the proprietaries of these bones, or what bodies these ashes made up, were a question above Antiquarism. Not to be resolved by man, nor easily perhaps by spirits, except we consult the Provinciall Guardians, or tutellary Observators. Had they made as good provision for their names, as they have done for their Reliques, they had not so grosly erred in the art of perpetuation. But to subsist in bones, and be but Pyramidally extant, is a fallacy in duration. Vain ashes, which in the oblivion of names, persons, times and sexes, have found unto themselves, a fruitlesse continuation, and onely arise unto late posterity, as Emblemes of mortal vanities; Antidotes against pride, vainglory, and madding vices. Pagan vainglories which thought the world might last for ever, had encouragement for ambition, and finding no *Atropos* unto the immortality of their names, were never dampt with the necessity of oblivion. Even old ambitions had the advantage of ours, in the attempts of their vainglories, who acting early, and before the probable Meridian of time, have by this time found great accomplishment of their designes, whereby the ancient *Heroes* have already outlasted their Monuments, and Mechanicall preservations. But in this latter Scene of time we cannot expect such Mummies unto our memories, when ambition may fear the Prophecy

(e) The puzling questions of *Tiberius* unto *Grammarians. Marcel. Donatus in Suet.*

(f) Κλυτὰ ἔνθεα νεκρῶν Hom.   (g) Job.

of *Elias*,[h] and *Charles* the fifth can never hope to live within two *Methusela's* of *Hector*.[i]

And therefore restlesse inquietude for the diuturnity of our memories unto present considerations, seems a vanity almost out of date, and superannuated peece of folly. We cannot hope to live so long in our names, as some have done in their persons, one face of *Janus* holds no proportion unto the other. 'Tis too late to be ambitious. The great mutations of the world are acted, or time may be too short for our designes. To extend our memories by Monuments, whose death we dayly pray for, and whose duration we cannot hope, without injury to our expectations, in the advent of the last day, were a contradiction to our beliefs. We whose generations are ordained in this setting part of time, are providentially taken off from such imaginations. And being necessitated to eye the remaining particle of futurity, are naturally constituted unto thoughts of the next world, and cannot excusably decline the consideration of that duration, which maketh Pyramids pillars of snow, and all that's past a moment.

Sir Thomas Browne

Hydriotaphia, Urne-Buriall, or, A Discourse of the
Sepulchrall Urnes lately found in Norfolk (1658)

THE CLOUDS OF GLORY

WILL you see the infancy of this sublime and celestial greatness? Those pure and virgin apprehensions I had from the womb, and that divine light wherewith I was born are the best unto this day, wherein I can see the Universe. By the Gift of God they attended me into the world, and by His

(h) That the world may last but six thousand years.

(i) Hector's fame lasting above two lives of Methuselah before that famous Prince was extant.

special favour I remember them till now. Verily they seem the greatest gifts His wisdom could bestow, for without them all other gifts had been dead and vain. They are unattainable by book, and therefore I will teach them by experience. Pray for them earnestly: for they will make you angelical and wholly celestial. Certainly Adam in Paradise had not more sweet and curious apprehensions of the world, than I when I was a child.

*

All appeared new, and strange at first, inexpressibly rare and delightful and beautiful. I was a little stranger, which at my entrance into the world was saluted and surrounded with innumerable joys. My knowledge was Divine. I knew by intuition those things which since my Apostasy, I collected again by the highest reason. My very ignorance was advantageous. I seemed as one brought into the Estate of Innocence. All things were spotless and pure and glorious: yea, and infinitely mine, and joyful and precious. I knew not that there were any sins, or complaints or laws. I dreamed not of poverties, contentions or vices. All tears and quarrels were hidden from mine eyes. Everything was at rest, free and immortal. I knew nothing of sickness or death or rents or exaction, either for tribute or bread. In the absence of these I was entertained like an Angel with the works of God in their splendour and glory, I saw all in the peace of Eden; Heaven and Earth did sing my Creator's praises, and could not make more melody to Adam, than to me. All Time was Eternity, and a perpetual Sabbath. Is it not strange, that an infant should be heir of the whole World, and see those mysteries which the books of the learned never unfold?

*

The corn was orient and immortal wheat, which never should be reaped, nor was ever sown. I thought it had stood from everlasting to everlasting. The dust and stones of the street were as precious as gold: the gates were at first the end of the world. The green trees when I saw them first through one of the gates transported and ravished me, their sweetness and unusual beauty made my heart to leap, and almost mad with ecstasy, they were such strange and wonderful things. The Men! O what venerable and reverend creatures did the aged seem! Immortal Cherubims! And young men glittering and sparkling Angels, and maids strange seraphic pieces of life and beauty! Boys and girls tumbling in the street, and playing, were moving jewels. I knew not that they were born or should die; But all things abided eternally as they were in their proper places. Eternity was manifest in the Light of the Day, and something infinite behind everything appeared: which talked with my expectation and moved my desire. The city seemed to stand in Eden, or to be built in Heaven. The streets were mine, the temple was mine, the people were mine, their clothes and gold and silver were mine, as much as their sparkling eyes, fair skins and ruddy faces. The skies were mine, and so were the sun and moon and stars, and all the World was mine; and I the only spectator and enjoyer of it. I knew no churlish proprieties, nor bounds, nor divisions: but all proprieties and divisions were mine: all treasures and the possessors of them. So that with much ado I was corrupted and made to learn the dirty devices of this world. Which now I unlearn, and become, as it were, a little child again that I may enter into the Kingdom of God.

Thomas Traherne
Centuries of Meditations (1908)

THE ARTIFICE OF ETERNITY

. . . SOME things the Angels do know by the dignity of their Nature, by their Creation, which we know not; as we know many things which inferior Creatures do not; and such things all the Angels, good and bad know. Some things they know by the Grace of their confirmation, by which they have more given them, then they had by Nature in their Creation; and those things only the Angels that stood, but all they, do know. Some things they know by Revelation, when God is pleased to manifest them unto them; and so some of the Angels know that, which the rest, though confirm'd, doe not know. By Creation, they know as his Subjects; by Confirmation, they know as his servants; by Revelation, they know as his Councel. Now, *Erimus sicut Angeli*, says Christ, *There we shall be as the Angels:* The knowledge which I have by Nature, shall have no Clouds; here it hath: that which I have by Grace, shall have no reluctation, no resistance; here it hath: That which I have by Revelation, shall have no suspition, no jealousie; here it hath: sometimes it is hard to distinguish between a respiration from God, and a suggestion from the Devil. There our curiosity shall have this noble satisfaction, we shall know how the Angels know, by knowing as they know. We shall not pass from Author, to Author, as in a Grammar School, nor from Art to Art, as in an University; but, as that General which Knighted his whole Army, God shall Create us all Doctors in a minute. That great Library, those infinite Volumes of the Books of Creatures, shall be taken away, quite away, no more Nature; those reverend Manuscripts, written with Gods own hand, the Scriptures themselves, shall be taken away, quite away; no more preaching, no more reading of Scriptures, and that great School-Mistress, Experience, and Observation shall be remov'd, no new thing to be done, and in an instant, I shall know more, then they all could reveal unto me. I shall know, not only as I know already, that a Bee-hive, that an Ant-hill is the same Book in *Decimo sexto*, as a Kingdom is in *Folio*, that a Flower that lives but a day, is an abridgment of that King, that lives out his threescore and ten yeers; but I shall know too, that all these Ants, and Bees, and Flowers, and Kings, and Kingdoms, howsoever they may be Examples, and Comparisons to one another, yet they are all as nothing, altogether nothing, less then nothing, infinitely less then nothing, to that which shall then be the subject of my knowledge, for, *it is the knowledge of the glory of God.*

John Donne

A Sermon Preached at the Spittle, Easter-
Monday, 1622, in *XXVI Sermons* (1661)

THE COURTSHIP OF THEAGENES AND STELLIANA[1]

"I MUST yield," replied Stelliana, "in the manner of expression, to you that have the advantages of wit and learning to clothe your conceptions in the gracefullest attire; but in reality of love I will never yield to you; for I take Heaven to witness, I have tasted no joy in this long night of absence, but what the thoughts of you have brought me; and have ever resolved no longer to live than I have had hope to enjoy your love." – "Oh, think not," answered Theagenes, "that when the heart speaks upon so serious and high a theme, wit or study can have any share in the contexture of what one saith; lovers can speak as effectually in silence, as by the help of weak words, which are but the overflowings of a passionate heart; for intellectual substances communicate themselves by their wills; and mine is so entirely drowned in yours, that

1. Digby and Venetia Stanley: see biographical note on Digby.

it moveth not but as you guide it. Yet dare I not to contend with you who loveth most; for I know that as you surpass me in all excellent faculties of a worthy soul, so you do in the perfection of love; yet in this I think I have much the advantage of you, that I love you as well as I can, and stretch all the powers of my soul to bring my love to the highest pitch that I may, since it hath a worthier object than it can raise itself unto; whereas, on the other side, you not finding in me worth enough to take up as much as you could bestow, must go with reservation; and thus I, by soaring up to perfections above me, do daily refine myself, whilst you are fain to let yourself down, unless it be when your contemplations, rolling like the heavens about their own centre, do make yourself their object." "Fie, fie," said Stelliana, "stop that mouth, which were it any other but whose it is, I would call it a sacrilegious mouth, that thus blasphemeth against the saint that I adore." And then went on with the story of her passed troubles for Theagenes; who, when she had ended, requited her with his.

Sir Kenelm Digby
Private Memoirs (1827). Written before 1633

THE ANGLER AND THE MILKMAID

Speakers: Piscator, and a Milkmaid's Mother.

Pisc. Nay, stay a little good Scholar, I caught my last *Trout* with a Worm, now I will put on a Minnow, and try a quarter of an hour about yonder trees for another, and so walk towards our Lodging. Look you Scholar, thereabout we shall have a bite presently, or not at all: Have with you (Sir!) o' my word I have hold of him. Oh it is a great loggerheaded *Chub*; Come, hang him upon that Willow twig, and lets be going, But turn out of the way a little, good Scholar, towards yonder high *honysuckle* hedg; there we'll sit and sing whilst this showr falls so gently upon the teeming earth, and gives yet a sweeter smell to the lovely flowers that adorn these verdant Meadows.

Look, under that broad *Beech-tree*, I sate down, when I was last this way a fishing, and the birds in the adjoyning Grove seemed to have a friendly contention with an Eccho, whose dead voice seemed to live in a hollow tree, near to the brow of that Primrose-hill; there I sate viewing the silver-streams glide silently towards their center, the tempestuous Sea; yet, sometimes opposed by rugged roots, and pebble stones, which broke their waves, and turned them into foam: and sometimes I beguil'd time by viewing the harmless Lambs, some leaping securely in the cool shade, whilst others sported themselves in the chearful Sun: and saw others craving comfort from the swoln Udders of their bleating Dams. As I thus sate, these and other sights had so fully possest my soul with content, that I thought as the Poet has happily exprest it:

> *I was for that time lifted above earth;*
> *And possest joys not promis'd in my birth,*

As I left this place, and entred into the next field, a second pleasure entertained me, 'twas a handsom milk-maid that had not yet attain'd so much age and wisdom as to load her mind with any fears of many things that will never be (as too many men too often do) but she cast away all care, and sung like a *Nightingale*: her voice was good, and the Ditty fitted for it; 'twas that smooth song, which was made by *Kit. Marlow*, now at least fifty years ago: and the Milk-maids Mother sung an answer to it, which was made by Sir *Walter Rawleigh* in his younger days.

They were old fashioned Poetry, but choicely good, I think much better than the strong lines that are now in fashion in this critical age. Look yonder! on my word, yonder they both be a milking again, I will give her the *Chub*, and perswade them to sing those two songs to us.

God speed you good woman, I have been a Fishing, and am going to *Bleak-Hall*, to my bed, and having caught more Fish than will sup my self and my friend, I will bestow this upon you and your daughter, for I use to sell none.

Milkw. Marry God requite you Sir, and we'll eat it chearfully: and if you come this way a Fishing two months hence, a grace of God I'le give you a Sillybub of new Verjuice in a new made Hay-cock, for it, And my *Maudlin* shall sing you one of her best *Ballads*, for she and I both love all *Anglers*, they be such honest, civil, quiet men; in the mean time will you drink a draught of *Red-Cows milk*, you shall have it freely.

Pisc. No, I thank you, but I pray do us a courtesie that shall stand you and your daughter in nothing, and yet we will think our selves still something in your debt; it is but to sing us a Song, that was sung by your daughter, when I last past over this Meadow, about eight or nine days since.

Milk. What Song was it, I pray? was it *Come Shepherds deck your herds*, or *As at noon* Dulcina *rested*; or, Phillida *flouts me*: or, *Chevy Chase*? or *Jonny Armstrong*? or *Troy Town*?

Pisc. No, it is none of those: it is a Song that your daughter sung the first part, and you sung the answer to it.

Milk. O, I know it now, I learn'd the first part in my golden age, when I was about the age of my poor daughter; and the latter part, which indeed fits me best now, but two or three years ago, when the cares of the World began to take hold of me: but you shall, God willing, hear them both, and sung as well as we can, for we both love Anglers. Come *Maudlin*, sing the first part to the Gentlemen, with a merry heart, and I'le sing the second, when you have done.

Izaak Walton

The Compleat Angler, Part I (1653).   Text
from the revised fifth edition (1676)

How Gargantua did eat up Six Pilgrims in a Sallet

THE Story requireth, that we relate [that] which happened unto six Pilgrims, who came from *Sebastian* near to *Nantes*: and who for shelter that night, being afraid of the Enemy, had hid themselves in the garden upon the chichling Pease, among the Cabbages and Lettices. *Gargantua* finding himself somewhat dry, asked whether they could get any Lettice to make him a Sallet; and hearing that there were the greatest and fairest in the Country (for they were as great as Plum-trees, or as Walnut-trees,) he would go thither himself, and brought thence in his hand what he thought good, and withal carried away the six Pilgrims, who were in so great fear, that they did not dare to speak nor cough.

Washing them therefore first at the Fountain, the Pilgrims said to one another softly, *What shall we do? we are almost drowned here amongst these Lettice, shall we speak? But if we speak, he will kill us for Spies:* And as they were thus deliberating what to do, *Gargantua* put them with the Lettice into a platter of the House, as large as the huge Tun of the *Cistertians*, which done, with Oil, Vinegar and Salt he eat them up, to refresh himself a little before Supper; and had already swallowed up five of the Pilgrims, the sixth being in the Platter, totally hid under a Lettice, except his Staff that appeared, and nothing else. Which *Grangousier* seeing, said to *Gargantua*, I think that is the Horn of a Shell-snail, do not eat it. Why not (said *Gargantua*) they are good all this Month, which he no sooner said, but, drawing up the Staff, and therewith taking up the Pilgrim, he eat him very well, then drank a terrible draught of excellent White-wine, and expected Supper to be brought up.

The Pilgrims, thus devoured, made shift to save themselves as well as they could, by withdrawing their bodies out of the reach of the Grinders of his Teeth, but could not escape from thinking they had been put in the lowest Dungeon of a Prison. And when *Gargantua* whiffed the great draught, they thought to have been drowned in his mouth, and the flood of Wine had almost carried them away into the Gulf of his Stomach. Neverthelesse skipping with their Staves, as St. *Michael*'s Palmers use to do, they shelter'd themselves from the danger of that Inundation, under the Banks of his Teeth. But one of them by chance, groping or sounding the Country with his staff, to try whether they were in safety or no, struck hard against the cleft of a hollow tooth, and hit the mandibulary Sinew, or nerve of the Jaw, which put *Gargantua* to very great pain, so that he began to cry for the rage that he felt. To ease himself therefore of his smarting ach, he called for his Tooth-picker, and rubbing towards a young Walnut-tree, unnestled you my Gentlemen Pilgrims.

For he caught one by the Legs, another by the scrip, another by the Pocket, another by the Scarf, another by the band of the Breeches, and the poor Fellow that had hurt him with the staff, him he hooked to him by the Codpiece, which snatch neverthelesse did him a great deal of good, for it broke upon him a pocky botch he had in the Groin, which grievously tormented him ever since they were past *Ancenis*. The Pilgrims thus dislodged ran away athwart the Plain a pretty fast pace, and the pain ceased, even just at the time when by *Eudemon* he was called to Supper, for all was ready. I will go then (said he) and piss away my misfortune, which he did in such a copious measure, that, the Urin taking away the Feet from the Pilgrims, they were carried along with the stream unto the bank of a tuft of Trees: Upon which, as soon as they had taken footing, and that for their self-preservation they had run a little out of the road, they on a sudden fell all six, except *Fourniller*, into a trap that had been made to take Wolves by a train; out of which they escaped nevertheless by the industry of the said *Fourniller*, who broke all the snares and ropes.

Being gone from thence, they lay all the rest of that night in a lodge near unto *Coudry*, where they were comforted in their Miseries, by the gracious words of one of their Company called *Sweertogo*, who shewed them that this adventure had been foretold by the Prophet *David*, Psalm. Quum exurgerent homines in nos, forte vivos deglutissent nos; when we were eaten in the Sallet, with Salt, Oil and Vinegar.

Sir Thomas Urquhart

Translation of *The Lives, Heroic Deeds & Sayings of*
Gargantua and his Son Pantagruel by Dr Francis Rabelais (1653)
Text from the complete Urquhart-Motteux Rabelais (1694)

MR FEARING

EVERY thing frightned him that he heard any body speak of, that had the least appearance of Opposition in it. I heard that he lay roaring at the *Slough* of *Despond*, for above a Month together, nor durst he, for all he saw several go over before him, venture, tho they, many of them, offered to lend him their Hand. *He would not go back again neither.* The Celestial City, he said he should die if he came not to it, and yet was dejected at every Difficulty, and stumbled at every Straw that any body cast in his way. Well, after he had layn at the *Slough of Despond* a great while, as I have told you; one sun-shine Morning, I do not know how, he ventured, and so got over. But when he was over, he would scarce believe it. He had, I think, a *Slough of Despond* in his Mind, a *Slough* that he carried every where with him, or else he could never have been as he was. So he came up to the Gate, you know what I mean, that stands at the head of this way, and there also he stood a good while before he would adventure to knock. When the Gate was opened he would give back, and give place to others, and say he was not worthy. For, for all he gat before some to the Gate, yet many of them went in before him. There the poor man would stand shaking and shrinking; I dare say it would have pitied ones heart to have seen him: *Nor would he go back again.* At last he took the Hammer that hanged on the Gate in his hand, and gave a small Rapp or two; then one opened to him, but he shrunk back as before. He that opened, stept out after him, and said, Thou trembling one, what wantest thou? with that he fell down to the Ground. He that spoke to him wondered to see him so faint. So he said to him, *Peace be to thee*; up, for I have set open the Door to thee; come in, for thou art blest. With that he gat up, and went in trembling, and when he was in, he was ashamed to show his Face. Well, after he had been entertained there a while, as you know how the manner is, he was bid go on his way, and also told the way he should take. So he came till he came to our House, but as he behaved himself at the Gate, so he did at my master the *Interpreters* Door. He lay thereabout in the Cold a good while, before he would adventure to call; *Yet he would not go back.* And the Nights were long and cold then. Nay he had a Note of *Necessity* in his Bosom to my Master, to receive him, and grant him the Comfort of his House, and also to allow him a stout and valiant Conduct, because he was himself so *Chicken-hearted* a Man; and yet for all that he was afraid to call at the Door. So he lay up and down thereabouts, till, poor man, he was almost starved; yea so great was his Dejection, that tho he saw several others for knocking got in, yet he was afraid to venture. At last, I think I looked out of the Window, and perceiving a man to be up and down about the Door, I went out to him, and asked what he was; but poor man, the water stood in his Eyes. So I perceived what he wanted. I went therefore in, and told it in the House, and we shewed the thing to our Lord; So he sent me out again, to entreat him to come in, but I dare say I had hard work to do it. At last he came in, and I will say that for my Lord, he carried it wonderful lovingly to him. There were but a few good bits at the Table, but some of it was laid upon his Trencher. Then he presented the *Note*, and my Lord looked thereon and said, His desire should be granted. So when he had bin there a good while, he seemed to get some Heart, and to be a little more Comfortable. For my Master, you must know, is one of very tender Bowels, especially to them that are afraid, wherefore he carried it so towards him, as might tend most to his Incouragement. Well, when he had had a sight of the things of the place, and was ready to take his Journey to go to the City, my Lord, as he did to *Christian* before, gave him a Bottle of Spirits, and some comfortable things to eat. Thus we set forward, and I went before him; but the man was but of few Words, only he would sigh aloud.

When we were come to where the three Fellows were hanged, he said, that he doubted that that would be his end also. Only he seemed glad when he saw the *Cross* and the Sepulcher. There I confess he desired to stay a little, to look; and he seemed for a while after to be a little *Cheary*. When we came at the Hill *Difficulty*, he made no stick at that, nor did he much fear the Lyons. For you must know that his Trouble *was not about such things as those*, his Fear was about his Acceptance at last.

I got him in at the House *Beautiful*, I think before he was willing; also when he was in, I brought him acquainted with the Damsels that were of the Place, but he was ashamed to make himself much for Company, he desired much to be alone, yet he always loved good talk, and often would get behind the *Skreen* to hear it; he also loved much to see *ancient* things, and to be *pondering* them in his Mind. He told me afterwards, that he loved to be in those two Houses from which he came last, to wit, at the Gate, and that of the *Interpreters*, but that he durst not be so bold to ask.

When we went also from the House *Beautiful*, down the Hill, into the Valley of *Humiliation*, he went down *as well as ever I saw man in my Life*, for he cared not how mean he was, so he might be happy at last. Yea, I think there was a kind of Sympathy betwixt that Valley and him: For I never saw him better in all his Pilgrimage, than when he was in that Valley.

Here he would lye down, embrace the Ground, and kiss the very Flowers that grew in this Valley. He would now be up every Morning by break of Day, tracing, and walking to and fro in this Valley.

But when he was come to the entrance of the Valley of the Shadow of death, I thought I should have lost my Man; not for that he had any Inclination *to go back*, that he alwayes abhorred, but he was ready to dye for Fear. O, the *Hobgoblins* will have me, the *Hobgoblins* will have me, cried he; and I could not beat him out on't. He made such a noyse, and such an outcry here, that, had they but heard him, 'twas enough to encourage them to come and fall upon us.

But this I took very great notice of, that this Valley was as quiet while he went thorow it, as ever I knew it before or since. I suppose, those Enemies here, had now a special Check from our Lord, and a Command not to meddle until Mr. *Fearing* was pass'd over it.

It would be too tedious to tell you of all; we will therefore only mention a Passage or two more. When he was come at *Vanity Fair*, I thought he would have fought with all the men in the Fair; I feared there we should both have been knock'd o' th' Head, so hot was he against their Fooleries; upon the inchanted Ground, he also was very wakeful. But when he was come at the *River* where was no Bridge, there again he was in a heavy Case; now, now he said he should be drowned for ever, and so never see that Face with Comfort, that he had come so many miles to behold.

And here also I took notice of what was very remarkable,

the Water of *that River* was lower at *this* time, than ever I saw it in all my Life; so he went over at last, not much above *wet-shod*. When he was going up to the Gate, Mr *Great-heart* began to take Leave of him, and to wish him a good Reception above; So he said, *I shall, I shall*. Then parted we asunder and I saw him no more.

John Bunyan

The Pilgrim's Progress . . . The Second Part (1684)

Text from the second edition of 1686

A Pike and Little Fishes

THE *Roches, Daces, Gudgeons* and the whole Fry of *Little Fishes* met in Councel once, how to deliver themselves from the Tyranny of the *Pike*; with a Protestation, at the same time, *one and all*, to give over Spawning, and utterly to extinguish the whole Race: unless their Posterity might be better Secur'd against the Out-rage of That Unnatural Monster.

The Substance of This Complaint was digested into a Petition to *Jupiter*, who divided his Answer into Two Articles. First, says he, as to your Fancy of a Total Failure, Nature has made it absolutely Impossible: Beside that your Consumption is in some sort Necessary, for if there were not *Destroying* on the *One* hand, as well as *Encreasing*, on the *Other*, the Whole World would be too Little for any one Species of Creatures.

And then again for the Voracious Humour of the Pike, there is no Room left for Reasoning in the Case: for it is a Resolution founded in the Laws of Providence and Nature, that the Stronger shall Govern: over and above, that Tyranny is no New Thing in This World, and whoever shall pass by *Transmigration* into a *Pike*, will go the same way to work Himself too.

The MORAL

We have here the Lively Image of a Popular *League*, and *Complaint* against *Arbitrary Power*: that is to say; against Government it self, under the Scandal of That Odious Imputation; though but in the Exercise of an Authority according to the very Order and Instinct of Nature: And what's the Grievance at last? The *Pike* devours the *Little Fishes*, and the *Fry* have a Mind to *starve* the *Pike*: the One being but the Humour of the Multitude; and the other the Ordinance and Appointment of an Almighty Creator.

It is but natural to follow This Expostulation with a Menace; and the One just as Reasonable as the Other. And what does all This amount to now, but a Threat rather to Destroy the whole Race of *Little Fishes* at a Blow, then to lay them at the Mercy of the *Pike*, to be eaten-up Piece-meal? Now the *Pike* has not only Reason on his side, but Prescription also, and Authority, against the Clamorous Envy of an Impetuous Rabble. And at worst, where Arguments cannot prevail, he does himself right by Force, which is a Remedy that holds among Men, as well as among Fishes.

Sir Roger L'Estrange
Fables and Storyes Moralized (1699)

An Antiquary

HEE is a man strangely thriftie of Time past, and an enemie indeed to his Maw, whence hee fetches out many things when they are now all rotten and stinking. Hee is one that hath that unnaturall disease to bee enamour'd of old age, and wrinckles, and loves all things (as Dutchmen doe Cheese) the better for being mouldy and worme-eaten. He is of our Religion, because wee say it is most ancient; and yet a broken Statue would almost make him an Idolater. A great admirer he is of the rust of old Monuments, and reades onely those Characters, where time hath eaten out the letters. Hee will goe you forty miles to see a Saints Well, or ruin'd Abbey: and if there be but a Crosse or stone foot stoole in the way, hee'l be considering it so long, till he forget his iourney. His estate consists much in shekels, and Roman Coynes, and hee hath more Pictures of Cæsar, then *Iames* or *Elizabeth*. Beggers coozen him with musty things which they have rak't from dunghils, and he preserves their rags for precious Reliques. He loves no Library, but where there are more Spiders volums then Authors, and lookes with great admiration on the Antique worke of Cob-webs. Printed bookes he contemnes, as a novelty of this latter age; but a Manu-script he pores on everlastingly, especially if the cover be all Moth-eaten, and the dust make a Parenthesis betweene every Syllable. He would give all the Bookes in his Study (which are rarities all) for one of the old Romane binding, or sixe lines of *Tully* in his owne hand. His chamber is hung commonly with strange Beasts skins, and is a kind of Charnel-house of bones extraordinary, and his discourse upon them, if you will heare him shall last longer. His very atyre is that which is the eldest out of fashion, and his hat is as antient as the tower of Babel. He never lookes upon himself till he is gray hair'd, and then he is pleased with his owne Antiquity. His Grave do's not fright him, for he ha's been us'd to Sepulchers, and hee likes Death the better, because it gathers him to his Fathers.

John Earle

Micro-cosmographie. Or, A Peece of the World
Discovered; in Essayes and Characters (1628)

ANOTHER ANTIQUARY

Is one that has his Being in this Age, but his Life and Conversation is in the Days of old. He despises the present Age as an Innovation, and slights the future; but has a great Value for that, which is past and gone, like the Madman, that fell in Love with *Cleopatra*. He is an old frippery-Philosopher, that has so strange a natural Affection to worm-eaten Speculation, that it is apparent he has a Worm in his Skull. He honours his Forefathers and Fore-mothers, but condemns his Parents as too modern, and no better than Upstarts. He neglects himself, because he was born in his own Time, and so far off Antiquity, which he so much admires; and repines, like a younger Brother, because he came so late into the World. He spends the one half of his Time in collecting old insignificant Trifles, and the other in shewing them, which he takes singular Delight in; because the oftener he does it, the further they are from being new to him. All his Curiosities take place of one another according to their Seniority, and he values them not by their Abilities, but their Standing. He has a great Veneration for Words that are stricken in Years, and are grown so aged, that they have out-lived their Employments – These he uses with a Respect agreeable to their Antiquity, and the good Services they have done. He throws away his Time in enquiring after that which is past and gone so many Ages since, like one that shoots away an Arrow, to find out another that was lost before. He fetches things out of Dust and Ruins, like the Fable of the chymical Plant raised out of its own Ashes. He values one old Invention, that is lost and never to be recovered, before all the new ones in the World, tho' never so useful. The whole Business of his Life is the same with his, that shows the Tombs at *Westminster*, only the one does it for his Pleasure, and the other for Money. As every Man has but one Father, but two Grand-Fathers and a World of Ancestors; so he has a proportional Value for Things that are antient, and the further off the greater.

Samuel Butler

The Genuine Remains in Verse and Prose (1759)

The Good Schoolmaster

THERE is scarce any profession in the Common-wealth more necessary, which is so slightly performed. The reasons whereof I conceive to be these: first, young scholars make this calling their refuge, yea perchance before they have taken any degree in the University, commence Schoolmasters in the countrey, as if nothing else were required to set up this profession but onely a rod and a ferula. Secondly, others who are able use it onely as a passage to better preferment, to patch the tents in their present fortune, till they can provide a new one, and betake themselves to some more gainfull calling. Thirdly, they are disheartned from doing their best with the miserable reward which in some places they receive, being Masters to the children, and slaves to their parents. Fourthly, being grown rich, they grow negligent, and scorn to touch the school, but by the proxie of an Usher. But see how well our Schoolmaster behaves himself.

His genius inclines him with delight to this profession. Some men had as lieve be schoolboyes as Schoolmasters, to be tyed to the school as Coopers Dictionary, and Scapula's Lexicon are chained to the desk therein; and though great scholars, and skilfull in other arts, are bunglers in this: But God of his goodnesse hath fitted severall men for severall callings, that the necessities of Church, and State, in all conditions may be provided for. So that he who beholds the fabrick thereof may say, God hewed out this stone, and appointed it to lie in this very place, for it would fit none other so well, and here it doth most excellent. And thus God mouldeth some for a Schoolmasters life, undertaking it with desire and delight, and discharging it with dexterity and happy successe.

He studieth his scholars natures as carefully as they their books: and ranks their dispositions into severall forms. And though it may seem difficult for him in a great school to descend to all particulars, yet experienced Schoolmasters may quickly make a Grammar of boyes natures, and reduce them all (saving some few exceptions) to these generall rules.

1 Those that are ingenious and industrious. The conjunction of two such Planets in a youth presage much good unto him. To such a lad a frown may be a whipping, and a whipping a death: yea where their Master whips them once, shame whips them all the week after. Such natures he useth with all gentlenesse.

2 Those that are ingenious and idle. These think with the hare in the fable, that running with snails (so they count the rest of their school-fellows) they shall come soon enough to the Post, though sleeping a good while before their starting. Oh, a good rod would finely take them napping.

3 Those that are dull and diligent. Wines the stronger they be the more lees they have when they are new. Many boyes are muddy-headed till they be clarified with age, and such afterwards prove the best. Bristoll diamonds are both bright, and squared and pointed by Nature, and yet are soft and worthlesse; whereas orient ones in India are rough and rugged naturally. Hard rugged and dull natures of youth acquit themselves afterwards the jewells of the countrey, and therefore their dulnesse at first is to be born with, if they be diligent. That Schoolmaster deserves to be beaten himself, who beats

Bristoll diamonds] rock-crystal found in Clifton limestone

Nature in a boy for a fault. And I question whether all the whipping in the world can make their parts which are naturally sluggish, rise one minute before the houre Nature hath appointed.

4 Those that are invincibly dull and negligent also. Correction may reform the latter, not amend the former. All the whetting in the world can never set a rasours edge on that which hath no steel in it. Such boyes he consigneth over to other professions. Shipwrights and boatmakers will choose those crooked pieces of timber, which other carpenters refuse. Those may make excellent merchants and mechanicks which will not serve for Scholars.

He is able, diligent, and methodicall in his teaching; not leading them rather in a circle then forwards. He minces his precepts for children to swallow, hanging clogs on the nimblenesse of his own soul, that his Scholars may go along with him.

Thomas Fuller

The Holy State . . . (1642)

A Letter to an Actress

Thomas Otway to Elizabeth Barry (c. 1677).

It is *Pleasure* to think how *fair* you are, tho' at the same time worse then *Damnation*, to think how *cruel*: Why should you tell me you have *shut* your Heart up *for ever*? It is an Argument *unworthy* of your self, sounds like *Reserve*, and not so much *Sincerity*, as sure I may claim even from *a little* of your *Friendship*. Can your *Age*, your *Face*, your *Eyes*, and your *Spirit* bid Defiance to that *sweet Power*? No, you know better to what end *Heaven* made you, know better how to manage *Youth* and *Pleasure* than to let them die, and pall upon your Hands. 'Tis *me*, 'tis only *me*, you have barr'd your *Heart* against. My

Sufferings, my Diligence, my Sighs, Complaints, and Tears are of no power with your *haughty* Nature; yet sure you might at least vouchsafe to *pity* them, not shift me off with *gross*, *thick*, *home-spun* Friendship, the common *Coin* that passes betwixt worldly *Interests*: must that be my *Lot*! Take it, *Ill natur'd*, take it, and give it to *him* who would waste his *Fortune* for you, give it the *Man* would fill your Lap with *Gold*, court you with Offers of vast rich *Possessions*, give it the *Fool* that hath nothing but his *Money* to plead for him: *Love* will have a much nearer *Relation*, or none. I ask for *glorious Happiness*; you bid me welcome to your *Friendship*; it is like seating me at your *Side-table*, when I have the best Pretence to your *Right hand* at the Feast. I *love*, I *dote*, I am *mad*, and know no measure, nothing but *Extreams* can give me ease; the kindest *Love*, or most provoking *Scorn*: Yet even your *Scorn* would not perform the Cure, it might indeed take off the Edge of *Hope*, but damn'd *Despair* will gnaw my *Heart* for ever. If then I am not *odious* to your Eyes, if you have *Charity* enough to value the *Well-being* of a Man that holds you dearer then you can the *Child* your *Bowels* are most *fond of*, by that sweet *Pledge* of your *first* softest *Love* I *charm* and here *conjure* you to pity the distracting *Pangs* of mine; pity my unquiet *Days* and restless *Nights*; pity the *Frenzy* that has half possest my *Brain* already, and makes me write to you thus *ravingly*: The *Wretch* in *Bedlam* is more at peace than I am! And if I must never possess the *Heav'n* I wish for, my next *Desire* is, (and sooner the better) a clean-swept *Cell*, a merciful *Keeper*, and your *Compassion*, when you find me there.

Think and be Generous.

Thomas Otway

Familiar Letters by Lord Rochester and Others (1697)

A Country Justice

Characters:

Rains, Bevil, Woodly, Men of Wit and Pleasure. Clodpate, A Country Justice, a publick-spirited, politick, discontented Fop, an immoderate hater of London, and a lover of the Country above measure, a hearty true English coxcomb.

Scene: Epsom

Clodp. O Mr. *Woodly*, how is it? You drink no Waters; but have you had your other Mornings draught yet?

Wood. Yes, I never leave off my Evenings draught till it becomes my Mornings draught.

Clodp. Mr. *Rains* and *Bevill*, gad save ye; how de'e like the Country? is't not worth a hundred of old *Sodom* yonder? good Horses, good Dogs, good Ale, hah –

Rains. Good Wine, good Wit, and fine Women, may I take it, compare with them.

Clodp. I find you'l never leave that place of sin and sea-coal, give me drink for all that, that breeds no Gout; a wholsome plain Wench, that will neither bring my body to the Surgeons hands, nor my Land to the Scrivners: and for Wit, there is such a stir amongst you, who has it, and who has it not, that we honest Country Gentlemen begin to think there's no such thing, and have hearty Mirth and good old Catches amongst us, that do the business every whit as well.

Rains. He's in the right.

Clodp. But Mr. *Woodly*, how do you like my Dapple Mare?

Wood. Not comparable to a Hackney Coach.

Clodp. But she shall run with e're a Hackney Coach in *England* for all that, or e're a Horse in your stable, weight him and inch him.

Wood. I would not keep a running horse, though a running horse would half keep me.

Bev. We are for *London* to morrow; shall we have your company?

Clodp. Ud's bud, I go to *London*! I am almost sick at *Epsom*, when the wind sits to bring any of the smoak this way, and by my good will would not talk with a man that comes from thence till he hath ayr'd himself a day or two.

Wood. Why, there's no Plague.

Clodp. There's Pride, Popery, Folly, Lust, Prodigality, Cheating Knaves, and Jilting Whores; Wine of half a crown a quart, and Ale of twelve pence, and what not.

Rains. This is a terrible regiment you have muster'd; but neither the Priests nor the Women will ravish you; nor are you forc'd to take the Wine, as the *French* are their Salt, there are twelve penny Ordinaries.

Clodp. Ay, and Cards and false Dice, and Quarrels, Hectors and reform'd Officers to borrow a Crown, and beat a man that refuses it, or asks for't again; besides, I'le sum you up the beastly pleasures of the best of ye.

Wood. What are those?

Clodp. Why, to sit up drunk till three a clock in the morning, rise at twelve, follow damn'd French Fashions, get dress'd to go to a damn'd Play, choak your selves afterwards with dust in Hide-park, or with Sea-coal in the Town, flatter and fawn in the drawing room, keep your Wench, and turn away your Wife, Gods-ooks.

Bev. The Rogue is a tart and witty whorson.

Clodp. I was at *Sodom* at eighteen, I thank 'em, but now I serve my Country, and spend upon my Tenants what I get amongst them.

Rains. And so, indeed, are no better than their Sponge, which they moisten only to squeeze again. But what important service do you do your Country?

Clodp. S'bud I – why I am Justice of *Quorum* in *Sussex*, and this County too, and I make the Surveyors mend the High ways; I cause Rogues to be whipt for breaking fences or pilling trees, especially if they be my own; I swear Constables and the like.

Bev. But is this all?

Clodp. No: I call Over-seers for the Poor to an account, sign Rates, am a Game-keeper, and take away Guns and Greyhounds, bind fellows to the Peace, observe my monthly Meeting, am now and then an Arbitrator, and License Ale-houses, and make people bury in Flannel, to encourage the Woollen Manufacture; which never a Justice of Peace in *England* does but I.

Wood. Look you, what would you have?

Clodp. Besides, I am drunk once a week at my Lord Lieutenants; and at my own house spend not scurvy French kick-shaws, but much Ale and Beef, and Mutton, the Manufactures of the Country.

Bev. The Manufactures of the Country, that's well.

Rains. Ay, and, I warrant, by the vertue of that, can bring as many wide mouth'd Rogues to Ball and holloa for a Knight of the shire, as any man.

Clodp. Ay gods-ooks can I.

Rains. That men should be such infinite Coxcombs to live scurvily to get reputation among thick-scull'd Peasants, and be at as great a distance with men of wit and sense, as if they were another sort of Animals.

Bev. 'Tis fit such fools should govern and do the drudgery of the world, while reasonable men enjoy it.

Thomas Shadwell
Epsom-Wells (1673)

MELANTHA'S WORD-HOARD

Characters: Melantha and Philotis, her maid.

Enter Philotis *with a paper in her hand.*

Mel. O, are you there, Minion? And, well are not you a most precious damsel, to retard all my visits for want of language, when you know you are paid so well for furnishing me with new words for my daily conversation? Let me die, if I have not run the risque already, to speak like one of the vulgar; and if I have one phrase left in all my store that is not thrid-bare & *usé*, and fit for nothing but to be thrown to Peasants.

Phil. Indeed, Madam, I have been very diligent in my vocation; but you have so drain'd all the *French* Plays and Romances, that they are not able to supply you with words for your daily expences.

Mel. Drain'd? What a word's there!
Epuisée, you sot you. Come, produce your morning's work.

Phil. 'Tis here, Madam. [*Shows the Paper.*

Mel. O, my *Venus*! fourteen or fifteen words to serve me a whole day! Let me die, at this rate I cannot last till night. Come, read your works: twenty to one half of 'em will not pass muster neither.

Phil. Sottises. [*Reads.*

Mel. Sottises: *bon.* That's an excellent word to begin withall: as for example; He, or she said a thousand *Sottises* to me. Proceed.

Phil. Figure: as what a *figure* of a man is there!
Naive and *naiveté*.

Mel. Naive! as how?

Phil. Speaking of a thing that was naturally said; it was so *naive*: or such an innocent piece of simplicity; 'twas such a *naiveté*.

Mel. Truce with your interpretations: make haste.

Phil. Foible, *Chagrin*, *Grimace*, *Embarrassè*, *Double entendre*,
Equivoque, *Eclaircissement*, *Suittè*, *Beveue*, *Facòn*, *Panchant*,
Coup d'etourdy, and *Ridicule*.

Mel. Hold, hold; how did they begin?

Phil. They began at *Sottises*, and ended *en Ridicule*.

Mel. Now give me your Paper in my hand, and hold you my
glass, while I practise my postures for the day.

[*Melantha laughs in the Glass.*

How does that laugh become my face?

Phil. Sovereignly well, Madam.

Mel. *Sovereignly!* Let me die, that's not amiss. That word
shall not be yours; I'll invent it, and bring it up my self:
my new Point Gorget shall be yours upon't: not a word of
the word, I charge you.

Phil. I am dumb, Madam.

Mel. That glance, how sutes it with my face?

[*Looking in the Glass again.*

Phil. 'Tis so *languissant!*

Mel. *Languissant!* that word shall be mine too, and my last
Indian-Gown thine for't. That sigh?   [*Looks again:*

Phil. 'Twill make many a man sigh, Madam. 'Tis a meer
Incendiary.

Mel. Take my Guimp Petticoat for that truth. If thou hast
more of these phrases, let me die but I could give away all
my Wardrobe, and go naked for 'em.

Phil. Go naked? Then you would be a *Venus*, Madam. O
Jupiter! what had I forgot? this Paper was given me by
Rhodophil's Page.

Mel. [*Reading the Letter*] – Beg the favour from you, – Grati-
fie my passion – so far – assignation – in the Grotto – behind
the Terras – clock this evening – Well, for the *Billets doux*
there's no man in *Sicily* must dispute with *Rhodophil*; they
are so *French*, so *gallant*, and so *tendre*, that I cannot resist the
temptation of the assignation. Now go you away, *Philotis*;

it imports me to practise what I shall say to my Servant when I meet him. [*Exit* Philotis.] *Rhodophil*, you'll wonder at my assurance to meet you here; let me die, I am so out of breath with coming, that I can render you no reason of it. Then he will make this *repartee*; Madam, I have no reason to accuse you for that which is so great a favour to me. Then I reply, But why have you drawn me to this solitary place? let me die, but I am apprehensive of some violence from you. Then, says he; Solitude, Madam, is most fit for Lovers; but by this fair hand — Nay, now I vow you're rude. Sir. O fie, fie, fie; I hope you'l be honourable? – You'd laugh at me if I should, Madam – What do you mean to throw me down thus? Ah me! ah, ah, ah.

Enter Polydamas, Leonidas, *and Guards.*

O *Venus*! the King and Court. Let me die but I fear they have found my *foible* and will turn me into *ridicule*.

[*Exit running.*

John Dryden
Marriage-à-la-Mode (1673)

A LOVE SCENE

Characters: Dorimant, Harriet.

Dor. That demure curt'sy is not amiss in jest, but do not think in earnest it becomes you.
Har. Affectation is catching, I find; from your grave bow I got it.
Dor. Where had you all that scorn, and coldness in your look?
Har. From nature, Sir, pardon my want of art:
I have not learnt those softnesses and languishings
Which now in faces are so much in fashion.

Dor. You need 'em not, you have a sweetness of your own, if you would but calm your frowns and let it settle.

Har. My Eyes are wild and wandring like my passions
And cannot yet be ty'd to Rules of charming.

Dor. Women indeed have commonly a method of managing those messengers of Love: now they will look as if they would kill, and anon they will look as if they were dying. They point and rebate their glances, the better to invite us.

Har. I like this variety well enough; but hate the set face that always looks as it would say Come love me. A woman, who at Playes makes the Doux yeux to a whole Audience, and at home cannot forbear 'em to her Monkey.

Dor. Put on a gentle smile, and let me see, how well it will become you.

Har. I am sorry my face does not please you as it is, but I shall not be complaisant and change it.

Dor. Though you are obstinate, I know 'tis capable of improvement, and shall do you Justice Madam, if I chance to be at Court, when the Critiques of the Circle pass their judgment; for thither you must come.

Har. And expect to be taken in pieces, have all my features examin'd, every motion censur'd, and on the whole be condemn'd to be but pretty, or a Beauty of the lowest rate. What think you?

Dor. The Women, nay the very lovers who belong to the Drawing-room will malitiously allow you more than that; they always grant what is apparent, that they may the better be believ'd when they name conceal'd faults they cannot easily be disprov'd in.

Har. Beauty runs as great a risque expos'd at Court as wit does on the Stage, where the ugly and foolish, all are free to censure.

Dor. aside]. I love her, and dare not let her know it, I fear sh'as an ascendant o're me and may revenge the wrongs I have done her sex.

Think of making a party Madam, love will engage. [*To her.*

Har. You make me start! I did not think to have heard of Love from you.

Dor. I never knew what 'twas to have a settled Ague yet, but now and then have had irregular fitts.

Har. Take heed, sickness after long health is commonly more violent and dangerous.

Dor. I have took the infection from her, and feel the disease now spreading in me –   [*Aside.*
Is the name of love so frightful that you dare not stand it?
[*To her.*

Har. 'Twill do little execution out of your mouth on me, I am sure.

Dor. It has been fatal –

Har. To some easy Women, but we are not all born to one destiny; I was inform'd you use to laugh at Love, and not make it.

Dor. The time has been, but now I must speak –

Har. If it be on that Idle subject, I will put on my serious look, turn my head carelessly from you, drop my lip, let my Eye-lids fall and hang half o're my Eyes – Thus – While you buz a speech of an hour long in my ear, and I answer never a word! Why do you not begin?

Dor. That the company may take notice how passionately I make advances of Love! and how disdainfully you receive 'em.

Har. When your Love's grown strong enough to make you bear being laugh'd at, I'll give you leave to trouble me with it. Till when pray forbear, Sir.

Enter Sir Fopling *and others in Masques.*

Sir George Etherege
*The Man of Mode, or, S*ʳ *Fopling Flutter* (1676)[1]

1. The 1676 text's printing of prose as verse has been corrected, following the edition by H. F. Brett-Smith (Oxford, 1927).

The Plain-Dealing Philosophy

Characters:

Manly: Of an honest, surly, nice humor, suppos'd first, in the time of the Dutch *War, to have procur'd the Command of a Ship, out of Honour, not Interest; and choosing a Sea-life, only to avoid the World.*
Freeman: Manly's Lieutenant, a Gentleman well Educated, but of a broken Fortune, a Complyer with the Age.

Scene: London

Free. But what, will you see no Body? not your Friends?

Man. Friends – I have but one, and he, I hear, is not in Town; nay, can have but one Friend, for a true heart admits but of one friendship, as of one love. But in having that Friend, I have a thousand, for he has the courage of men in despair, yet the diffidency and caution of Cowards; the secresie of the Revengeful, and the constancy of Martyrs; one fit to advise, to keep a secret: to fight and dye for his Friend. Such I think him; for I have trusted him with my Mistress in my absence: and the trust of Beauty, is sure the greatest we can shew.

Free. Well, but all your good thoughts are not for him alone? (I hope:) pray, what d'ye think of me for a Friend?

Man. Of thee! Why, thou art a *Latitudinarian* in Friendship, that is, no Friend; thou dost side with all Mankind, but wilt suffer for none. Thou art indeed like your *Lord Plausible*, the Pink of Courtesie, therefore hast no Friendship: for Ceremony, and great Professing, renders Friendship as much suspected, as it does Religion.

Free. And no Professing, no Ceremony at all in Friendship, were as unnatural and as undecent as in Religion; and there is hardly such a thing as an honest Hypocrite, who professes himself to be worse than he is, unless it be your self; for, though I cou'd never get you to say you were my Friend, I know you'll prove so.

Man. I must confess, I am so much your Friend, I wou'd not deceive you; therefore must tell you (not only because my heart is taken up) but according to your rules of Friendship, I cannot be your Friend.

Free. Why pray?

Man. Because he that is (you'll say) a true Friend to a man, is a Friend to all his Friends; but you must pardon me, I cannot wish well to Pimps, Flatterers, Detractors, and Cowards, stiff nodding Knaves, and supple pliant kissing Fools: now, all these I have seen you use, like the dearest Friends in the World.

Free. Hah, hah, hah – What, you observ'd me, I warrant, in the Galleries of *Whitehall*, doing the business of the place! Pshaw, Court Professions, like Court Promises, go for nothing, man. But, faith, cou'd you think I was a Friend to all those I hugg'd, kiss'd, flatter'd, bow'd to? Hah, ha –

Man. You told 'em so, and swore it too; I heard you.

Free. Ay, but, when their backs were turn'd, did I not tell you they were Rogues, Villains, Rascals, whom I despis'd, and hated?

Man. Very fine! But what reason had I to believe you spoke your heart to me, since you profess'd deceiving so many?

Free. Why, don't you know, good Captain, that telling truth is a quality as prejudicial, to a man that wou'd thrive in the World, as square Play to a Cheat, or true Love to a Whore! Wou'd you have a man speak truth to his ruine? You are severer than the Law, which requires no man to swear against himself; you wou'd have me speak truth against my self, I warrant, and tell my promising Friend, the Courtier, he has a bad memory?

Man. Yes.

Free. And so make him remember to forget my business; and

I shou'd tell the great Lawyer too, that he takes oftner Fees
to hold his tongue, than to speak!

Man. No doubt on't.

Free. Ay, and have him hang, or ruine me, when he shou'd
come to be a Judge, and I before him. And you wou'd have
me tell the new Officer, who bought his Employment lately,
that he is a Coward?

Man. Ay.

Free. And so get my self cashiered, not him, he having the
better Friends, though I the better Sword. And I shou'd
tell the Scribbler of Honour, that Heraldry were a prettier
and fitter Study for so fine a Gentleman, than Poetry!

Man. Certainly.

Free. And so find my self maul'd in his next hir'd Lampoon.
And you wou'd have me tell the holy Lady too, that she
lies with her Chaplain?

Man. No doubt on't.

Free. And so draw the Clergy upon my back, and want a good
Table to Dine at sometimes. And by the same reason too,
I shou'd tell you that the world thinks you a Mad-man,
a Brutal, and have you cut my throat, or worse, hate me!
What other good success of all my *Plain-dealing* cou'd I
have, than what I've mentioned?

Man. Why, first, your promising Courtier wou'd keep his
word, out of fear of more reproaches, or at least wou'd
give you no more vain hopes: your Lawyer wou'd serve
you more faithfully; for he, having no Honor but his
Interest, is truest still to him he knows suspects him: The
new Officer wou'd provoke thee to make him a Coward,
and so be cashier'd, that thou, or some other honest Fellow,
who had more courage than money, might get his place:
the Noble Sonneteer wou'd trouble thee no more with his
Madrigals: the praying Lady wou'd leave off railing at
Wenching before thee, and not turn away her chamber-

maid for her own known frailty with thee: and I, instead of hating thee, shou'd love thee, for thy *Plain-dealing*; and in lieu of being mortifi'd, am proud that the World and I think not well of one another.

Free. Well, Doctors differ. You are for *Plain-dealing*, I find; but against your particular Notions, I have the practice of the whole World. Observe but any Morning what people do when they get together on the *Exchange*, in *Westminster-hall*, or the Galleries in *Whitehall*.

Man. I must confess, there they seem to rehearse *Bays*'s grand Dance: here you see a *Bishop* bowing low to a gaudy *Atheist*; a Judge, to a Door-keeper; a great Lord, to a Fishmonger, or a Scrivener with a Jack-chain about his neck; a Lawyer, to a Serjeant at Arms; a velvet *Physician*, to a thredbare *Chymist*; and a supple Gentleman Usher, to a surly Beef-eater; and so tread round in a preposterous huddle of Ceremony to each other, whil'st they can hardly hold their solemn false countenances.

Free. Well, they understand the World.

Man. Which I do not, I confess.

Free. But, sir, pray believe the Friendship I promise you, real, whatsoever I have profest to others: try me, at least.

Man. Why, what wou'd you do for me?

Free. I wou'd fight for you.

Man. That you wou'd do for your own Honour: but what else?

Free. I wou'd lend you money, if I had it.

Man. To borrow more of me another time. That were but putting your money to Interest, a Usurer wou'd be as good a Friend. But what other piece of Friendship?

Free. I wou'd speak well of you to your Enemies.

Man. To encourage others to be your Friends, by a shew of gratitude: but what else?

Jack-chain] chain of the 'jack', which turned the spit in roasting meat; here used sarcastically, for mayoral chain

Free. Nay, I wou'd not hear you ill spoken of behind your back, by my Friend.

Man. Nay, then thou'rt a Friend indeed; but it were unreasonable to expect it from thee, as the World goes now: when new Friends, like new Mistresses, are got by disparaging old ones.

William Wycherley
The Plain-Dealer (1677)

CONDITIONS AND PROVISOS

Characters: Millamant and Mirabell.

Mir. . . . Do you lock your self up from me, to make my search more Curious? Or is this pretty Artifice Contriv'd, to Signifie that here the Chase must end, and my pursuit be Crown'd, for you can fly no further. –

Mill. Vanity! No – I'll fly and be follow'd to the last moment, tho' I am upon the very Verge of Matrimony, I expect you shou'd solicite me as much as if I were wavering at the grate of a Monastery, with one foot over the Threshold. I'll be solicited to the very last, nay and afterwards.

Mir. What, after the last?

Mill. O, I should think I was poor and had nothing to bestow, If I were reduc'd to an Inglorious ease; and free'd from the Agreeable fatigues of solicitation.

Mir. But do not you know, that when favours are conferr'd upon Instant and tedious Sollicitation, that they diminish in their value, and that both the giver loses the grace, and the receiver lessens his Pleasure?

Mill. It may be in things of common Application; but never sure in Love. O, I hate a Lover, that can dare to think, he draws a moments air, Independent on the Bounty of his Mistress. There is not so Impudent a thing in Nature, as

the sawcy look of an assured man, Confident of Success.
The Pedantick arrogance of a very Husband, has not so
Pragmatical an Air. Ah! I'll never marry, unless I am first
made sure of my will and pleasure.

Mit. Wou'd you have 'em both before Marriage? Or will you
be contented with the first now, and stay for the other 'till
after grace?

Mill. Ah don't be Impertinent – My dear Liberty, shall I
leave thee? My faithful Solitude, my darling Contemplation, must I bid you then Adieu? ay-h adieu. – my morning
thoughts, agreeable wakings, indolent slumbers, all ye *dou-
ceurs*, ye *Someils du Matin adieu* – I can't do't, 'tis more than
Impossible – positively *Mirabell*, I'll lye a Bed in a morning
as long as I please.

Mir. Then I'll get up in a morning as early as I please.

Mill. Ah! Idle Creature, get up when you will – And dee
hear, I won't be call'd names after I'm Married; positively
I won't be call'd Names.

Mir. Names!

Mill. Ay as Wife, Spouse, My dear, Joy, Jewel, Love, Sweet
heart, and the rest of that Nauseous Cant, in which Men
and their Wives are so fulsomely familiar, – I shall never
bear that, – Good *Mirabell* don't let us be familiar or fond,
nor kiss before folks, like my Lady *Fadler* and Sr. *Francis*:
Nor goe to *Hide-Park* together the first *Sunday* in a New
Chariot, to provoke Eyes and Whispers; And then never be
seen there together again; as if we were proud of one another
the first Week, and asham'd of one another ever After. Let
us never Visit together, nor go to a Play together, But let
us be very strange and well bred: let us be as strange as if
we had been married a great while; and as well bred as if
we were not marri'd at all.

Mir. Have you any more Conditions to offer? Hitherto your
demands are pretty reasonable.

Mill. Trifles, – As liberty to pay and receive visits to and from whom I please, to write and receive Letters, without Interrogatories, or wry Faces on your part. To wear what I please; and choose Conversation with regard only to my own taste; to have no obligation upon me to converse with Wits that I don't like, because they are your acquaintance; or to be intimate with Fools, because they may be your Relations. Come to Dinner when I please, dine in my dressing room when I'm out of humour without giving a reason. To have my Closet Inviolate; to be sole Empress of my Tea-table, which you must never presume to approach without first asking leave. And lastly where ever I am, you shall always knock at the door before you come in. These Articles subscrib'd, If I continue to endure you a little longer, I may by degrees dwindle into a Wife.

Mir. Your bill of fare is something advanc'd in this latter account. Well, have I Liberty to offer Conditions – that when you are dwindl'd into a Wife, I may not be beyond Measure enlarg'd into a Husband?

Mill. You have free leave; propose your utmost, speak and spare not.

Mir. I thank you. *Inprimis* then, I Covenant that your acquaintance be General; that you admit no sworn Confident, or Intimate of your own Sex; No she friend to skreen her affairs under your Countenance and tempt you to make tryal of a Mutual Secresie. No Decoy-Duck to wheadle you a *fop* – *scrambling* to the Play in a Mask – then bring you home in a pretended fright, when you think you shall be found out. – And rail at me for missing the Play, and disappointing the Frolick which you had to pick me up and prove my Constancy.

Mill. Detestable *Inprimis*! I go to the Play in a Mask!

Mir. Item, I Article, that you shall continue to like your own Face, as long as I shall. And while it passes Current with me, that you endeavour not to new Coin it. To which end, together with all Vizards for the day, I prohibit all Masks for the Night, made of oil'd-skins and I know not what – Hog's-bones, Hare's-gall, Pig-water, and the marrow of a roasted Cat. In short, I forbid all Commerce with the Gentlewoman in *What-de-call-it*-Court. *Item*, I shut my doors against all Bauds with Baskets, and penny-worths of *Muslin*, *China*, *Fans*, *Atlases*, &c. – *Item*, when you shall be Breeding –

Mill. Ah! Name it not.

Mir. Which may be presum'd, with a blessing on our endeavours –

Mill. Odious endeavours!

Mir. I denounce against all strait-laceing, Squeezing for a Shape, 'till you mold my boy's head like a Sugar-loaf; and instead of a Man-child, make me the Father to a Crooked-billet. Lastly to the Dominion of the *Tea-Table*, I submit. – But with *Proviso*, that you exceed not in your province; but restrain your self to Native and Simple *Tea-Table* drinks, as *Tea*, *Chocolate* and *Coffee*. As likewise to Genuine and Authoriz'd *Tea-Table* talk, – such as mending of Fashions, spoiling Reputations, railing at absent Friends, and so forth – but that on no account you encroach upon the mens prerogative, and presume to drink Healths, or toste fellows; for prevention of which, I banish all *foreign Forces*, all Auxiliaries, to the *Tea-Table*, as *Orange-Brandy*, all *Anniseed*, *Cinamon*, *Citron* and *Barbado*'s-Waters, together with *Ratifia* and the most noble Spirit of *Clary*, – but for *Couslip-Wine*, *Poppy-Water*, and all *Dormitives*, those I allow, – these *proviso's* admitted, in other things I may prove a tractable and complying Husband.

Mill. O horrid *Proviso's*! filthy strong waters! I toste fellows, Odious Men! I hate your Odious *proviso's*.

Mir. Then wee're agreed. Shall I kiss your hand upon the

Contract? and here comes one to be a witness to the Sealing of the Deed.

Enter Mrs. Fainall.

Mill. *Fainall*, what shall I do? shall I have him? I think I must have him.

Mrs. *Fain.* Ay, ay, take him, take him, what shou'd you do?

Mill. Well then – I'll take my Death I'm in a horrid fright – *Fainall*, I shall never say it – well – I think – I'll endure you.

Mrs *Fain.* Fy, fy, have him, have him, and tell him so in plain terms: For I am sure you have a mind to him.

Mill. Are you? I think I have – and the horrid Man looks as if he thought so too – Well, you ridiculous thing you, I'll have you, – I won't be kiss'd, nor I won't be thank'd – here kiss my hand tho' – so hold your tongue now, and don't say a Word.

William Congreve
The Way of the World (1700)

IV

THE CRITICISM OF THE ARTS

What to Read and How to Write

Be conversant in the *Speeches, Declarations* and *Transactions* occasioned by the *late Wars*: out of which more naturall and *usefull knowledge* may be sucked, then is ordinarily to be found in the mouldy Records of Antiquity. . . .

A *few Books* well studied, and throughly digested, nourish the understanding more, then hundreds but gargled in the mouth, as ordinary Students use: And of these *Choyce* must be had answerable to the *Profession* you intend: For a States-man, *French Authors* are best, as most fruitfull in *Negotiations* and *Memoires*, left by Publick Ministers, and by their Secretaries published after their deaths: Out of which you may be able to unfold the Riddles of all States: None making more faithfull Reports of things done in all Nations, than *Embassadors*; who cannot want the *best Intelligence*, because their Princes Pensioners unload in their Bosomes all they can discover. . . .

Propose not them for patterns, who make all places *rattle*, where they come with *Latine and Greek*; For *the more you seem to have borrowed from Books, the poorer you proclaime your naturall Parts*, which can only be properly called yours:

Follow not the tedious Practice of such as seek *Wisdome* onely in *Learning*: not attainable but by *Experience* and *Naturall Parts. Much Reading*, like a too-great repletion, stopping up, the Accesse of a nearer, newer and quicker *Invention* of your own. And for *Quotations*, they resemble *Sugar in wine*, marring the naturall taste of the liquor, if it be good; if bad, that of it self: such *patches* rather making the *rent* seem greater, by an interruption of the stile, then less, if not so neatly ap-plyed as to fall-in without *drawing*: Nor is any *Thiefe* in this kind sufferable, who comes not off, like a *Lacedæmonian*, without discovery.

Spend no time in reading, much less writing, *Strong-lines: which like tough meat, aske more paines and time in chewing, than can be recompensed by all the nourishment they bring.*

Bookes flatly writ debase your stile; the like may be truly objected to *weak Preachers* and *ignorant Company.* Pennes Im-proving, like childrens leggs, proportionally to their *Exer-cise* . . . This appeared in the late King *Charles*, who, after his more imperious destiny had placed him under the Tutorage of an unavoidable necessity, attained a *Pen* more Majesticall, than the *Crown* he had lost. . . .

The way to *Elegancy of stile*, is to employ your pen upon every Errand; and the more triviall and dry it is, the more Brains must be allowed for Sauce: Thus by checking all or-dinary Invention, your Reason will attain to such an habit, as not to dare to present you but with what is excellent; and if void of Affectation, it matters not how meane the subject is, There being the same Exactness observed, by good Archi-tects, in the structure of the Kitchin, as the Parlour.

When business or Complement calls you to *write Letters*, Consider what is fit to be said, were the Party present, and set down That.

Avoid *Words* and *Phrases* likely to be learned in base Com-pany: lest you fall into the Error, the late Archbishop *Laud* did; who though no ill speaker, yet blunted his repute by saying in the *Star-Chamber*, *Men entred the Church as a tinker and his Bitch do an Alehouse.*

Francis Osborn
Advice to a Son (1658). Text from the
sixth edition of 1658

STYLE

IT is the Excellency of Speaking, and Writing, to do it Close; and in Words accomodate to the Intention; and I would yet have somewhat more to be signify'd, than is Deliver'd: It being also a Mark of Strength, and Solidity of Judgment. . . . As to forc'd *Metaphors*, and wild *Hyperbole's*, I would leave them to the *Poets*. And I am utterly against Fooling with Tinckling Conceipts, and Sounds: Not that I would wholly forbid the use of *Hyperboles*; which, although they exceed the Truth, may yet be a means, by things Incredible, to bring us unto things Credible. And there may be great use made also of *Parables*: For the way of Application does usually more affect the Mind, than the down-right Meaning. That Speech which gains upon the Passions, is much more Profitable than that which only works upon the Judgment. *Chrysippus* was a Great Man, and of an Acute Wit; but the Edge of it was so fine, that every thing turn'd it; and he might be said, in truth, rather to Prick the Subject that he handled, than to Pierce it Through.

As it is not for the Honour of a *Philosopher* to be Solicitous about Words, I would not have him negligent neither: But, let him speak with Assurance, and without Affectation. If we can, let our Discourses be Powerful; but however, let them be Clear. I like a Composition that is Nervous, and Strong; but yet I would have it Sweet, and Gracious withal. There are many things, I know, that please well enough in the De-livery, and yet will hardly abide the Test of an Examination. But, that Eloquence is Mischievous, that diverts a Man from Things to Words; and little better than a Prostitution of Letters. For, what signifies the Pomp of Words, or the Jumb-ling of Syllables, to the making up of a Wise Man?

Sir Roger L'Estrange
Seneca's Morals, by way of abstract . . . (1678)

WIT

WIT is the laborious, and the lucky resultances of thought, having towards its excellence (as we say of the strokes of Painting) as well a happinesse, as care. It is a Web consisting of the subtilest threads, and like that of the *Spider*, is considerately woven out of our selves; for a *Spider* may be said to consider, not only respecting his solemnesse and tacite posture (like a grave Scout in ambush for his Enemy) but because all things done, are either from consideration or chance; and the works of Chance are accomplishments of an instant, having commonly a dissimilitude; but hers are the works of time, and have their contextures alike.

Wit is not onely the luck and labour, but also the dexterity of the thought; rounding the world like the Sun with unimaginable motion; and bringing swiftly home to the memory universall surveyes. It is the Souls *Powder* which when supprest (as forbidden from flying upward) blows up the restraint; and loseth all force in a farther ascension towards Heaven (the region of God) and yet by nature is much lesse able to make any inquisition downward towards Hell, the Cell of the Devill; but breaks through all about it (as farre as the utmost it can reach) removes, uncovers, makes way for Light, where darknesse was inclosed, till great bodies are more examinable by being scattered into parcels; and till all that find its strength (but most of mankind are strangers to *Wit*, as *Indians* are to *Powder*) worship it for the effects as derived from the Deity. It is in Divines Humility, Exemplarinesse, and Moderation: in States-men, Gravity, Vigilance, Benigne Complacency, Secrecy, Patience, and Dispatch. In Leaders of Armies, Valor, Painfulnesse, Temperance, Bounty, Dexterity in Punishing and Rewarding, and a sacred Certitude of promise: It is in Poets a full comprehension of all recited in all these; and an ability to bring those comprehensions into action, when they shall so farre forget the true measure of what is of greatest consequence to humanity, (which are things righteous, pleasant, and usefull) as to think the delights of greatnesse equal to that of Poesie; or the Chiefs of any Profession more necessary to the World then excellent Poets. Lastly, though *Wit* be not the envy of ignorant Men, 'tis often of evill Statesmen, and of all such imperfect great spirits, as have it in a lesse degree then Poets: for though no man envies the excellence of that which in no proportion he ever tasted (as men cannot be said to envy the condition of Angels) yet we may say the Devill envies the Supremacy of God, because he was in some degree partaker of his Glory.

That which is not, yet is accounted *Wit*, I will but slightly remember; which seems very incident to imperfect youth and sickly age; Young men (as if they were not quite delivered from Child-hood whose first exercise is Language) imagine it consists in the Musick of words, and believe they are made wise by refining their speech above the vulgar Dialect: which is a mistake almost as great as that of the people, who think Oratours (which is a title that crowns at riper years those that have practised the dexterity of tongue) the ablest men; who are indeed so much more unapt for governing, as they are more fit for Sedition: and it may be said of them as of the Witches of *Norway*, who can sell a Storm for a *Doller*, which for ten thousand they cannot allay. From the esteem of speaking they proceed to the admiration of what are commonly called *Conceits*, things that sound like the knacks or toyes of ordinary *Epigrammatists*: and from thence, after more conversation and variety of objects, grow up to some force of *Fancy*; Yet even then, like young Hawks, they stray and fly farre off; using their liberty as if they would ne're return to the Lure; and often goe at check ere they can make a steddy view, and know their game.

Sir William Davenant
A Discourse upon Gondibert . . . (1650)

goe at check] forsake the quarry and fly at a baser game

PREACHERS ORNATE AND MEAN

IT seems also not very easie, for a Man in his Sermon to learn his Parishioners how to dissolve Gold; of what, and how the stuff is made. Now, to ring the Bells, and call the People on purpose together, would be but a blunt business; but to do it neatly, and when no Body look'd for it, that's the rarity and art of it. Suppose then, that he takes for his text that of *St. Matthew, Repent ye, for the Kingdom of God is at hand*. Now tell me, Sir, do you not perceive the Gold to be in a dismal fear, to curl and quiver at the first reading of these words. It must come in thus: *The blotts and blurrs of our sins must be taken out by the* Aqua-fortis *of our Tears; to which* Aqua-fortis *if you put a fifth part of* Sal-Almoniack, *and set them in a gentle heat, it makes* Aqua-Regia, *which dissolves Gold*. And now 'tis out. Wonderfull are the things that are to be done by the help of metaphors and similitudes! And I'll undertake, that with a little more pains and consideration, out of the very same words, he could have taught the People how to make Custards, Marmalade, or to stew Prunes. But pray, why the *Aqua-fortis* of Tears? For, if it so falls out, that there should chance to be neither *Apothecary* nor *Druggist* at Church, there's an excellent Jest wholly lost . . . I cannot but consider with what understanding the People sighed and cryed, when the Minister made for them this Metaphysical Confession: *Omnipotent All; Thou art only: Because thou art All, and because thou only art: As for us, we are not, but we seem to be, and only seem to be, because we are not; for we be but Mites of Entity, and Crumbs of something;* and so on: As if a company of Countrey People were bound to understand *Suarez*, and all the *School-Divines*.

And as some are very high and learned in their attempts; so others there be who are of somewhat too mean and dirty imaginations: Such was he, who goes by the name of *Parson Slip-stocking:* Who preaching about the Grace and Assistance of God, and that of our selves we are able to do nothing; advised his Beloved to take him in this plain Similitude. *A Father calls his Child to him, saying, Child pull of this Stocking: The Child mightily joyful, that it should pull off Fathers Stocking, takes hold of the Stocking, and tuggs, and pulls, and sweats, but to no purpose, for Stocking stirs not, for it is but a Child that pulls: Then the Father bids the Child to rest a little, and try again; so then the Child sets on again, tuggs again, and pulls again, and sweats again, but no Stocking comes, for Child is but Child: Then at last the Father, taking pitty upon his Child, puts his hand behind, and slips down the Stocking, and off comes the Stocking: Then how does the Child rejoyce? for Child have pull'd off Father's Stocking. Alas, poor Child! It was not Childs strength, it was not Childs sweating that got off the Stocking, but it was the Fathers hand behind that slipt down the Stocking.* Even so – Not much unlike to this was he, that preaching about the Sacrament and Faith, makes Christ a *Shop-keeper*; telling you that *Christ is a Treasury of all Wares and Commodities:* And thereupon, opening his wide throat, cryes aloud, *Good People, what do you lack? what do you buy?*

John Eachard

*The Grounds and Occasions of the Contempt
of the Clergy and Religion* (1670)

OF PREACHING

THE *excess* which is the *defect of preaching*, has made the *Pulpit* slighted, I mean, the much bad *Oratory* we find it guilty of. 'Tis a wonder to me, how men can *preach so little*, and so *long*: so *long a time*, and so *little matter*: as if they thought to please, by the inculcation of their vain *Tautologies*. I see no reason, that so high a *Princess* as *Divinity* is, should be presented to the *people* in the *sordid rags* of the *tongue*: nor that *he* which speaks from the *Father of languages*, should deliver his

Embassage in an *ill one*. A man can never speak *too well*, where he speaks not *too obscure*. Long and distended *clauses*, are both tedious to the *ear*, and difficult for their retaining. A *Sentence* well couch'd, takes both the *sense* and the *understanding*. I love not those *Cart-rope speeches*, that are longer then the memory of man can fathom. I see not, but that *Divinity*, put into apt *significants*, might ravish as well as *Poetry*. The waighty *lines* men find upon the *Stage*, I am perswaded, have been the *lures* to draw away the *Pulpits followers*. We complain of drowziness at a *Sermon*; when a *Play* of a doubled length, leads us on still with alacrity. But the fault is not all in our selves. If we saw *Divinity* acted, the *gesture* and *variety* would as much invigilate. But it is too high to be personated by *Humanity*. The *Stage* feeds both the *ear* and the *eye*: and through this *latter sense*, the Soul drinks deeper draughts, Things *acted*, possess us more, and are too more retainable. then the *passable tones* of the *tongue*. Besides, here we meet with more *composed language*: The *Dulcia sermonis*, moulded into curious phrase; though 'tis to be lamented, such *wits* are not set to the right *tune*, and consorted to *Divinity*; who without doubt, well deckt, will cast a far more radiant *lustre*, then those *obscene scurrilities*, that the *Stage* presents us with, though oe'd and spangled in their *gawdiest tyre*. At a *Sermon* well dress'd, what *understander* can have a motion to *sleep*? *Divinity* well ordered, casts forth a *bait*, which angles the soul into the *ear*: and how can that close when such a guest sits in it? They are *Sermons* but of baser metal, which *lead* the eyes to Slumber. . . . And this is *Seneca's* opinion: *Fit words* are better then *fine ones*: I like not those that are *in-judiciously* made; but such as be *expressively significant*: that lead the *mind* to something, beside the naked *term*. And he that speaks thus, must not look to speak thus every day. A *kem'b Oration* will cost both *sweat* and the *rubbing of the brain*. And *kemb'd* I wish it, not *frizzled*,

     invigilate] arouse   *o'ed*] decorated with circular patterns

nor *curl'd*. *Divinity* should not *lasciviate*. *Unwormwooded Jests*
I like well; but they are fitted for the *Tavern*, then the Majesty
of a *Temple*. *Christ* taught the *People* with *Authority*. *Gravity*
becomes the *Pulpit*. *Demosthenes* confest he became an *Orator*,
by spending more *Oyl* then *Wine*. This is too fluid an *Element*
to beget *substantials*. *Wit*, procur'd by *wine*, is, for the most
part, like the *sparklings* in the *cup*, when 'tis filling: they *brisk*
it for a moment, but dye immediately.

Owen Felltham

'Of Preaching' (1628). Text from the revised eighth
edition of Resolves: Divine, Moral, Political (1661)

A Short View of Letter-writing

To Sr I. S. *at his House* Leeds *Castle*.

SIR, It was a quaint difference the Ancients did put 'twixt a
Letter and an *Oration*, that the one should be attird like a
Woman, the other like a Man: The latter of the two is allowed
large side robes, as long periods, parentheses, similes, examples, and other parts of Rhetoricall flourishes: But a Letter
should be short coated, and close couchd, a Hungerlin becomes a Letter more handsomely than a gown. Indeed we
should write as we speake, and that's a true familiar Letter
which expresseth on's Mind, as if he were discoursing with
the party in succinct and short tearms. The *Tongue*, and the
Pen, are both of them interpreters of the mind, but I hold
the *Pen* to be the more faithfull of the two: The Tongue
in udo posita, being in a moyst slippery place may fayle and
falter in her sudden extemporall expressions, but the *Pen*
having a greater advantage of premeditation, is not so subject to errour, and leaves things behind it upon firme and
authentic record. Now *Letters*, though they be capable of

Hungerlin] a short furred robe

any Subject, yet they may be restraind to these five heads; *Narratory*, *Obiurgatory*, *Consolatory*, *Monitory*, *or Congratulatory*, The first consists of relations, The second of reprehensions, the Third of comfort, the last two of counsell and joy: There are some who in lieu of Letters write *Homelies*, they preach when they should Epistolize, There are others that turn them to tedious tractates, this is to make Letters degenerate from their true nature. Some modern Authors there are, who have expos'd their *Letters* to the world, but most of them, I meane among your Latin Epistolizers, go fraighted with meer *Bartholomew* ware, listed with pedantic shredds of School-boy verses. Others there are among our next transmarine neighbours, who write in their own vulgar language, but their stile is so soft and fleshy, that their Letters may be said to be like bodies without sinews, they have neither art nor arteries in them; They have a kind of feminine, and lank hectic expressions made up of a bombast of words, and smooth affected Complement: I cannot well away with such sleazie stuff, with such cobweb-compositions, where there is no strength of matter, nothing for the Reader to carry away with him, that may enlarge the notions of his soule. One shall hardly find an apothegm, example, simile, or any thing of Philosophy, History, or solid knowledge in a hundred of them: Insomuch that it may be sayed of them, what was said of the Eccho – Vox est, praetereáque nihil.

I return you your *Balzac* by this bearer, and when I found those Letters, wherein he is so familiar with his King, so flat, I forbore to read him further: So I am.

Your most affectionate servit^r.

J. H.

James Howell
A New Volume of Letters ... (1647)

Bartholomew ware] knick-knacks   *listed*] bordered   *sleazie*] flimsy

POETIC ABILITIES AND THEIR USE

THESE abilities, wheresoever they be found, are the inspired guift of God rarely bestow'd, but yet to some (though most abuse) in every Nation: and are of power beside the office of a pulpit, to inbreed and cherish in a great people the seeds of vertu, and publick civility, to allay the perturbations of the mind, and set the affections in right tune, to celebrate in glorious and lofty Hymns the throne and equipage of Gods Almightinesse, and what he works, and what he suffers to be wrought with high providence in his Church, to sing the victorious agonies of Martyrs and Saints, the deeds and triumphs of just and pious Nations doing valiantly through faith against the enemies of Christ, to deplore the general relapses of Kingdoms and States from justice and Gods true worship. Lastly, whatsoever in religion is holy and sublime, in vertu amiable, or grave, whatsoever hath passion or admiration in all the changes of that which is call'd fortune from without, or the wily suttleties and refluxes of mans thoughts from within, all these things with a solid and treatable smoothnesse to paint out and describe. Teaching over the whole book sanctity and vertu through all the instances of example with such delight to those especially of soft and delicious temper who will not so much as look upon Truth herselfe, unlesse they see her elegantly drest, that whereas the paths of honesty and good life appear now rugged and difficult, though they be indeed easy and pleasant, they would then appeare to all men both easy and pleasant though they were rugged and difficult indeed. And what a benefit this would be to our youth and gentry, may be soon guest by what we know of the corruption and bane which they suck in dayly from the writings and interludes of libidinous and ignorant Poetasters, who having scars ever heard of that which is the main consistence of a true poem, the choys of such persons as they ought to introduce, and what is morall and decent to each one, doe for the most part lap up vitious principles in sweet pils to be swallow'd down, and make the tast of vertuous documents harsh and sowr. But because the spirit of man cannot demean it selfe lively in this body without some recreating intermission of labour, and serious things, it were happy for the Common wealth, if our Magistrates, as in those famous governments of old, would take into their care, not only the deciding of contentious Law cases and brauls, but the managing of our publick sports, and festival pastimes, that they might be, not such as were autoriz'd a while since, the provocations of drunkennesse and lust, but such as may inure and harden our bodies by martial exercises to all warlike skil and performance, and may civilize, adorn and make discreet our minds by the learned and affable meeting of frequent Academies, and the procurement of wise and artfull recitations sweetned with eloquent and gracefull inticements to the love and practice of justice, temperance and fortitude, instructing and bettering the Nation at all opportunities, that the call of wisdom and vertu may be heard every where, as *Solomon* saith, *She crieth without, she uttereth her voice in the streets, in the top of high places, in the chief concours, and in the openings of the Gates.* Whether this may not be not only in Pulpits, but after another persuasive method, at set and solemn Paneguries, in Theaters, porches, or what other place, or way may win most upon the people to receiv at once both recreation, & instruction, let them in autority consult. The thing which I had to say, and those intentions which have liv'd within me ever since I could conceiv my self any thing worth to my Countrie, I return to crave excuse that urgent reason hath pluckt from me by an abortive and foredated discovery. And the accomplishment of them lies not but in a power above mans to promise; but that none hath by more studious ways endeavour'd, and with more unwearied spirit that none shall, that I dare almost averre of my self, as farre as life and free leasure will extend, and that the Land had once infranchis'd her self from this impertinent yoke of prelaty, under whose inquisitorius and tyrannical duncery no free and splendid wit can flourish. Neither doe I think it shame to covenant with any knowing reader, that for some few yeers yet I may go on trust with him towards the payment of what I am now indebted, as being a work not to be rays'd from the heat of youth, or the vapours of wine, like that which flows at wast from the pen of some vulgar Amorist, or the trencher fury of a riming parasite, nor to be obtain'd by the invocation of Dame Memory and her Siren daughters, but by devout prayer to that eternall Spirit who can enrich with all utterance and knowledge, and sends out his Seraphim with the hallow'd fire of his Altar to touch and purify the lips of whom he pleases: to this must be added industrious and select reading, steddy observation, insight into all seemly and generous arts and affaires, till which in some measure be compast, at mine own peril and cost I refuse not to sustain this expectation from as many as are not loath to hazard so much credulity upon the best pledges that I can give them.

John Milton
The Reason of Church-governement Urg'd
against Prelaty (1642)

CHRISTIAN POETRY

AMONGST all holy and consecrated things which the *Devil* ever stole and alienated from the service of the *Deity*; as *Altars*, *Temples*, *Sacrifices*, *Prayers*, and the like; there is none that he so universally, and so long usurpt, as *Poetry*. It is time to recover it out of the *Tyrants* hands, and to restore it to the *Kingdom* of

God, who is the *Father* of it. It is time to *Baptize* it in *Jordan*, for it will never become clean by bathing in the *Waters of Damascus*. There wants, methinks, but the *Conversion* of *That*, and the *Jews*, for the accomplishing of the *Kingdom of Christ*. And as men before their receiving of the *Faith*, do not without some carnal reluctancies, apprehend the *bonds* and *fetters* of it, but finde it afterwards to be the truest and greatest *Liberty*: It will fare no otherwise with this *Art*, after the *Regeneration* of it; it will meet with wonderful variety of new, more beautiful, and more delightful *Objects*; neither will it want *Room*, by being *confined to Heaven*. There is not so great a *Lye* to be found in any *Poet*, as the vulgar conceit of men, that *Lying* is *Essential* to good *Poetry*. Were there never so wholesome *Nourishment* to be had (but, alas, it breeds nothing but *Diseases*) out of these boasted *Feasts* of *Love* and *Fables*; yet, methinks, the unalterable continuance of the *Diet* should make us *Nauseate* it: For it is almost impossible to serve up any *new Dish* of that kinde. They are all but the *Cold-meats* of the *Antients*, new-heated, and new set forth. I do not at all wonder that the old *Poets* made some rich crops out of these grounds; the heart of the *Soil* was not then wrought out with continual *Tillage*: But what can we expect now, who come a *Gleaning*, not after the first *Reapers*, but after the very *Beggars*? Besides, though those mad stories of the *Gods* and *Heroes*, seem in themselves so ridiculous; yet they were then the *whole Body* (or rather *Chaos*) of the *Theologie* of those times. They were believed by all but a few *Philosophers*, and perhaps some *Atheists*, and served to good purpose among the *vulgar* (as pitiful things as they are) in strengthening the authority of *Law* with the terrors of *Conscience*, and expectation of certain rewards, and unavoidable punishments. There was no other *Religion*, and therefore *that* was better then *none at all*. But to us who have no need of them, to us who deride their *folly*, and are wearied with their *impertinencies*, they ought to appear no better arguments for *Verse* then those of their worthy Successors, the *Knights Errant*. What can we imagine more proper for the ornaments of *Wit* or *Learning* in the story of *Deucalion*, then in that of *Noah*? why will not the actions of *Sampson* afford as plentiful matter as the *Labors* of *Hercules*? why is not *Jeptha's Daughter* as *good a woman* as *Iphigenia*? and the friendship of *David* and *Jonathan* more worthy celebration, then that of *Theseus* and *Perithous*? Does not the passage of *Moses* and the *Israelites* into the *Holy Land*, yield incomparably more Poetical variety, then the voyages of *Ulysses* or *Æneas*? Are the obsolete threadbare tales of *Thebes* and *Troy*, half so stored with great, heroical, and supernatural actions (since *Verse* will needs *finde* or *make* such) as the wars of *Joshua*, of the *Judges*, of *David*, and divers others? Can all the *Transformations* of the *Gods*, give such copious hints to flourish and expatiate on, as the true *Miracles* of *Christ*, or of his *Prophets* and *Apostles*? What do I instance in these few particulars? All the *Books* of the *Bible* are either already most admirable and exalted pieces of *Poesie*, or are the best *Materials* in the world for it.

Abraham Cowley
Preface to *Poems* (1656)

POETRY ANCIENT AND MODERN

... WHAT Honour and Request the antient Poetry has Lived in, may not only be Observed from the Universal Reception and Use in all Nations from *China* to *Peru*, from *Scythia* to *Arabia*, but from the Esteem of the Best and the Greatest Men as well as the Vulgar. Among the *Hebrews*, *David* and *Solomon* the Wisest Kings, *Job* and *Jeremiah* the Holiest Men, were the best Poets of their Nation and Language. Among the *Greeks*, the Two most renowned Sages and Law-givers were

Lycurgus and *Solon*, whereof the Last is known to have excelled in Poetry, and the First was so great a Lover of it, That to his Care and Industry we are said (by some Authors) to owe the Collection and Preservation of the loose and scattered Pieces of *Homer*, in the Order wherein they have since appeared. *Alexander* is reported neither to have Travelled nor Slept, without those admirable Poems always in his Company. *Phalaris*, that was Inexorable to all other Enemies, Relented at the Charms of *Stesichorus* his Muse. Among the *Romans*, the Last and Great *Scipio*, passed the soft Hours of his Life in the Conversation of *Terence*, and was thought to have a Part in the composition of his Comedies. *Cæsar* was an Excellent poet as well as Orator, and Composed a Poem in his Voyage from *Rome* to *Spain*, Relieving the Tedious Difficulties of his March with the Entertainments of his Muse. *Augustus* was not only a Patron, but a Friend and Companion of *Virgil* and *Horace*, and was himself, both an Admirer of Poetry, and a pretender too, as far as his Genius would reach, or his busy Scene allow. 'Tis true, since his Age we have few such Examples of great Princes favouring or affecting Poetry, and as few perhaps of great Poets deserving it. Whether it be that the fierceness of the *Gothick* Humors, or Noise of their perpetual Wars frighted it away, or that the unequal mixture of the Modern Languages would not bear it; Certain it is, That the great Heighths and Excellency both of Poetry and Musick, fell with the *Roman* Learning and Empire, and have never since recovered the Admiration and Applauses that before attended them. Yet such as they are amongst us, they must be confest to be the Softest and Sweetest, the most General and most Innocent Amusements of common Time and Life. They still find Room in the Courts of Princes and the Cottages of Shepherds. They serve to Revive and Animate the dead Calm of poor or idle Lives, and to Allay or Divert the violent Passions and Perturbations of the greatest and the busiest Men. And both these Effects are of equal use to Humane Life; for the Mind of Man is like the Sea, which is neither agreable to the Beholder nor the Voyager, in a Calm or in a Storm, but is so to both, when a little Agitated by gentle Gales; and so the Mind, when moved by soft and easy Passions or Affections. I know very well, that many who pretend to be Wise by the Forms of being Grave, are apt to despise both Poetry and Musick, as Toys and trifles too light for the Use or Entertainment of serious Men. But whoever find themselves wholly insensible to these Charms, would I think do well, to keep their own Counsel, for fear of Reproaching their own Temper, and bringing the Goodness of their Natures, if not their Understandings, into Question: It may be thought at least an ill Sign, if not an ill Constitution, since some of the Fathers went so far, as to esteem the Love of Musick a Sign of Predestination, as a thing Divine, and Reserved for the Felicities of Heaven it self. While this World lasts, I doubt not, but the Pleasure and Request of these Two Entertainments, will do so too, and happy those that content themselves with these or any other so Easy and so Innocent, and do not trouble the World or other Men, because they cannot be quiet themselves, though no body hurts them.

When all is done, Humane Life is at the greatest and the best, but like a froward Child, that must be Play'd with and Humor'd a little, to keep it quiet, till it falls asleep, and then the Care is over.

Sir William Temple

'Upon Poetry' in Miscellanea: the Second Part (1690)
Text from the revised third edition (1692)

OVID AND CHAUCER – AND COWLEY

THE Vulgar Judges, which are Nine Parts in Ten of all Nations, who call Conceits and Jingles Wit, who see *Ovid* full of them, and *Chaucer* altogether without them, will think me little less than mad for preferring the *Englishman* to the *Roman*: Yet, with their leave, I must presume to say, that the Things they admire are only glittering Trifles, and so far from being Witty, that in a serious Poem they are nauseous, because they are unnatural. Wou'd any Man who is ready to die for Love, describe his passion like *Narcissus*? Wou'd he think of *inopem me copia fecit*, and a Dozen more of such Expressions, pour'd on the Neck of one another, and signifying all the same Thing? If this were Wit, was this a Time to be witty, when the poor Wretch was in the Agony of Death; This is just *John Littlewit* in *Bartholomew Fair*, who had a Conceit (as he tells you) left him in his Misery; a miserable Conceit. On these Occasions the Poet shou'd endeavour to raise Pity; But instead of this, *Ovid* is tickling you to laugh. *Virgil* never made use of such Machines, when he was moving you to commiserate the Death of *Dido*: He would not destroy what he was building. *Chaucer* makes *Arcite* violent in his Love, and unjust in the Pursuit of it: Yet when he came to die, he made him think more reasonably: He repents not of his Love, for that had alter'd his Character; but acknowledges the Injustice of his Proceedings, and resigns *Emilia* to *Palamon*. What would *Ovid* have done on this Occasion? He would certainly have made *Arcite* witty on his Death-bed. He had complain'd he was farther off from Possession, by being so near, and a thousand such Boyisms, which *Chaucer* rejected as below the Dignity of the *Subject*. They who think otherwise, would by the same Reason prefer *Lucan* and *Ovid* to *Homer* and *Virgil*, and *Martial* to all Four of them. As for the Turn of Words, in which *Ovid* particularly excels all Poets; they are sometimes a Fault, and sometimes a Beauty, as they are us'd properly or improperly; but in strong Passions always to be shunn'd, because Passions are serious, and will admit no Playing. The *French* have a high Value for them; and I confess, they are often what they call Delicate, when they are introduc'd with Judgment; but *Chaucer* writ with more Simplicity, and follow'd Nature more closely, than to use them. I have thus far, to the best of my Knowledge, been an upright Judge betwixt the Parties in Competition, not medling with the Design nor the Disposition of it; because the Design was not their own; and in the disposing of it they were equal. It remains that I say somewhat of *Chaucer* in particular.

In the first place, As he is the father of *English* Poetry, so I hold him in the same Degree of Veneration as the *Grecians* held *Homer*, or the *Romans Virgil*: He is a perpetual Fountain of good Sense; learn'd in all Sciences; and therefore speaks properly on all Subjects: As he knew what to say, so he knows also when to leave off; a Continence which is practis'd by few Writers, and scarcely by any of the Ancients, excepting *Virgil* and *Horace*. One of our late great Poets[1] is sunk in his Reputation, because he cou'd never forgive any conceit which came in his way; but swept like a Drag-net, great and small. There was plenty enough, but the Dishes were ill sorted; whole Pyramids of Sweet-meats, for Boys and Women; but little of solid Meat, for Men: All this proceeded not from any want of Knowledge, but of Judgment; neither did he want that in discerning the Beauties and Faults of other Poets; but only indulg'd himself in the Luxury of Writing; and perhaps knew it was a Fault, but hop'd the Reader would not find it. For this Reason, though he must always be thought a great Poet, he is no longer esteem'd a good Writer: and for Ten Impressions which his Works have had in so many successive Years, yet at present a hundred Books are scarcely purchas'd once a Twelvemonth: For, as my last Lord *Rochester* said, though somewhat profanely, *Not being of God, he could not stand*.

Chaucer follow'd Nature every where; but was never so

1. Cowley.

bold to go beyond her: And there is a great Difference of being *Poeta* and *nimis Poeta*, if we may believe *Catullus*, as much as betwixt a modest Behaviour and Affectation. The Verse of *Chaucer*, I confess, is not Harmonious to us; but 'tis like the Eloquence of one whom *Tacitus* commends, it was *auribus istius temporis accommodata*; they who liv'd with him, and some time after him, thought it Musical; and it continues so even in our Judgment, if compar'd with the Numbers of *Lidgate* and *Gower* his Contemporaries: There is the rude Sweetness of a *Scotch* Tune in it, which is natural and pleasing, though not perfect. 'Tis true, I cannot go so far as he who publish'd the last Edition of him[1]; for he would make us believe the Fault is in our Ears, and that there were really Ten Syllables in a Verse where we find but Nine: But this Opinion is not worth confuting; 'tis so gross and obvious an Errour, that common Sense (which is a Rule in every thing but Matters of Faith and Revelation) must convince the Reader, that Equality of Numbers in every Verse which we call *Heroick*, was either not known, or not always practis'd in *Chaucer*'s Age. It were an easie Matter to produce some thousands of his Verses, which are lame for want of half a Foot, and sometimes a whole one, and which no Pronunciation can make otherwise. We can only say, that he liv'd in the Infancy of our Poetry, and that nothing is brought to Perfection at the first. We must be Children before we grow Men. There was an *Ennius*, and in process of Time a *Lucilius*, and a *Lucretius*, before *Virgil* and *Horace*; even after *Chaucer* there was a *Spencer*, a *Harrington*, a *Fairfax*, before *Waller* and *Denham* were in being: And our Numbers were in their Nonage till these last appear'd.

John Dryden

Preface to *Fables Ancient and Modern* ... (1700)

1. T. Speght, whose edition appeared in 1597 and 1602.

SHAKESPEARE AND BOMBAST

... BOMBAST is commonly the delight of that Audience, which loves Poetry, but understands it not: and as commonly has been the practice of those Writers, who not being able to infuse a natural passion into the mind, have made it their business to ply the ears, and to stun their judges by the noise. But *Shakespear* does not often thus; for the passions in his Scene between *Brutus* and *Cassius* are extreamly natural, the thoughts are such as arise from the matter, and the expression of 'em not viciously figurative. I cannot leave this Subject before I do justice to that Divine Poet, by giving you one of his passionate descriptions: 'tis of *Richard* the Second when he was depos'd, and led in Triumph through the Streets of *London* by *Henry* of *Bullingbrook*: the painting of it is so lively, and the words so moving, that I have scarce read any thing comparable to it, in any other language. Suppose you have seen already the fortunate Usurper passing through the croud, and follow'd by the shouts and acclamations of the people; and now behold King *Richard* entring upon the Scene: consider the wretchedness of his condition, and his carriage in it; and refrain from pitty if you can.

> As in a Theatre, the eyes of men
> After a well-grac'd Actor leaves the Stage,
> Are idly bent on him that enters next,
> Thinking his prattle to be tedious:
> Even so, or with much more contempt, mens eyes
> Did scowl on *Richard*: no man cry'd God save him:
> No joyful tongue gave him his welcom home,
> But dust was thrown upon his Sacred head,
> Which with such gentle sorrow he shook off,
> His face still combating with tears and smiles
> (The badges of his grief and patience)
> That had not God (for some strong purpose) steel'd

> The hearts of men, they must perforce have melted,
> And Barbarism it self have pity'd him.

To speak justly of this whole matter; 'tis neither height of thought that is discommended, nor pathetic vehemence, nor any nobleness of expression in its proper place; but 'tis a false measure of all these, something which is like 'em, and is not them: 'tis the *Bristol-stone*, which appears like a Diamond; 'tis an extravagant thought instead of a sublime one; 'tis roaring madness instead of vehemence; and a sound of words instead of sence. If *Shakespear* were stript of all the Bombast in his passions, and dress'd in the most vulgar words, we should find the beauties of his thoughts remaining; if his embroideries were burnt down, there would still be silver at the bottom of the melting-pot: but I fear (at least, let me fear it for my self) that we who Ape his sounding words, have nothing of his thought, but are all out-side; there is not so much as a dwarf within our Giants cloaths. Therefore, let not *Shakespear* suffer for our sakes; 'tis our fault, who succeed him in an Age which is more refin'd, if we imitate him so ill, that we coppy his failings only, and make a virtue of that in our Writings, which in his was an imperfection.

John Dryden
'... the Grounds of Criticism in Tragedy'
in *Troilus and Cressida* ... (1679)

Thoughts on 'Othello'

ONE might think that the General should not glory much in this action, but make an hasty work on't, and have turn'd his Eyes away from so unsouldierly an Execution: yet is he all pause and deliberation; handles her as calmly: and is as careful of her Souls health, as it had been her *Father Confessor. Have you prayed to Night*, Desdemona? But the suspence is necessary, that he might have a convenient while so to *roul his Eyes*, and so to *gnaw* his *nether lip* to the spectators. ...

So much ado, so much stress, so much passion and repetition about an Handkerchief! Why was not this call'd the *Tragedy of the Handkerchief*? What can be more absurd than (as *Quintilian* expresses it) *in parvis litibus has Tragœdias movere*? We have heard of *Fortunatus his Purse*, and of the *Invisible Cloak*, long ago worn threadbare and stow'd up in the Wardrobe of obsolete Romances: one might think, that were a fitter place for this Handkerchief, than that it, at this time of day, be worn on the Stage, to raise every where all this clutter and turmoil. Had it been *Desdemona's* Garter, the Sagacious Moor might have smelt a Rat: but the Handkerchief is so remote a trifle, no Booby, on this side *Mauritania*, cou'd make any consequence from it. . . .

Then for the *unraveling of the Plot*, as they call it, never was old deputy Recorder in a Country Town, with his spectacles in summoning up the evidence, at such a puzzle: so blunder'd, and be doultefied; as is our Poet, to have a good riddance: And get the *Catastrophe* off his hands.

What can remain with the Audience to carry home with them from this sort of Poetry, for their use and edification? how can it work, unless (instead of settling the mind, and purging our passions) to delude our senses, disorder our thoughts, addle our brain, pervert our affections, hair our imaginations, corrupt our appetite, and fill our head with vanity, confusion, *Tintamarre*, and Jingle-jangle, beyond what all the Parish Clarks of *London*, with their *old Testament* farces, and interludes, in *Richard* the seconds time cou'd ever pretend to? Our only hopes, for the good of their Souls, can be, that these people go to the Playhouse, as they do to Church, to sit still, look on one another, make no reflection, nor mind the Play, more than they would a Sermon.

There is in this Play, some burlesk, some humour, and ramble of Comical Wit, some shew, and some *Mimickry* to

hair] harass

divert the spectators: but the tragical part is, plainly none other, than a Bloody Farce, without salt or savour.

Thomas Rymer
A Short View of Tragedy . . . (1693)

FRENCH AND ENGLISH DRAMATIC CONVENTIONS

A CONTINUED gravity keeps the spirit too much bent; we must refresh it sometimes, as we bait upon a journey, that we may go on with greater ease. A Scene of mirth mix'd with Tragedy has the same effect upon us which our musick has betwixt the Acts and that we find a relief to us from the best Plots and language of the Stage, if the discourses have been long. I must therefore have stronger arguments ere I am convinc'd, that compassion and mirth in the same subject destroy each other; and in the mean time cannot but conclude, to the honour of our Nation, that we have invented, increas'd and perfected a more pleasant way of writing for the Stage then was ever known to the Ancients or Moderns of any Nation, which is Tragicomedie.

And this leads me to wonder why *Lisideius*[1] and many others should cry up the barrenness of the French Plots above the variety and copiousness of the English. Their plots are single, they carry on one design which is push'd forward by all the Actors, every Scene in the Play contributing and moving towards it: Ours, besides the main design, have under plots or by-concernments, of less considerable Persons, and Intrigues, which are carried on with the motion of the main Plot: just as they say the Orb of the fix'd Stars, and those of the Planets, though they have motions of their own, are whirl'd about by the motion of the *primum mobile*, in which

1. One of the other speakers in the colloquy.

they are contain'd: that similitude expresses much of the English Stage: for if contrary motions may be found in Nature to agree; if a Planet can go East and West at the same time; one way by virtue of his own motion, the other by the force of the first mover, it will not be difficult to imagine how the under Plot, which is onely different, not contrary to the great design, may naturally be conducted along with it.

Eugenius[1] has already shown us, from the confession of the French Poets, that the Unity of Action is sufficiently preserv'd, if all the imperfect actions of the Play are conducing to the main design; but when those petty intrigues of a Play are so ill order'd that they have no coherence with the other, I must grant *Lisideius* has reason to tax that want of due connexion; for Co-ordination in a Play is as dangerous and unnatural as in a State. In the mean time he must acknowledge our variety, if well order'd, will afford a greater pleasure to the audience.

As for his other argument, that by pursuing one single Theme they gain an advantage to express and work up the passions, I wish any example he could bring from them would make it good: for I confess their verses are to me the coldest I have ever read: Neither indeed is it possible for them, in the way they take, so to express passion, as that the effects of it should appear in the concernment of an Audience: their Speeches being so many declamations, which tire us with the length; so that instead of perswading us to grieve for their imaginary Heroes, we are concern'd for our own trouble, as we are in the tedious visits of bad company; we are in pain till they are gone. When the French Stage came to be reform'd by Cardinal *Richelieu*, those long Harangues were introduc'd, to comply with the gravity of a Churchman. Look upon the *Cinna* and the *Pompey*; they are not so properly to be called Playes, as long discourses of reason of State: and *Polieucte* in matters of Religion is as solemn as the long

1. Another speaker in the colloquy.

stops upon our Organs. Since that time it is grown into a custome, and their Actors speak by the Hour-glass, as our Parsons do; nay, they account it the grace of their parts, and think themselves disparag'd by the Poet, if they may not twice or thrice in a Play entertain the Audience with a Speech of an hundred or two hundred lines. I deny not but this may sute well enough with the French; for as we, who are a more sullen people, come to be diverted at our Playes; they, who are of an ayery and gay temper come thither, to make themselves more serious: And this I conceive to be one reason why Comedy is more pleasing to us, and Tragedies to them. But to speak generally, it cannot be deny'd that short Speeches and Replies are more apt to move the passions and beget concernment in us then the other: for it is unnatural for any-one in a gust of passion to speak long together, or for another in the same condition, to suffer him, without interruption. Grief and Passion are like floods rais'd in little Brooks by a sudden rain; they are quickly up, and if the concernment be powr'd unexpectedly in upon us, it overflows us: But a long sober shower gives them leisure to run out as they came in, without troubling the ordinary current. As for Comedy, Repartee is one of its chiefest graces; the greatest pleasure of the Audience is a chase of wit kept up on both sides, and swiftly manag'd. And this our forefathers, if not we, have had in *Fletchers* Playes, to a much higher degree of perfection than the French Poets can arrive at.

John Dryden

Of Dramatick Poesie, an Essay (1668)

ALTERATIONS OF TASTE

IN a Play-house, every thing contributes to impose upon the Judgment; the Lights, the Scenes, the Habits, and, above all, the Grace of Action, which is commonly the best where there is the most need of it, surprize the Audience, and cast a mist upon their Understandings; not unlike the cunning of a Juggler, who is always staring us in the face, and overwhelming us with gibberish, onely that he may gain the opportunity of making the cleaner conveyance of his Trick. But these false Beauties of the Stage are no more lasting than a Rainbow; when the Actor ceases to shine upon them, when he guilds them no longer with his reflection, they vanish in a twinkling. I have sometimes wonder'd, in the reading, what was become of those glaring Colours which amaz'd me in *Bussy Damboys*[1] upon the Theatre: but when I had taken up what I suppos'd, a fallen Star, I found I had been cozen'd with a Jelly: nothing but a cold dull mass, which glitter'd no longer than it was shooting: A dwarfish thought dress'd up in gigantick words, repetition in aboundance, looseness of expression, and gross Hyperboles; the Sense of one line expanded prodigiously into ten: and to sum up all, uncorrect English, and a hideous mingle of false Poetry and true Nonsense; or, at best, a scantling of wit which lay gasping for life, and groaning beneath a Heap of Rubbish. A famous modern Poet us'd to sacrifice every year a *Statius* to *Virgil*'s Manes: and I have Indignation enough to burn a *D'amboys* annually, to the memory of *Johnson*. But now, My Lord, I am sensible, perhaps too late, that I have gone too far: for I remember some verses of my own *Maximin* and *Almanzor* which cry, Vengeance upon me for their Extravagance, and which I wish heartily in the same fire with *Statius* and *Chapman*: All I can say for those passages, which are I hope not many, is, that I knew they were bad enough to please, even when I writ them: but I repent of them amongst my Sins: and if any of their fellows intrude by chance into my present Writings, I draw a stroke over all those *Dalilahs* of the Theatre; and am resolv'd

1. A tragedy by George Chapman (1607).

I will settle my self no reputation by the applause of fools. 'Tis not that I am mortified to all ambition, but I scorn as much to take it from half-witted Judges, as I shou'd to raise an Estate by cheating of Bubbles. Neither do I discommend the lofty style in Tragedy which is naturally pompous and magnificent: but nothing is truly sublime that is not just and proper. If the Ancients had judg'd by the same measures which a common Reader takes, they had concluded *Statius* to have written higher than *Virgil*: for,

Quæ superimposito moles geminata Colosso,

carries a more thundring kind of sound than,

Tityre tu patulæ recubans sub tegmine fagi:

yet *Virgil* had all the Majesty of a lawfull Prince; and *Statius* onely the blustring of a Tyrant. But when men affect a Vertue which they cannot reach, they fall into a Vice, which bears the nearest resemblance to it. Thus an injudicious Poet who aims at Loftiness runs easily into the swelling puffie style, because it looks like Greatness. I remember, when I was a Boy, I thought inimitable *Spencer* a mean Poet, in comparison of *Sylvester*'s *Dubartas*: and was rapt into an ecstasie when I read these lines:

Now, when the Winter's keener breath began
To Chrystallize the Baltick Ocean;
To glaze the Lakes, and bridle up the Floods,
And periwig with Snow the bald-pate Woods:

I am much deceiv'd if this be not abominable fustian, that is, thoughts and words ill sorted, and without the least relation to each other: yet I dare not answer for an Audience, that they wou'd not clap it on the Stage: so little value there is to be given to the common cry, that nothing but Madness can please Mad-men, and a Poet must be of a piece with the Spectators, to gain a reputation with them. But, as in a room,

contriv'd for State, the height of the roof shou'd bear a proportion to the Area; so, in the Heightnings of Poetry, the
strength and vehemence of Figures shou'd be suited to the
Occasion, the Subject, and the Persons. All beyond this is
monstrous; 'tis out of nature, 'tis an excrescence, and not a
living part of Poetry.

John Dryden
Dedication of *The Spanish Fryar* (1681)

BIOGRAPHICAL NOTES

Aubrey, John (1626–97), antiquarian and friend of Hobbes, discovered the prehistoric remains at Avebury in 1648 and was an early member of the Royal Society. From 1667 associated with Anthony à Wood in the project for a collective biography of Oxford men.

Barclay, Robert (1648–90), leading Quaker theologian, joined the Friends in 1667 and was associated with Fox [q.v.] and Penn. His *Apology*, with other writings, remains a standard exposition of Quaker principles, and first appeared in Latin in 1676.

Baxter, Richard (1615–91), became famous for his preaching at Kidderminster; an opponent of Cromwell, working for the spread of moderate rational nonconformity. Chief works: *Saints Everlasting Rest* (1650), *Reliquiæ Baxterianæ* (1696).

Boyle, Hon. Robert (1627–91), the 'father of chemistry'; leading member of the Royal Society, his interests extended to the whole range of scientific enquiry. Experiments with the air-pump from 1659, 'Boyle's Law,' 1662, work on colours, fluids and the relation of science to religion.

Brooke, Lord – See Greville.

Browne, Sir Thomas (1605–82). After graduation as a physician at Leyden he settled at Norwich in 1637; knighted, 1671. Chief works: *Religio Medici* (1643), *Pseudodoxia Epidemica* (1646), *Urn Burial* and *Garden of Cyrus* (1658), *Christian Morals* (1716).

Bunyan, John (1628–88). Served in the Parliamentary army, 1644–7; baptized in the Ouse, 1653; a Baptist preacher from 1655. In Bedford Gaol (1661–72) he wrote *Grace Abounding* (1666); Minister at Bedford from 1672; again in gaol (1675) where he wrote *Pilgrim's Progress I*. Other works include *Life and Death of Mr Badman* (1680), *Holy War* (1682), *Pilgrim's Progress II* (1684).

Burnet, Gilbert (1643–1715), Bishop of Salisbury from 1689, political ecclesiastic, the 'Buzzard' of Dryden's *Hind and Panther, III*. Chief works: *History of the Reformation* (1679–1714), *Life of Sir Matthew Hale* (1682), *Exposition of the Thirty-Nine Articles* (1699), *History of his Own Time* (published 1724–34).

Burton, Robert (1577–1640). A Leicestershire man, he was vicar of St Thomas's, Oxford, from 1616, and also of Segrave, Leics., from 1630. He continued to revise *The Anatomy of Melancholy* (1621) in later editions, but appears to have written nothing else.

Butler, Samuel (1612–80), author of *Hudibras* (1663–78), a mock-heroic poem against the Presbyterians and Independents; he received a pension for it from Charles II. Also satirized the Royal Society in verse and wrote miscellaneous prose works.

Clarendon, Edward Hyde, first Earl of (1609–74). Supported Charles I in Parliament from 1641; Lord Chancellor and chief minister to Charles II from 1658; Chancellor of Oxford University, 1660–7. Fell from power in 1667 and died in exile. His *History of the Rebellion* and his *Life* of himself were written during the Commonwealth and after his fall.

Congreve, William (1670–1729), greatest of the Restoration comic dramatists; wrote his four comedies (*The Old Bachelor*, *The Double Dealer*, *Love for Love*, *The Way of the World*) before 1700, a tragedy, *The Mourning Bride* (produced 1697) and a prose romance, *Incognita* (1691).

Cotton, Charles (1630–87), poet and patron of poets, was distantly related to Col. Hutchinson [q.v.]. Chief works: *Scarronides* (1664), a burlesque of *Aeneid I*; supplement to Walton's *Compleat Angler* (1676); lyrical and miscellaneous poems (1689).

Cowley, Abraham (1618–67), poet and essayist, Royalist spy and admirer of the Royal Society. His poetry includes *The Mistress* (1647), *Davideis*, a Christian epic, and *Pindarique Odes* (1656).

Cromwell, Oliver (1599–1658), Lord Protector, 1653–8. For his writings consult *The Writings and Speeches of Oliver Cromwell*, ed. Abbott (Cambridge, Mass., 1937–47).

Culverwel, Nathanael (d. 1651?), Cambridge Platonist and Fellow of Emmanuel College. Chief work: *The Light of Nature* (1652).

Davenant, Sir William (1606–68), dramatist from 1629 and poet laureate from 1638, he was also a leading figure in the early Restoration theatre. Chief works: *Platonic Lovers* (1636), *Love and Honour* (1634), *Siege of Rhodes* (1656), *Gondibert* [an epic] (1651).

Digby, Sir Kenelm (1603–65), sailor, diplomatist, author of the first learned commentary on Spenser (1644), member of the Royal

Society, a Roman Catholic. His *Private Memoirs* are a disguised account of his courtship of Venetia Stanley (on whom see Aubrey's *Brief Lives*). See Aubrey on p. 57.

Donne, John (1572–1631). Donne's love poetry was mostly written when he was a younger man; a promising worldly career was spoilt by his marriage to the niece of his employer Sir T. Egerton, Lord Keeper, 1601. Ordained, 1615, Reader in Divinity at Lincoln's Inn from 1616, Dean of St Paul's from 1621. His poems were mostly printed posthumously after 1633, and so were the sermons for which he was equally renowned in his life-time.

Dryden, John (1631–1700). He published his critical writings mainly as prefaces to his plays and poetry, except for the *Essay on Dramatic Poesy* (1668); his verse satire came largely after 1678, and he occupied his last years with translations.

Eachard, John (1636?–97), Master of Catharine Hall, Cambridge, from 1675. Chief works: *Grounds and Occasions of the Contempt of the Clergy* (1670) and his reply to a critic of this book (1671); two witty dialogues criticizing Hobbes [q.v.], 1672, 1673.

Earle, John (1601–65). A Yorkshireman, tutor to Prince Charles and in exile with him, he became Bishop of Worcester, 1662, and then of Salisbury, 1663. Besides *Microcomographie* (1628 and later enlarged editions), wrote occasional poems, and sermons.

Etherege, Sir George (?1635–91). Began his career as a playwright with *The Comical Revenge* (1664). The interesting letters he wrote during his three and a half years as James II's envoy at Ratisbon have been printed as *The Letter Book of Sir George Etherege* (1928).

Evelyn, John (1620–1706). Evelyn's *Memoirs*, a complete account of his life, reveal the breadth of his interests as connoisseur, traveller, architect and gardener, also expressed in numerous prose works published during his life-time, such as *Fumifugium* (1661), *Sculptura* (1662), *Sylva* (1664), *Acetaria* [on salads] (1699).

Felltham, Owen (1602?–68). Lived mainly at Great Billing, his estate in Northamptonshire. Moralist and prose-stylist, he published the first edition of the *Resolves* when he was eighteen; also wrote occasional poetry including an ode to the memory of Jonson.

Fiennes, Celia or Cecilia (1662–1741), grand-daughter of the first Viscount Saye and Sele, came of a notable Hampshire Roundhead and Nonconformist family. A keen social observer with up-to-date tastes, her *Journeys* provide the best description of the late seventeenth-century English scene.

Fox, George (1624–91), founder of the Society of Friends. His chief work, the *Journal*, was first issued in 1694 by T. Ellwood, who edited and expurgated it.

Frank, Mark (1613–64). Fellow of Pembroke College and Master from 1662. Sermons published posthumously in 1672.

Fuller, Thomas (1608–61), historian and antiquarian, he held various livings in the Church of England. Chief works: *Holy State and Profane State* (1642), *History of the Holy War* [on the Crusades] (1643), *Church History of Britain* (1655), *Worthies of England* (1662).

Glanvill, Joseph (1636–80), F.R.S., Rector of the Abbey Church at Bath from 1666, chaplain in ordinary to Charles II from 1672. Chief works: *Vanity of Dogmatizing* (1661; revised as *Scepsis Scientifica*, 1665); *Plus Ultra, or the Progress and Advancement of Knowledge* (1668); *Sadducismus Triumphatus* [on witchcraft] (1681).

Goodwin, John (1594?–1665). One of the first clergymen to support the Parliamentary cause in 1642, he was a schismatic in Presbyterian eyes and known as the 'Great Red Dragon of Coleman Street' (he was Vicar of St Stephen's, Coleman St). Wrote much theological controversy.

Greville, Robert, second Lord Brooke (1608–43). Philosopher and Parliamentary General, he was a cousin of Fulke Greville the poet, who adopted him; killed in an attack at Lichfield. Chief works: *The Nature of Truth* (1640); *A Discourse* [upon] *Episcopacie* (1641).

Hacket, John (1592–1670). Chaplain to Archbishop Williams and then to James I, took a prominent part in the episcopacy controversy. Bishop of Coventry and Lichfield from 1661, restored Lichfield Cathedral.

Halifax, George Savile, first Marquess of (1633–95). A moderating influence during Charles II's reign, President of the Council under James II, but later opposed toleration of Catholics; Lord Privy Seal under William and Mary. Chief works: *The Character of a Trimmer* (written 1685); *The Character of Charles II* (printed 1750). See Burnet on p. 72.

Halkett, Lady Anne (1622–99). Daughter of Charles I's secretary,

married Sir J. Halkett (d. 1676) in 1656. Her autobiography, besides foreshadowing Jane Austen's novels, tells how she nursed
wounded soldiers at Dunbar (1650) and helped the Duke of York
to escape from London disguised as a woman (1648).

Harrington, James (1611–77). Travelled widely in Europe and was
impressed by the Venetian constitution. The Rota Club was formed
in 1659, after the publication of his masterpiece *Oceana*, for discussion of his 'classical republican' ideas.

Herbert of Cherbury, Lord (1583–1648). Metaphysical poet, historian, inventor, and philosopher, his famous *Autobiography* dis-
plays the least attractive aspect of George Herbert's brother. Other
works include poems (1608–31), *De Veritate* (1624), *History of
Henry VIII* (1649).

Hobbes, Thomas (1588–1679). Spent many years at Chatsworth as
tutor to the Cavendishes, then travelled and lived abroad, meeting
foreign savants; tutor to Prince Charles in exile, but the highly
controversial masterpiece *Leviathan* (1651) made him unpopular
and he went back to Chatsworth. Was often at court during the
Restoration. See Aubrey on p. 67, and Burnet on p. 135.

Hooke, Robert (1635–1703), F.R.S., experimental philosopher. Assisted Boyle at Oxford; curator of experiments for the Royal
Society from 1662, Professor of Geometry at Gresham College
from 1665, Secretary of the Royal Society, 1677–82. Argued with
Newton on light, wrote on astronomy, gravity, earthquakes, etc.,
and developed scientific apparatus.

Howell, James (1594?–1666). Held various government posts, but
was imprisoned as a Royalist during the Commonwealth. Chief
works: *Epistolæ Ho-elianæ* (1645–55); *Instructions for Foreign Travel*
(1642, 1650).

Hutchinson, Lucy (1620–?75). Daughter of the Lieutenant of the
Tower of London, married Col. Hutchinson (1615–64) in 1638.
He was Parliamentary Governor of Nottingham, then its M.P.
and one of Charles I's judges. Owes his fame to Lucy who em-
bodies in her account of him the Puritan gentlemanly ideal.

Lapthorne, Richard. Known only as the London agent of a Devonshire squire and bibliophile Richard Coffin (1622–98), to whom he
wrote a series of weekly newsletters, 1683–95.

L'Estrange, Sir Roger (1616–1704). Tory journalist, periodical-publisher and translator; knighted in 1685, he was imprisoned in the next reign. Translated Erasmus, Quevedo, Aesop, Josephus, etc.

Lilburne, John (1614–57). 'Free-Born John', the best-known Leveller leader, dramatized his life and sufferings and set out the Leveller complaints and principles in over a hundred tracts, many written in prison.

Lister, Martin (1638?–1712), F.R.S., zoologist, mineralogist, etc. Practised medicine at York, 1670–83, M.D.Oxon, 1684, Fellow of the Royal College of Physicians, 1687. His chief work is on shells, *Historia. . .Conchyliorum* (1685–92).

Locke, John (1632–1704). Held University posts at Oxford, then from 1667 physician to first Earl Shaftesbury [q.v.]; exiled because of supposed complicity in Shaftesbury's plots, 1684; held government posts under William III. Chief works: *Letters concerning Toleration* (1689–92), *Human Understanding* (1690), *Treatises of Government* (1690); *On Education* (1693).

Marvell, Andrew (1621–78). Tutor to the daughter of Lord Fairfax at Nun Appleton House, Yorks., 1650–3; Milton's assistant in the Latin secretaryship, 1657–9; M.P. for Hull, 1659–78. Besides his famous poems, he wrote verse satires and in *The Rehearsal Transpros'd* argued for the rights of conscience and dissent.

Milton, John (1608–74). Milton's prose was mostly written 1641–60 between his earlier and later poetic periods. He was appointed Secretary for Foreign Tongues to the Council of State in 1649. For his prose, consult the Columbia edition (New York, 1931–8).

Mundy, Peter (fl. 1600–67), a Cornishman, traveller and trader in Europe, India, China and Japan. His extensive journals, illustrated with pen and ink drawings, were begun about 1620.

Nayler, James (1617?–60). Wakefield Quaker apostle, converted by Fox [q.v.] in 1651, he was cruelly punished for 'horrid blasphemy' in 1656. Wrote many tracts and pamphlets.

Newton, Sir Isaac (1642–1727). Master of the Mint from 1699; President of the Royal Society from 1703. Theory of light and colours first communicated to the Royal Society in 1672. *Optics* (1704) is his chief English work; his masterpiece, *Philosophiæ Naturalis Principia Mathematica* (1686–7) is in Latin.

Osborn, Francis (1593–1659). Roundhead in sympathy, he held a legal post under the Commonwealth. His very popular *Advice to a Son* was admired by Pepys and Boswell, though not by Dr Johnson. Also wrote political essays of a republican cast.

Osborne, Dorothy (1627–95). The courtship of Dorothy and William Temple [q.v.] was begun when she was twenty-one and he twenty; their marriage, delayed by opposition on the part of families politically divided, took place in 1654. Her letters were written 1652–4.

Otway, Thomas (1652–85). Otway's unrequited passion for Elizabeth Barry (1658–1713), who acted in his plays, endured many years. Chief works: verse-tragedies, *The Orphan* (performed 1680), *Venice Preserved* (performed 1682); two-part comedy, *The Soldier's Fortune* (1680/3).

Overton, Richard (fl. 1646). Perhaps the ablest Leveller writer, published anti-Presbyterian tracts as 'Martin Marpriest' before he joined with Lilburne [q.v.] in 1646. Implicated in projected Leveller rising of 1655 he fled to Flanders. His *Arraignment of Mr Persecution* (1645) anticipates *Pilgrim's Progress* in allegorical method.

Oxinden, Henry (1608–70). The Oxinden papers, as edited by D. Gardiner (2 vols., 1933, 1937), give a continuous picture of the life of a county family up to 1670.

Parker, Henry (1604–52). He sided with the Presbyterians in the Civil War but afterwards became an Independent. Held various legal and secretarial posts in the Army and Parliament from 1645 and wrote many political pamphlets.

Pepys, Samuel (1633–1703). His diary, begun in 1660, was ended in 1669 owing to his fear of blindness. Held government posts from about 1660; Secretary to the Admiralty, 1673–79 and 1684–88. The diary remained unpublished in cipher until 1825 and has not yet been printed in full.

Ray, John (1627–1705), 'father of English natural history', son of a blacksmith, held posts at Trinity, Cambridge, until 1662; ordained, 1660. Travelled in England and abroad for scientific material and wrote series of pioneer catalogues of fauna and flora in Latin and collections of English proverbs. *The Wisdom of God* was written during his Cambridge period.

Raymond, Thomas (1610?–81?). Clerked in London, then soldiered in the Netherlands; secretary to the Ambassador at Venice, 1634–6; Keeper of the Records of State, 1660–1. Only work: the *Autobiography*.

Rochester, John Wilmot, second Earl of (1648–80). Poet and libertine, a favourite at Charles's court, he was attended on his deathbed by Bp Burnet [q.v.] who published an account of his repentance. Chief work: amorous and satirical poetry, especially 'A Satire against Mankind' (1675).

Rymer, Thomas (1641–1713), archivist and neo-classical critic; translated Rapin and wrote *The Tragedies of the Last Age* (1678) and *A Short View of Tragedy* (1692). As historiographer to the king (1692) he produced *Foedera* (1704–35), a collection of the letters, treaties, etc., between English kings and foreign states up to 1654.

Selden, John (1584–1654), jurist, antiquary, orientalist, friend of Jonson, Camden, Drayton. Works include: *Titles of Honour* (1614), *De Diis Syriis* (1617), *History of Tythes* (1617). M.P.(1621–49), against the Crown and relied upon by Parliamentarians as a legal and historical authority (in prison, 1629–31).

Shadwell, Thomas (1642?–92). Dryden's target in 'MacFlecknoe' (1678), 'The Medal', and 'Absalom and Achitophel II' (1682), Shadwell succeeded him as poet laureate in 1688. Wrote a large number of Jonsonian prose comedies, including *Epsom Wells* (1673), *Bury Fair* (1689).

Shaftesbury, Anthony Ashley Cooper, first Earl of (1621–83), led the Parliamentary opposition to Cromwell and then the anti-Catholic movement at the Restoration, instigating the plan to exclude the Duke of York [James II] from the throne; the 'Achitophel' of Dryden's poem.

Sloane, Sir Hans (1660–1753), physician, secretary to the Royal Society, 1693–1712, Pres. R. Coll. Physicians, 1719–35, correspondent with many scientists; his collections of papers and specimens became Sloane's Museum, from which the British Museum arose.

Smith, John (1618–52). Cambridge Platonist, pupil of Whichcote (on whom see p. 134), studied at Emmanuel and taught at Queens' Coll. *Select Discourses* (1660) is his only work.

Sprat, Thomas (1635–1713). Interested in science at Oxford, he was a

friend of Wren and Cowley and helped to found the Royal
Society. Dean of Westminster from 1683, Bishop of Rochester
from 1684. Chief works: *History of the Royal Society* (1667); *Life of
Cowley* (1668).

Taylor, Jeremy (1613–67), protégé and chaplain of Laud and later of
the Earl of Carbery at Golden Grove, Carmarthenshire. Bishop of
Down and Connor from 1660 and Vice-chancellor of Trinity
Coll., Dublin. Chief works: collections of sermons (1651–3),
Liberty of Prophesying (1647), *The Great Exemplar* (1649), *Holy Living*
(1650), *Holy Dying* (1651), *Ductor Dubitantium* (1660).

Temple, Sir William (1628–99). Married Dorothy Osborne [q.v.];
English envoy at the Hague, where between 1675 and 1677 he
negotiated the marriage of Mary and William of Orange. At
Moor Park, Surrey, from 1689 Swift was a member of his house-
hold. Chief work: *Miscellanea* (1680–1701).

Tillotson, John (1630–94), a Yorkshireman from Halifax, ordained
1661, preacher at Lincoln's Inn from 1664, chaplain to Charles II,
Dean of Canterbury, 1672, of St Paul's, 1689, Archbishop of
Canterbury, 1691. First collection of his sermons appeared in
1694. See Burnet on p. 137.

Traherne, Thomas (1637?–74). Rector of Credenhill, Herefordshire,
from 1657, and then private chaplain to Sir O. Bridgeman, Lord
Keeper. Chief works: poems (first printed 1903, standard edition
1932); *Christian Ethicks* (1675); *Centuries of Meditations* (1908).

Urquhart, Sir Thomas (1611–60), of Cromarty. Knighted by Charles
I for his opposition to the Covenanters, he was captured at the
Battle of Worcester (1651) but released by Cromwell's order.
Famous as translator of the first three books of Rabelais (1653,
1693), he also projected a Universal Language and wrote mathe-
matical works.

Walton, Izaak (1593–1683). Free of the Ironmongers' Company, he
kept a shop in Donne's Fleet St parish until about 1644, and knew
many Anglican divines. After 1660 lived at Winchester with Bp
Morley, where he knew Cotton [q.v.]. Chief works: *Lives*
('Donne', 1640; 'Wotton', 1651; 'Hooker', 1665; 'Herbert', 1670;
rev. coll. editions, 1670, 1675; 'Sanderson', 1678, rev. 1681);
Compleat Angler, 1653, rev. 1655.

Walwyn, William (fl. 1649). A London tradesman, was one of Lilburne's [q.v.] chief associates from 1647. Had the most attractive and enquiring temper amongst the Levellers. Of his many pamphlets, the one against the Presbyterian T. Edwards (1646) shows him at his best.

Winstanley, Gerrard (1609–?60). Member of the Merchant Taylors Company, ruined in the Civil War slump, he settled at Cobham, and in 1649–50 led the Diggers' attempt to till common land and establish communal farms, to the fury of the local landlords and parsons, who suppressed the movement by force. Wrote many pamphlets (first collected ed., 1941).

Wycherley, William (1640–1716). First educated in France, he soon left Oxford to join the London fashionable world and was the lover of the king's mistress, the Duchess of Cleveland (on whom see pp. 70–1). In old age, a friend of Pope. His plays (*Love in a Wood, The Gentleman Dancing-Master, The Plain Dealer, The Country Wife*) were all acted and printed in the 1670s.

INDEX OF AUTHORS

ACKNOWLEDGEMENTS

FOR permission to quote extracts from their publications we are indebted to:

Messrs G. Bell & Sons Ltd, publishers of Pepys' *Diary* edited by Henry B. Wheatley; Basil Blackwell, publisher of Sir George Etherege's *Works* edited by H. F. Brett-Smith; Messrs Jonathan Cape Ltd, publishers of Richard Lapthorne's *Portledge Papers* edited by R. J. Kerr and I. C. Duncan; the Clarendon Press, publishers of the Earl of Clarendon's *Life* and *History of the Rebellion and Civil Wars*, of John Aubrey's *Brief Lives* edited by A. Clark, and of *The Letters of Dorothy Osborne to William Temple* edited by G. C. Moore Smith; Messrs Constable & Co. Ltd, publishers of *The Oxinden Letters* edited by D. Gardiner; the Cresset Press Ltd, publishers of Celia Fiennes' *Journeys* edited by Christopher Morris; Messrs Percy Dobell, publishers of Thomas Traherne's *Centuries of Meditations* edited by B. Dobell; the Hakluyt Society, publishers of *The Travels of Peter Mundy in Europe and Asia* edited by Sir R. C. Temple; the Library of the Society of Friends and the Cambridge University Press, publishers of George Fox's *Journal* edited by Norman Penney; Messrs Routledge & Kegan Paul, publishers of Lucy Hutchinson's *Memoirs of Colonel Hutchinson* edited by Sir C. H. Firth; the Royal Historical Society, publishers of the *Autobiography* of Thomas Raymond edited by G. Davies and the *Autobiography* of Anne, Lady Halkett edited by J. G. Nichols; and the Selden Society, publishers of John Selden's *Table-Talk* edited by Sir F. Pollock.

A Guide to English Literature

EDITED BY BORIS FORD

The series is not a *Bradshaw* or *Whitaker's Almanack* of information; nor has it been designed on the lines of the standard Histories of Literature. It is intended for those many thousands of general readers who accept with genuine respect what is known as our 'literary heritage', but who might none the less hesitate to describe intimately the work of such writers as Pope, George Eliot, Langland, Marvell, Yeats, Tourneur, Hopkins, Crabbe, or D. H. Lawrence, or to fit them into any larger pattern of growth and development. It is with such readers in mind that this guide to the history and traditions of our literature, this contour-map to the literary scene, has been planned. It attempts to draw up an ordered account of literature that is concerned, first and foremost, with value for the present, and this as a direct encouragement to people to read for themselves.

THE AGE OF CHAUCER

A 290

The first volume covers the period from Chaucer to Spenser. It includes two general surveys of the literature of the period, one on poetry and the other on prose; an account of the social context of the literature of the time; and a series of essays dealing in detail with individual writers and works. It also contains an appendix of biographies and bibliographies, and a specially edited anthology of medieval texts that are otherwise virtually inaccessible to the general reader, texts such as the complete versions of the great alliterative poem *Sir Gawayne and the Grene Knight*.

A Guide to English Literature

THE AGE OF SHAKESPEARE

A 291

The second volume in the series covers Shakespeare's own life-time. It contains a long general survey of the English literary renaissance, and also an account of the social context of literature in the period. Then there follows a number of essays which consider in detail the work and importance of individual dramatists and poets and prose-writers, but above all the dramatists, for this was their age: five of the essays are devoted to Shakespeare's plays alone. Finally it contains an appendix giving short author-biographies and, in each case, standard editions of author's works, critical commentaries, and lists of books for further study and reference.

FROM DONNE TO MARVELL

A 325

The third volume covers the period from John Donne to Andrew Marvell. It begins with a survey of the background to English literature from 1603 to 1630, followed by a survey of the literature itself. The rest of the book is made up of a series of essays dealing in detail with Donne, the poems of Ben Jonson, Herbert and the devotional poets, the Cavalier poets, Milton, Marvell, Hobbes, Bunyan, and Cowley. In addition, the volume contains an appendix of biographies and bibliographies.